Global Democracy,
Social Movements,
and Feminism

Feminist Theory and Politics

Virginia Held and Alison Jaggar, Series Editors

Global Democracy, Social Movements, and Feminism

Catherine Eschle

Westview
PRESS

A Member of the Perseus Books Group

Copyright © 2001 by Catherine Eschle

Published in 2001 in the United States of America by Westview Press, 5500 Central Avenue, Boulder, Colorado 80301-2877, and in the United Kingdom by Westview Press, 12 Hid's Copse Road, Cumnor Hill, Oxford OX2 9JJ, A Member of Perseus Books Group.

Find us on the World Wide Web at www.westviewpress.com

Library of Congress Cataloging-in-Publication Data
Eschle, Catherine.
    Global democracy, social movements, and feminism / Catherine Eschle.
        p.   c.m.
    Includes bibliographical references and index.
    ISBN 0-8133-9149-0
    1. Democracy.   2. Social movements.   3. Feminism.   4. Globalization.   I. Title.
JC423.E68   2000
909.82′9—dc21   00-043989

The paper used in this publication meets the requirements of the American National Standard for Permanence of Paper for Printed Library Materials Z39.48-1984.

PERSEUS
POD
ON DEMAND   10   9   8   7   6   5   4   3

For my grandmothers,
Florence Eschle and Joan Martin
—much loved and much missed

Contents

Tables

Acknowledgments

This book began life as a doctoral thesis, written at the University of Sussex between 1995 and 1999. I would like to express my gratitude and affection to all participants in the Feminist Theory Reading Group at Sussex during this period, especially Charlotte Adcock, Jo Littler, Bridget Byrne, Paramjit Rai, Niamh Moore, Andrea Hammel, and Jude Reddaway. The group was a source of real intellectual and emotional sustenance during the highs and lows of postgraduate study. It made the D.Phil. journey a less solitary one. Particular thanks are due to Bridget and Paramjit, who read sections of the thesis for me while they were both on holiday! Thanks also to my thesis supervisors. Jan Aart Scholte's energy and commitment were crucial in getting the project off the ground; over the subsequent three years, Martin Shaw and Fiona Robinson were unfailingly kind, patient, and constructive. Norman MacLeod proofread the entire thesis with scrupulous attention to detail and in a very short period of time, for which I am very grateful. I would also like to acknowledge the financial support of the Economic and Social Research Council.

Several other people played an important role in encouraging me to turn the thesis into a book. Dymphna Evans has my heartfelt thanks for her help in getting a publication proposal together and for our subsequent conversations about this project. Sarah Warner at Westview Press and Alison Jaggar, co-editor of this series, took the book on and have been very encouraging and enthusiastic about it. I would also like to thank four people who read and engaged with the manuscript at a late stage in its development: V. Spike Peterson and another Westview reviewer who remained anonymous, and my D.Phil. examiners, William Outhwaite and Judith Squires. All offered considered, incisive advice. Judith and Spike, in particular, understood exactly what I was trying to do. They cut straight through to the weaknesses of the argument and were more than generous in their support of its stronger points. I have done my best to take on board many of their comments here; any defects that remain are, of course, entirely my own responsibility.

Finally, this book owes most to my parents, John and Sheila Eschle, and to my partner, Neil Stammers. They have all provided constant love and support. I realize increasingly that Mum and Dad have been a central inspiration behind my research. Their involvement in peace activism and other kinds of radical politics, and their continuing passionate engagement with the world, have had a profound effect on their community and friends and on the ideas I have tried to express here. Neil has nurtured me through the five years of this project and has always been fired with enthusiasm about it. I want to thank him for reading and commenting on numerous drafts, for putting up with my preoccupations, for keeping me fed and taking me on holiday—and for countless other kindnesses. I hope that some of the spark of our conversations together is reflected in this book.

Catherine Eschle

Introduction

This book explores the relationship between social movements and democracy in social and political thought. It does so in the context of arguments about the exclusions and mobilizations generated by gender hierarchies and the impact of globalization. Two interrelated questions are considered. What is the role and significance of movements in democracy according to social and political theorists? Conversely, in what ways do movements disrupt the assumptions of social and political theorists and point toward alternative understandings and practices of democracy? These questions are examined with a particular focus on feminism, which is both a social movement and a range of theoretical approaches, and which has struggled at length with the problems and possibilities of democracy.

The impetus for this inquiry has been provided by rising concern in social and political thought about the weaknesses of contemporary democracy—despite the near worldwide hegemony that democracy seems to have achieved in recent years. Of particular significance is an apparent "convergence of views . . . that a major culprit in the hollowing out of democratic institutions and the growing incapacity of democratic states to direct their own future is the intensity of contemporary globalization" (McGrew 1997b: 234). Processes identified as key here include innovations in communications and transport technology; the unification and increasing autonomy of the global economy; the proliferation of suprastate political institutions; and the homogenization, fragmentation, and interpenetration of cultural forms. Many analysts believe that such processes are leading to the diffusion of democracy in a particularly weak form and producing disjunctures between the sources of power and those affected by them. This may be exacerbating the disaffection of citizens who feel unable to exercise control over the forces affecting their lives. It may also be encouraging their mobilization in ways that bypass conventional, state-centric politics.

The other major source of concern behind this book is the feminist claim that women are consistently marginalized within democratic ideas and institutions. Carole Pateman puts it more forcefully (1989: 210): "For feminists, democracy has *never* existed; women have never been and still are not admitted as full and equal members and citizens in any country known as a democracy." In response, feminists continue to strive for inclusion on a more equal basis and to construct alternative democratic forms through mobilization in movement politics.

Thus both of these arguments about gender inequalities and globalization encourage an interest in social movements both as a response to the limitations of democracy and as a source of new democratic possibilities.

Some discussion of definitions is needed here, given that the term *social movement* remains heavily contested. The earliest systematic approach to movement activity defined its field in terms of "crowd psychology" and "collective behavior," with mobilization seen as a sign of social dysfunction and stigmatized as extra-institutional and irrational. More recently, "resource mobilization" theorists have interpreted social movements as the rational result of individuals coming together to pursue collective interests. Factors identified as causal in this approach include the availability of social resources and the capacity of entrepreneurial organizers to access them. "Political opportunity structures" theorists build on these rationalist foundations but focus on changes in the political context. More specifically, they examine the role played by the consolidation of the state in encouraging movements to expand to national size and to develop a statist orientation, and they look at the opportunities opened up to movements by the subsequent maneuvering for power among political elites. In contrast, the "new social movement" (NSM) school argues that there have been profound changes in recent activism as both a product of deep structural change in late modernity and a response to it. Movements are understood to have become diffuse in form and broadly cultural in orientation, aiming to constrain state and economic power rather than to gain access to it (for critical comparative surveys of social movement theory, see Scott 1992: 1–80; Cohen and Arato 1992: ch. 10; Tarrow 1998: 10–25; Foweraker 1995: 1–35).

My understanding of social movements differs somewhat from all of the above. First, I see movements as a form of collective action-in-process. As Alberto Melucci has argued, movements are not "unified empirical datum" or "personages" pursuing preformed social interests and able to act with a single will; rather, they are ongoing constructions of collective action and identity, always in progress (Melucci 1989: 18–19, 24–36; 1996a: 13–21). Second, movements are distinguished from other forms of collective action by mass participation. This can be short-lived or relatively sustained and it can take the form of the demonstrations emphasized by collective behavior theorists, the lobbying tactics stressed by proponents of the resource mobilization approach, or the more latent forms of cultural activity identified by NSM theorists. This brings me to a third feature of movements. They are heterogeneous constructions, encompassing diverse organizational forms, ideological positions, and forms of collective identity. Fourth, movements aim to achieve social change. This broad aspiration can encompass a variety of ideological positions and political strategies within and between movements, ranging from reaction to revolution.

Defining movements in this way complicates the task of considering their relationship to democracy in social and political thought. Movements can no longer be assessed as if they all shared a single ideology or goal. Conservative commentators have often presumed that all movement activity is hostile to democracy and destabilizes it. Their fears have been particularly aroused by the "mob," left radicalism, fascism, and, most recently, Islamic fundamentalism. Other kinds of social movement activity, from civil rights demonstrations to the direct action of suffragettes, have been tarred with the same brush. Radical analysts have just as readily slipped into idealized images of movements as intrinsically progressive forces for democracy. Their theories and political hopes have focused historically on workers' struggles and more recently on "new" social movements. Yet what about Islamists, fascists, and other ostensibly anti-democratic bogeymen? Is it possible to construct an understanding of the relationship between democracy and movements that can take on board their diversity of goals?

The first step must be to draw an analytical distinction between the diverse goals pursued by movements and the movement form they share. Yet even here it is necessary to be careful. The organizational heterogeneity of movements means that any account of their democratic role cannot simply focus on, for example, the activities of formal organizations within the system or, alternatively, on the "mob." It would be necessary to include both and everything in between, including the submerged networks of cultural innovation embedded in everyday life to which Melucci, in particular, draws attention (1989: 58–80). It must then be asked whether established traditions in social and political thought are capable of taking on board these different organizational manifestations of movements. Does movement complexity point toward the need to rethink existing democratic frameworks? If so, precisely which movement goals and aspects of movement structure could contribute to the reconstruction of democracy? Can these challenge or overcome marginalization arising from gender hierarchies and globalization processes?

Answering these questions requires devoting attention to the debates and dynamics of specific movements. In this book, consideration of the democratic implications of the movement form in general are combined with analysis of the feminist movement in particular.[1] Here another set of definitional debates arises. Rosalind Delmar puts forward a "base-line definition" of a femin*ist* as "someone who holds that women suffer discrimination because of their sex" and that this necessitates "a radical change . . . in the social, economic and political order" (1986: 8). Delmar's refusal to translate this into a definition of the collective undertaking of femin*ism* is instructive, based on a belief that such a move is precluded by the differences between self-identified feminists (1986: 9–11). Yet, as we shall see, social movements are typically riven by differences and yet can still be said to have some collective existence and impact. Delmar is also worried that a definition of feminism will necessarily rest on a fixed notion of "women" as both object and subject of struggle when the meaning of this category is contested (1986: 27–28). However, this proposition can be accepted without abandoning all attempts to define feminism and its connection to women. As Denise Riley has argued, feminists need to entertain the possibility that "'women' is indeed an unstable category, that this instability has a historical foundation, and that feminism is the site of the systematic fighting-out of that instability" (1988: 5).

Finally, Delmar is concerned about the "overstrict identification of feminism with a women's movement," a problem rooted in "a definition of feminism as *activity*" (1986: 23). I would argue that Delmar is in danger here of falling into the converse and equally problematic tendency to identify feminism with *ideas*, contrasting it with the activities of the "women's movement," which may or may not be feminist in orientation. Both formulations, though widespread, are confusing. Women have predominated in a wide variety of movements, relatively few of which have been consciously feminist in orientation. Feminist ideas may have germinated in the work of lone thinkers, who were sometimes participants in male-dominated radical movements, but later developments took place within the context of great surges of collective action by women for women (e.g., Rowbotham 1992; Banks 1986). This brings me to a "base line definition" of feminism as a set of ideas *and* practices, generated by a social movement of women and aiming to challenge the disadvantages faced by women and to contest and reconstruct women's identities.[2]

Some feminists have adopted social movement theory to analyze the movement in which they are participants. The resource mobilization approach has been frequently invoked (Evans 1979; Chafetz and Dworkin 1986; Ryan 1992) with a turn more recently to political opportunities structures theory (Costain 1992; Katzenstein 1987; Gelb 1989). Advocates of both have concentrated on feminism in North American and European contexts. Further, NSM theorists, many of whom are not explicitly feminist-identified, have stressed the role of feminism as one of a wave of late modern movements in the West, struggling for largely symbolic and cultural stakes. There is some dispute among NSM theorists over whether feminism also retains a distinctive attachment to more conventional, less defensive political goals (Melucci 1989: 93–95; 1996a: 133–144; Habermas 1981: 34–35; Cohen and Arato 1992: 548–556). All of these approaches have been the subject of feminist criticism. Attention has been drawn to long-term continuities in feminism that challenge its categorization as "new." The contextual importance of changes in structures of gender hierarchy has been stressed, along with the significance of emotion and affinity in building and sustaining mobilization (Roseneil 1995: 15–19; Taylor 1983: 435; 1995; Fraser 1987: 52–55). Clearly the feminist movement disrupts existing categorizations and singular histories.

Nonetheless, I want to sketch here what I would stress is a partial history of the emergence and development of feminism that emphasizes its intimate relationship to democratic theory and practice. Wendy Brown has warned against the tendency to "freight" feminism with "a strong democratic ambition": "While some feminists may be radical democrats, no ground exists for marking such a political posture as either indigenous or consequent to the diverse attachments traveling under feminism's name" (Brown, W. 1995: x). I agree that feminism is not intrinsically democratic and that not all feminists are democrats, but I would insist that there is an important relationship here. There are three dimensions to this relationship.

First, at certain historical moments, feminism has arisen as a response to women's exclusion from liberal democracy or their marginalization within it. Thus the development of the "first wave" of feminism in the West was partly mobilized by anger at the fact that women were not included in evolving liberal institutions. It eventually coalesced around the struggle for the vote. In the third world, and more recently in East Central Europe, women have mobilized extensively in anti-colonial, anti-authoritarian struggles only to face the subsequent retrenchment and even worsening of gendered access to the post-transition, liberal democratic polity. This has encouraged many to pursue their goals through autonomous feminist organization.

Second, feminist activism has arisen as a response to the subordination of women within leftist movements supposedly offering an alternative to liberal democracy. The more radical wing of the so-called second wave of feminism in the West was stimulated in part by the trivialization of women's concerns and their confinement to lower-status roles within the "New Left" movement, despite its rhetoric of egalitarian democracy. A similar dynamic continues to lead to autonomous feminist organizing in diverse contexts worldwide.

Third, democratic shortfalls within the feminist movement itself have shaped its development. Despite an explicit preoccupation with overcoming mechanisms of exclusion to enable women to speak for themselves, the historical dominance of white, western, middle-class, hetero-sexual, able-bodied women in the feminist movement has encouraged the spurious universalization of what are actually limited and relatively privileged experiences. This has marginalized the lived realities of work-ing-class, black, Asian, third world, lesbian, and disabled women. The ef-fort to articluate these realities and to pursue the distinctive political agendas arising from them has tended to encourage the fragmentation and diversification of feminist organization.

This threefold connection of feminism to democracy is, arguably, unique among movements and has generated a large, diverse, and reflex-ive literature. Of course, this is not the only reason why I focus on femi-nism here; my interest is personal and political. I write as a white, west-ern, middle-class, university-educated woman whose family life, personal relationships, academic interests, and social options have been shaped by feminism in important ways. This book would not have been written had it not been for the manner in which feminism has helped me to see the world. It represents, in part, an effort to contribute to debates within the movement over the challenges that women still face and the kind of strategies feminists should adopt. It is also intended to illustrate the vital relevance of feminist theory and practice for social and political thought and for movement activism more generally.

In exploring the implications of feminism for thinking about the rela-tionship between social movements and democracy, this book must span several disciplinary and methodological chasms. The first is between the "malestream"[3] of academia and feminist argument, the latter remaining largely ghettoized within the confines of feminist theory or women's studies. There are several reasons for this ghettoization. The historic dominance of men in the academy hardly needs underlining and has re-sulted in an "androcentric" skew to much theorizing. By this I mean that theory has largely been written by men and it reflects male standpoints. Male roles and experiences—for example as citizens, parliamentary rep-resentatives, party activists, workers, or movement organizers—have been the norm. Social and political thought is also "masculinist" in that it tends to reflect and elevate the values of "autonomy, separation, distance and control" associated in the West with the masculine (Jayaratne and Stewart 1992: 89). These values shape both the normative content of the-ory and the processes by which it is constructed. This leads, for example, to assumptions about the rationality and detachment of political actors and political scientists. Values traditionally associated with the feminine, such as emotional involvement and partiality, are neglected and even derogated. This has reinforced the exclusion of those designated the bearers of emotion, including women, from the pursuit of knowledge (Jaggar 1989; Lloyd 1989; Peterson 1992a: 191–196).

In response, feminists have questioned the detachment of the individual from social context and family life. They have challenged the downgrading of emotional motivation in political life and of political motivation in academic research. They have drawn attention to the invisibility of women in formal public life and to their relatively high levels of participation in social movements and community activism. Their efforts can have profound implications for "malestream" theoretical frameworks. For example, they encourage the radical reconceptualization of what democracy is and how social movements operate.

A second disciplinary and methodological chasm that this book attempts to bridge is that dividing sociology from politics. This division is predicated on a narrow understanding of the subject matter of both disciplines. Politics is elided with the operations of state institutions, whereas society is understood as the realm of everyday interactions, values, culture, and organizations that are, or ought to be, essentially separated from the state and its machinations (Giddens 1985: 22–31; Agnew, J. 1994: 68–69; Walker, R. B. J. 1995: 312). In line with this view, the study of democracy has been confined to the discipline of politics. Work has focused largely on the institutional manifestation of democracy, downplaying its social and cultural roots and effects. Conversely, movements have mostly been studied within sociology. They have been defined as primarily social, emerging as political actors only when they interact with or have an impact on the institutions and policies of the state and political society. It is at this point that the two spheres of the social and political are seen to be connected to a certain extent and that we find some convergence between sociological and political analysis. Most notably, political opportunity structures theory bridges sociology and political science in its focus on repertoires of movement action and their relationship to changing state structures (e.g., Tarrow 1998).

The argument in this book presupposes that the overlap between movements and democracy is much more extensive than such an approach allows, because the overlap between the social and the political is much more extensive. The dominant tendency toward an institutional, statist approach to politics as separate from society has long been the focus of criticism from certain academic traditions, most notably elitism, marxism, and feminism. These traditions have given rise to an alternative understanding of politics as "a process of negotiation or struggle over the distribution of power" that can reach deep into society (Squires 1999: 3, 7). As Judith Squires recognizes, the "more extensive power-based conception of the political both emerges from, and makes possible, the feminist challenge to the orthodoxy of politics" (1999: 9). This challenge is the subject of Chapters 3 and 4 of this book. I want to emphasize here that the power-based approach also enables the recognition of both the social dimension of political ideas and institutions and the political dimension of social interactions. This book is particularly concerned with the overlaps between social and political *theory*, rather than with the quantification or comparison of movement activity and modes of democracy typical of empirical sociological analysis and political science. The umbrella term *social and political thought* is used throughout to encompass all systematic reflection on the purposes and problems of human interaction, power relationships, and collective decision-making procedures, and on the possibilities (if any) for change. Bringing sociological and political analysis together in this way makes it clear that political concepts like democracy can be generated and institutionalized through social struggle and that movements can themselves be sources of democratic ideas and practices.

A third divide that this book attempts to cross separates the study of life *within* states from life *between* them. This separation is distinctive to the modern period. The premodern, feudal system of "overlapping loyalties and allegiances, geographically interwoven jurisdictions and political enclaves" (Camilleri 1990: 13) was glued together by hierarchical political and religious frameworks that transcended geographical boundaries. The rise of the modern nation-state system was accompanied by the pluralization and enclosure of politics, culture, and morality. Although cosmopolitan thinkers have stressed that there remain fundamental continuities between life within and beyond the state, their arguments have been overshadowed by the rise of state-centric, nationalist discourses taking both a "progressivist" and a "pessimistic" form.[4] Progressivist discourse "defends the state's place as a site for the realization of an ethical political community" (Linklater and Macmillan 1995: 5). In contrast, pessimists lament the divided and imperfect human condition but insist on the impossibility of significant change. These discourses have been entrenched in academia through the interventions of state elites in the academy, codified in the development of academic disciplines and reified by the positivistic turn across those disciplines in the mid–twentieth century (Agnew, J. 1994: 69; Walker and Mendlovitz 1990: 7). Outside pockets of philosophical and theological debate, and until the advent of arguments about globalization, the status of state boundaries and national community ceased being a question for academic inquiry and became its accepted backdrop. This is characterized by Jan Aart Scholte (1996: 48) in terms of a pervasive "methodological nationalism," which "holds that all social relations come packaged in national/ state/country units that divide the world into neatly distinguishable 'societies.'" Thus many sociologists have simply assumed that social movements end at state boundaries, treating them as discrete national phenomena. Further, most democratic theorists have believed that:

democracies can be treated as essentially self-contained units; that democracies are clearly demarcated one from another; that change within democracies can be understood largely with reference to the internal structures and dynamics of national democratic polities; and that democratic politics is itself ultimately an expression of the interplay between forces operating within the nation-state. (Held, D. 1991: 139)

Such assumptions receive confirmation in the discipline of international relations (IR), the very establishment of which was predicated on a distinction between the ordered life within states and the "anarchy" between them. The latter technically indicates absence of centralized government equivalent to that within a state. With its implications of lawlessness and terror, the term also implicitly constitutes relations between states as a realm of disorder and violence (Ashley 1988; Falk 1978; Walker, R. B. J. 1993). The dominant approaches within the discipline have begun their inquiries from this point, with the optimism of liberals about the possibility of mitigating anarchy through democratization within states and cooperation or institution building between them, eclipsed by the "realist" insistence that anarchy, and the dynamic of state competition that it encourages, cannot be transcended (e.g., Carr 1939; Morgenthau 1978; Waltz 1959, 1979; Gilpin 1986; Doyle 1983, 1986; Smith, M. J. 1992). The notion of an international or global dimension to democracy in the realist view is at best laughable, at worst dangerous—but mostly simply unthinkable. Realists have dismissed social movements as ineffectual and "utopian" in the face of *realpolitik* (Lynch 1994: 592–599) or simply ignored them as existing beyond the purview of the discipline.

Nonetheless, the global dimension of democracy and movement activity has been receiving increasing attention in a small but growing body of work by IR theorists, political theorists, and sociologists concerned about the impact of globalization. A variety of reconstructive schemes have been put forward that aim to strengthen the form in which democracy is globalized or to extend it beyond state borders. Many attempt to provide a role for social movements in that process. Most such schemes, however, continue to neglect feminist concerns about the marginalization of women in democracy, thus raising the specter of replicating old exclusions on a grander scale.

On the other hand, most feminist theoretical efforts to reconstruct democratic theory, the institutions of the state, and feminist activism to make them more inclusive of women remain limited by methodological nationalist and statist assumptions. Alternatively, they may be reliant on mystifying claims about the transborder, transcendental affinities of women. Feminist movement practices appear to be outrunning feminist conceptualizations on this issue. For example, the UN-sponsored International Women's Year in 1975 and the ensuing Decade for Women encouraged the collation of information about women on a global scale and led to the legitimization and proliferation of feminist groups and the transnational networks linking them together. I suggest in Chapter 6 that the UN Decade, despite its undoubted limitations, also aided the development of a sophisticated strand of feminist organizing that rejects both methodological nationalism and simplistic cosmopolitanism in its search for more genuinely democratic modes of participation in global politics.

Although this development has not yet received the consideration it deserves in feminist literature, some relevant analytical advances have emerged in feminism over the last few decades. For one thing, feminist engagement with the theorization and delivery of "development," frequently referred to as the Women in Development movement, or WID, has encouraged extensive consideration of the gendered impact of global economic and cultural forces. It has led to the proliferation of analyses of third world women's lives and, arguably, brought third world feminist contributions to feminist strategizing to the foreground (e.g., Boserup 1989; Sen and Grown 1987; Newland 1988; Goetz 1988; Mohanty 1991b; Chowdhury 1995; Pearson and Jackson 1999). Further, the WID movement and its critics have been very influential on the emergence of feminist voices within the discipline of IR. Feminists have contributed to the growing attacks on realism and positivism within the discipline by illuminating the androcentric and masculinist underpinnings of their hegemony. They have also cast a critical light on feminist debates about women, gender, and feminist activism by placing these in a global context (e.g., Enloe 1988; Whitworth 1989; Tickner 1992; Peterson 1992a; Peterson and Runyan 1999; Sylvester 1994; Zalewski 1994). To a large extent, WID and feminist IR have provided the analytical tools and political orientations that underlie my arguments here. What is more, a few pioneering analyses in feminist IR have dealt specifically with the question of the combined impact of gender hierarchies and globalization on democracy (Peterson 1995), and with the role this might open up for movements (Sylvester 1998; Dickenson 1997). Although I do not return to these analyses directly until much later, it should be noted here that they have influenced my general line of inquiry.

This book also draws upon assumptions about epistemology, method, and methodology that need to be made explicit.[5] For one thing, it adopts a modified form of "standpoint" epistemology. Standpoint theorists insist that all knowledge is mediated through a subject position. They claim that structures and relations of power impose continuities on those subject positions and the experiences to which they give rise. These structures and relations of power can be more profoundly perceived by those who experience life at their sharp end and who struggle against them.

My arguments here are thus founded on the notion that feminist women have had particular, complex experiences of democratic exclusion and negotiation, which generate insights into how social life could be made more democratic. These insights are partly attributable to the identity of most feminists as *women* and our disadvantaged positioning in society on that basis, albeit in ways stratified by ethnicity, nationality, and class. Recent modifications of standpoint theory have drawn attention to the fact that these differences between women produce multiple standpoints, although there remain sufficient continuities in the ways in which different women are materially and socially positioned to give rise to identifiable and overlapping social groupings and to distinctive, collective ways of looking at the world (Collins 1997: 375–379; Moya 1997: 137). Further, this modified version abandons the assumption that women reach the same view of the world, and that this is the most accurate view, simply by virtue of their overlapping locations. Rather, knowledge is achieved through oppositional struggle. This requires the formulation of challenges to conceptions of reality that uphold the status quo. It means that subordinated groups must systematize and interrogate their own world views and identify key forms of power and strategies for change (Moya 1997: 140–141). Thus I am arguing that it is specifically *the effort to construct a feminist movement* that has generated important arguments about both democracy and social movements.

What is more, I make a claim in this book that the arguments of black and third world feminists are particularly revealing about democracy and movements. There are enormous difficulties with this, not least in the use of the term *black and third world feminists,* a point to which I shall return. My point here is that commonalities in location and identification among black and third world women, and their efforts to act as feminists, give rise to thematic similarities in knowledge claims and particular insights. As Heidi Safia Mirza puts it:

> The invisibility of black women speaks of the separate narrative constructions of race, gender and class: in a racial discourse, where the subject is male; in a gendered discourse, where the subject is white; and a class discourse, where race has no place. It is because of these ideological blind spots that black women occupy a most critical place—a location whose very nature resists telling. In this critical space we can imagine questions that could not have been imagined before; we can ask questions that might not have been asked before. (Mirza 1997: 4)

Privileging black and third world feminist standpoints in this way could run the risk of falling into "unthinking celebrations of oppression, elevating the racially female voice into a metaphor for 'the good'" (Suleri

1996: 337). So it should be stressed that the knowledge to which the standpoints of black and third world feminists give rise is not the result of being the "most oppressed" social group. Rather, it is the result of being located at a particular conjuncture of oppression, of drawing on conceptual resources from outside the Eurocentric, academic "malestream" to explain that oppression, and of the struggle for clarity through movement activism (Harding 1997: 385). Further, it needs to be acknowledged that black and third world feminist arguments are not entirely unified and coherent but a site of contestation: "a sign that should be interrogated, a locus of contradictions" (Carby, quoted in Suleri 1996: 341). Finally, although I am privileging black and third world feminist theory as revealing a more accurate, or at least a "less false," picture of power relationships, I would also insist that the entirety of a dynamic and complex reality can never be fully and finally represented from one social location. Each standpoint remains, as Patricia Hill Collins puts it, a "partial perspective" that must be continually connected with the viewpoints of other groups and tested against them, in a process of an open-ended dialogue aimed at creating emancipatory knowledge (Collins 1990: 234–237).

Another epistemological assumption underpinning this book centers on the status and role of theory. The argument developed here rests on the belief that we can learn something about movements and democracy through reading theoretical texts about them. More specifically, it draws on *normative* and *critical* theory, which purports to tells us not only how democracy and social movements do operate, but how they could and should operate. Conversely, my argument assumes that the construction of theory should not be an abstracted undertaking involving the construction of internally coherent, logically compelling models with no anchor in actually existing social relations. As standpoint feminists and others have insisted, the boundary between theory and practice is a nebulous one. When we study "the real world" we do so with a conceptual, epistemological, and moral framework already in place, shaped by our location in structures and relations of power and informing what we look at and how we evaluate its significance. The reflexive consideration of our worldviews, and the ways in which they are confirmed or contested by the phenomena we set out to study, can lead to the production of a more or less systematic, logically cohesive, and normatively compelling body of writing we call theory. This can then influence how we act. Reading and writing theory is thus itself a form of social practice, both a product of and an intervention in the world. It cannot transcend contemporary power relations but it can reflect upon and challenge them (Sayer 1992: 12–16; Cox 1986: 207–210).

Sometimes the production of theory is also a kind of *social movement practice*, as academic thinkers attempt to identify and engage with a movement and further collective goals. This is precisely the kind of project that standpoint theorists are engaged in. More radically, participants in movements can generate theory collectively, in nonacademic terms. As Noël Sturgeon puts it:

> [S]ocial movements are involved in theorizing both the relations of power existing at particular conjunctures as well as previous traditions of opposition through their forms of action and their particular political rhetorics, and I call this aspect of movements *"direct theory."* (Sturgeon 1997: 5)

"Direct theory" needs to be taken more seriously by academics for its contribution to knowledge and generation of social change. It also demands critical interrogation, given the constraints placed on movements by the immediacy of their environment. The focus of this book on theoretical texts is thus intended as an intervention in both movement debates and academic analysis and a critical reflection on the links between the two.

To this end, the *method* of the book is to read and critically interrogate theoretical texts on democracy, social movements, and feminism. One methodological issue thus concerns the basis on which texts, traditions, and practices are assessed. The belief that theory is a social product and frequently a product of movement activity has encouraged me to place texts in the context of broader traditions of social and political thought, of changing historical backdrops, and of movement activity. The strengths and weaknesses of texts and theoretical traditions are drawn out by analyzing their internal logic and debates and by applying the insights of other texts and traditions. Further, each theoretical tradition is assessed in terms of the insights it reveals about the operations of power, the scope and location of democratic politics, and the nature of political agency and processes of change. Theory is also scrutinized for its account of movement activity, for the interests these accounts may or may not reflect, and for confirmation or contestation by movement activism. This demands attention to examples of movement practices.

A second methodological issue concerns the basis on which certain texts, movement practices, and themes are highlighted over others. No preexisting theoretical framework is applied systematically here other than in the form of a broad underlying commitment to feminist goals and approaches. Some guidelines are set in the opening questions of this introduction. To reiterate: What is the role and significance of social movements in democracy according to social and political theorists? How might movements disrupt the assumptions of social and political theorists and point to different ways of thinking about and practicing democracy? These questions demand investigation of approaches in social and political thought that bring to the foreground issues about democracy and social movements. More specific areas for inquiry emerge as the argument progresses. For example, problems with marxism point toward the need to examine the neglected tradition of anarchism. The limitations of most approaches to movements channel inquiry toward "constructivist" social movement theory. Difficulties with white western feminist thought encourage engagement with black and third world feminist critiques. It is inescapable, given the open-ended and interdisciplinary nature of this undertaking, that some detail may be sacrificed for breadth of discussion and that some relevant literatures and examples will be neglected. The conclusions reached are thus not intended as a final resolution of the issues discussed but rather as an opening to further debate.

The argument begins in Chapter 1 with an account of the ways in which democracy and social movements have been perceived in liberal, marxist, republican, and anarchist traditions of thought. The chapter puts these traditions into the context of the social institutions and historical ruptures of modernity, uncovering their shared "modernist" assumptions and the limitations these impose on the theorization of democracy and movement activity. Chapter 2 examines more recent innovations in social and political thought under the broad headings of postmarxism and postmodernism. These have given rise to analyses of social movements and democracy that start from a recognition of significant changes in the structures of modernity and thus in movement form and democratic practices. Although these analyses yield some insights, they also import several modernist assumptions and generate new epistemological and political problems. Furthermore, the literature examined in both these chapters neglects concerns about gender inequality and globalization.

So Chapter 3 turns to feminist arguments, looking at explanations of the marginalization of women in democracy and then at strategies to reconstruct democratic theory and incorporate women into the polity. Problems identified here lead, in Chapter 4, to a discussion of an alternative feminist trajectory of analysis, one concerned with democratization of the feminist movement itself. I focus on black and third world feminist critiques of racist exclusions in feminism and the democratic implications of their reconstructive efforts, particularly with regard to arguments about power, politics, agency, and change. These key arguments have one crucial limitation. They remain largely confined to national contexts, frequently stopping at the boundaries of states.

This leads in Chapter 5 to an examination of recent attempts to extend theories of democracy and social movements in the context of arguments about globalization. I look at liberal cosmopolitan approaches, the idea of global "demarchy," global versions of marxist theory, and globalized postmarxist and postmodernist alternatives. The affinities of this last approach with black and third world feminist concerns encourages, in Chapter 6, an attempt to synthesize feminist and globalization frameworks. The chapter documents the global nature of mechanisms marginalizing women in democracies and examines transnational innovations in feminist activism. Highlighting the limitations of feminist democratic and IR theory in dealing with these issues, the chapter turns again to feminist activism. More specifically, it looks at efforts to construct feminist activism across territorial borders on a more democratic basis and draws out the implications of these efforts for understanding power, politics, agency, and change. The conclusions that emerge point toward the possibility of a more democratic future for feminism. They also point toward an innovative understanding of democracy that is both global in scope and genuinely inclusive—and that has social movements at its heart.

Notes

1. Throughout this book, I am critical of theorists who look only at the analytical and political implications of "good" movements of which they approve, without specifying or scrutinizing the basis of that approval, while also ignoring the implications of "bad" movement activity. I recognize that my focus on feminism lays me open to similar charges. In my defense, I would reiterate that this book also considers the implications of the movement form more generally. Further, although my arguments about the movement form emerge in part through an interrogation of feminism, they are also shaped by readings of Melucci's social movement theory. Finally, I attempt to combine my general support of feminist aims and activities with an alertness to the differences and divisions within feminism, and to specify which strands of feminist praxis are important to the project of rethinking democracy, and why.

2. Many feminists would reject this emphasis on women as both the subject and object of feminist struggle. The object of feminism is increasingly recast as the contestation of gender, whether this is conceived as a struggle against the hierarchies implicit in gender relationships or as the destabilization of attempts to impose fixity on identity through gendered discourses. Nonetheless, it seems to me that these approaches usually retain an underlying political concern with the positioning of those people identified as women within gender relationships and discourses, and that this is what makes an argument about gender distinctively feminist. My insistence that feminism is also about the contestation of female identity highlights the fact that the category "women" has never been fixed within feminism but is continually contested and reconstructed, as Denise Riley has emphasized (1988). In addition, it should be stressed that the formulation above is not meant to suggest that men cannot be feminists and that they cannot

participate in the feminist movement. However, feminist mobilization that is not largely constituted by women would surely be a contradiction in terms, given the stress in feminist ideology on the need for women to mobilize collectively against their oppression and on the importance of self-representation.

3. "Feminist designation (coined by Mary Daly) for that body of thought perceived and judged *by (white educated) males* to constitute the 'mainstream'" (Kramarae and Trechler 1992: 244).

4. These state-centric discourses are more often discussed in terms of communitarianism, realism, or moral particularism, which are then juxtaposed to cosmopolitanism, idealism, or universalism (e.g., Brown, C. 1992; Clark, I. 1989). It seems to me that these categories are tied more tightly to specific debates and disciplines than are *progressivism* and *pessimism*; further, I want to draw attention to an important affective distinction *between* those who share the view that the state is the final source of political authority and the sole home of political community.

5. Here I am relying on Sandra Harding. Epistemology is "a theory of knowledge. It answers questions about who can be a knower (can women?); what tests beliefs must pass in order to be legitimated as knowledge . . . what kinds of things can be known." Method is "a technique for (or way of proceeding in) gathering evidence." Methodology is "a theory or analysis of how research does or should proceed" (Harding 1987a: 2–3).

1

Modernity, Social Movements, and Democracy

No practical component of ancient democracy has survived intact into the world in which we now live. . . . [W]hat has survived . . . is not simply a word, but also a diffuse and urgent hope.

(Dunn 1992: 256)

Introduction

Democracy has been both one of the greatest aspirations and achievements of modernity and one of its greatest disappointments. The passing of centuries between the collapse of the ancient Greek precursor and the reestablishment of democracy as a vital ideal and viable system makes its recent globalization all the more remarkable. The revival of democracy was achieved in part through the victories of social movements over entrenched interests. For those engaged in such struggles, ancient ideals of self-government, equality of citizens, and civic freedom clearly retained astonishing resonance. Yet as John Dunn recognizes, the liberal form of democracy most widely instituted in modernity retains only the most tenuous of connections with its ancient predecessor. Its contemporary hegemony may be due more to its effectiveness as a system of government in a mass, hierarchical, capitalist society, and its ability to weather movement demands for change, than to its imaginative appeal (Dunn 1992: 239–252). However, much social movement activism and academic theorizing continues to strive to recapture the imaginative appeal of democracy and to put alternative formulations into practice.

This chapter examines ideas about democracy and social movements springing from the four main political traditions in modernity: liberalism, marxism, republicanism, and anarchism. It looks at the ways in which each tradition deals with the nature of power, the location and scope of politics, the role of the political actor, and the possibility of social change. The analysis reveals that some liberals and marxists have carved out a positive, if limited, understanding of social movements and their democratic role, whereas other marxists, liberals, and most republicans are explicitly hostile to movement activity and systematically misrepresent and marginalize it. This tendency, I argue, points toward significant inadequacies in the theorization of democracy in each tradition and highlights the limitations of underlying modernist assumptions that these traditions all share. In contrast, proponents of anarchism offer an innovative, if flawed, approach to the relationship between democracy and movements, which challenges the parameters of modernist politics in ways that continue to inform contemporary movement activism. The chapter begins by specifying the framework of modernity, outlining the ways in which it has shaped both democracy and social movements and pointing to the continuities it has encouraged in apparently divergent traditions of social and political thought.

Epochal Change (1)

The Context of Modernity

Modernity is a highly contested concept. Perhaps the most important point to note is that "whenever we use the term modernity, we reiterate the claim that there is a huge gulf—a structural discontinuity—which separates the way the world used to be from the way it is now" (Rosenberg 1994: 1). The nature of this discontinuity has been variously characterized in terms of a shift from community to society, from organic to mechanical relations, from a society based on ascription to one based on achievement, or from feudal to capitalist social relations of production. Debate has tended to polarize around the question of whether the state or the economy is the primary source of power and social change. However, as Anthony Giddens argues (1990: 10–12), these orthodox ways of characterizing modernity are being met with an increasingly widespread skepticism. Many contemporary theorists emphasize instead that modernity is a multidimensional, multicausal, and interpenetrating set of social phenomena, emerging originally within Europe perhaps as early as the fifteenth century. It was decisively articulated in eighteenth-century Enlightenment texts, actively disseminated throughout the world, and reached its apogee in the middle decades of the twentieth century (e.g., Giddens 1990; Hall, S. 1992). Its main features can be described under the five headings discussed below.

i. The Economy. The capitalist economy is expanded worldwide, coercively and unevenly. A large-scale, industrial manufacturing base develops in the West, oriented toward mass production and consumption and organized in large-scale, mechanized, "Fordist" assembly lines. Populations concentrate in urban centers. Two major class groupings emerge: the property-owning bourgeoisie and the property-less proletariat, both stratified by ethnicity and gender and becoming more heterogeneous over time. States increasingly intervene in the management of the economy. Capitalism and industrialism are bolstered by ideologies of technological optimism and progress (e.g., Hall, J. 1985: 148–152, 171–179; Bradley 1992; Allen 1992a).

ii. The State. The means of waging war and raising taxes are monopolized and centralized by a single authority recognized as sovereign within a territory. State boundaries and institutions reflect and entrench hierarchical class arrangements; national cultural formations; and competitive, militaristic, interstate relations. This system is exported from Europe through imperialism and the subsequent diffusion of principles of self-determination. State regulative capacities and responsibilities for social provision gradually expand (e.g., Held, D. 1992a; McGrew 1992b; Watson, A. 1984).

iii. The Household and Family. The household/family unity shrinks in size. It is formally separated out from production processes through a hierarchical division of labor, which involves female responsibility for domestic work and male responsibility for economic provision, and which is underpinned by ideologies of women's domesticity and the home as sanctuary. Romantic love and sexual intimacy are emphasized as the foundations of marriage. Working-class women continue to combine domestic with productive work, in roles increasingly differentiated from those of men (e.g., Weeks 1981: 24–33, 201–214; Elliot 1986: 34–72, 77–82; Bradley 1992).

iv. Culture. Culture becomes secularized, rationalized, and individuated. Hierarchies emerge between the monumental and the ephemeral, high and popular art forms, masculine and feminine expression, western and non-western ways of life. Cultural dynamism is welcomed and form is increasingly emphasized over content. Cross-class lifestyle convergence is facilitated by mass production and consumption, the increasing reach of the media, and the consolidation of national identity (e.g., Bocock 1992: 120–133; Anderson 1991: 22–46; Harvey 1989: 10–38).

v. Ontology and Epistemology.   Notions of the self as unitary, self-contained, and competitively egoistic become dominant. Reality is largely understood to be external to the subject, comprehensible through objective observation and rational logic. Those people associated with such traits are privileged as actors and knowers. Simultaneously, universalizing discourses of truth, equality, and freedom proliferate into different domains (e.g., Touraine 1995; Hamilton 1992; Connolly 1988; Jaggar 1989; Lloyd 1989).

My account here is necessarily partial, even idiosyncratic. Other multidimensional approaches to modernity break it down into different analytical categories. For example, Giddens separates industrialism from capitalism and the surveillance dimension of the state from its military capacities (1990: 55–63). Few, though, draw attention to the household and family; this is a feminist-influenced addition. It should also be stressed that the precise details of the phenomena described are heavily contested. Modernity has been disseminated unevenly across time and space and has given rise to contradictory developments and counter-tendencies, including oppositional activisms and rejectionist theoretical formulations. Nonetheless, the above framework delineates significant trajectories and continuities in the development of modernity that help to contextualize the reemergence of democratic ideas and institutions.

The Reemergence of Democracy

The term *democracy* stems from the ancient Greek words *demos* (people) and *kratos* (rule) (Held, D. 1996: 1). A form of government bearing the label first emerged in Athens in the fifth century B.C. It should not be idealized, given that it was originally established by the aristocratic leader Kleisthenes to bolster his position in factional struggles (Dunn 1992: 240). It was also predicated on the political exclusion and labor of women and an enormous slave population, and it drew a sharp distinction between the rights accorded to Athenian-born men and others (Held, D. 1996: 13–15, 23–24). It was in these circumstances that a system of citizen self-rule was established: rule *by* the people, albeit with "the people" defined in narrow terms. All citizens were equally entitled to attend, vote, and speak at the Assembly. They were also expected to staff administrative, judicial, and military positions, mostly drawn by lot. This system of extensive civic participation aimed to achieve freedom of the individual and to sustain collective political agency (Dunn 1992: 241–242; Held, D. 1996: 15–23). It was also prone to manipulation by informal networks of influence, by those with rhetorical skill, and by emergent factions, and it could generate hasty, unreflective, and unstable decisions. Its duration for nearly two centuries may have been due more to military success than internal stability, with defeat in war eventually leading to collapse (Held, D. 1996: 25–28; Dunn 1992: 244).

Although democratic ideals continued to fire radical struggles from tenth-century millennial cults to the Levellers of the English Civil War, they were not systematically rearticulated and institutionalized until the end of the eighteenth century. It took another century and a half for democracy to be extended to the majority of the population in most western states, before accelerating in half a century to encompass most of the globe. What interests me here are the ways in which democracy was reconfigured by the context in which it was revived.

One important factor is the close relationship of modern democracy to the development and expansion of the industrial capitalist economy. Both share a common foundation in individuation and social mobility, the standardization of literacy and social skills, and the extension of civic rights and social autonomy (Lewis 1992: 27). However, a reductive account of democracy as a product of capitalism, or as straightforwardly functional for it, should be avoided. After all, capitalism continues to operate securely in authoritarian contexts. Democratic institutions emerged in certain contexts only after the protracted struggles of social groups who frequently hoped to mitigate or even transcend the capitalist order and who had to overcome the resistance of elites. Nonetheless, it is indisputable that the specifically liberal form of democracy that emerged in the course of the nineteenth century did not "challenge the *modus operandi* of capitalism or the economy of modern capitalism but rather helped to stabilize the socio-political conditions under which it operated" (Lewis 1992: 27). Exactly why this particular compromise emerged remains contested. The role of strategic alliances between elements of the bourgeoisie and working classes has been stressed by some (Lewis 1992: 27–28). Others have emphasized the significance of the prior development of liberal ideas about personhood and society. These had the potential for a radical political impact in authoritarian contexts but were not specifically democratic and, further, naturalized the operations of the market economy and class-divided society within which they were formulated (Barber 1984: 4–25; Macpherson 1977: 10–11, 20–24).

The state system has been another significant influence on modern democracy. In keeping with the aspiration to institutional differentiation characteristic of modern social life, democracy has been limited in scope to the sphere of the state. This has two dimensions. First, democracy has been channeled through, directed at, and played out in state institutions; the state may then act on economic, civic, and family life, but these domains have generally not themselves been constituted according to democratic principles. Second, democratic institutions end abruptly at the boundaries of the nation-state. The Janus-faced concept of sovereignty has played an important role here as the "point of intersection . . . separating community within from relations between states" (Walker, R. B. J. 1990: 171). The *external* dimension of sovereignty has changed over time from a claim about the absolute demarcation of distinct political authorities to a more conditional notion constrained by international law but still not dependent on democratic principles. The *internal* dimension of sovereignty has shifted from an assertion about the absolute power of the monarch to a claim that authority resides in the will of "the people," resulting in an irreducible tension between the demands of state and popular sovereignty (Held, D. 1995: 38–46, 73–98).

Nationalist ideology and identity have then played an important role in fixing the parameters of the people in terms of those within a clearly defined territory sharing ethnic and/or cultural commonalities. Democratic principles have encouraged increasing inclusivity within the national community, but they have not challenged its territorial boundaries. Further, militarism and war have frequently functioned to consolidate both national identities and democratic institutions. Citizenship has been tied to military participation, with the extension of compulsory service associated with the expansion of democratic rights to new constituencies and into new social and economic areas (Shaw 1997: 26–32). However, in contrast to ancient Greece, modern war has been perceived as an external matter, its operations largely removed from democratic scrutiny. In sum, the state appears to have triumphed over democracy, converting it "from unruly and incoherent master to docile and dependable servant" (Dunn 1992: 248).

The Rise of Social Movements

Alan Scott claims that social movements "are a product of 'modernity'" (1992: 130). This seems to me to be unduly restrictive. What of medieval millennial cults or groups active in the turmoil of the English Civil War, as mentioned earlier? Many such groups might meet the criteria laid down in the introduction, including mass participation, the formation of collective identity, and commitment to social change. The issue here may be definitional rather than historical. Certainly, my understanding of social movements does not confine them per se to the modern era.

However, it is undeniable that distinctive kinds of movements have developed in modernity. On this point, marxists stress the causal role of the change to a capitalist mode of production and the emergence of a property-less proletariat, working in urban concentrations and possessing the capacity for large-scale mobilization (e.g., Arrighi et al. 1989: 77–83). Others have developed more multidimensional analyses, emphasizing the role of urbanization, state consolidation, and technological innovation, particularly in print media, in enabling national-level and state-oriented movement organizing (Tarrow 1998: 43–67; Anderson 1991: 9–46). There is general agreement among most social movement theorists that the key forms of mobilization that have arisen in modernity are working-class movements and nationalist movements. The relative importance of each and their impact on modernity remain heavily contested. Although nationalist movements have been seen by many as a critical factor in the development of the state system and accompanying notions of identity and community, some marxists have highlighted their reactive and manipulated nature (Anderson 1991; Hobsbawm 1990). Marxists have emphasized instead the revolutionary potential of workers' movements, seeing them as potentially transformatory of modernity. In contrast, other commentators have characterized workers' movements as "integrative," increasingly located within the institutions of state and pursuing the reformist goals of material redistribution and political rights (Melucci 1992: 46; Scott 1992: 140–142). Scott insists that their legacy should not be underestimated:

> The impact of workers' movements on the institutions of contemporary capitalist societies can hardly be overstated, even if they did not, or could not, secure the ends imputed to them by orthodox marxists. Modern social democratic parties stem from nineteenth century workers' movements, while the welfare state has, in part at least, likewise been moulded by them. (Scott 1992: 130)

Modernist Assumptions in Social and Political Thought

Clearly, the analysis of social movements and democracy is as bound to modernity as movement practices and democratic institutions themselves. Indeed, much social and political thought that has touched on these issues could be called *modernist* in its commitment to the institutions and potentials of modernity.[1] At least four shared assumptions can be identified. First, there is a tendency to privilege one or two social institutions of modernity as the most important sources of power, usually the economy and/or state. These approaches to power can be described as *monist* or *parallelist*, to borrow terms from the work of black feminist theorist Deborah King (1988: 45, 51). Second, modernist traditions share spatial and bounded notions of politics and society. Democratic and social movement activity is largely understood to stop sharply at the boundaries of states. It is also located outside of the domestic sphere. The relationship of democracy and movements to economic life is, however, heavily disputed. Third, modernist traditions of thought draw on a view of the political actor as coherent, unitary, and rational. Debate then centers on the relationship of this individual to society and the likelihood and desirability of individuals coming together to pursue their goals collectively. Fourth, and finally, modernist approaches share a commitment to social change. In contrast to the circularity, stoicism, and deference to tradition found in premodern thought, society is seen as intrinsically dynamic. Both liberals and radicals consider it possible and necessary to control and direct this dynamism to further freedom and equality (Pieterse 1992: 7–8). Beyond this modernist commitment to progress, however, a major dichotomy emerges between reformist advocacy of incremental change and a revolutionary belief in transformatory social upheaval. Advocates of transformation have tended to stress the necessary role of movements, whereas opponents have been suspicious of them.[2] Modernists from both sides of the divide have tended to agree that the state is a key site and source of change.

All these assumptions have been subject to sustained criticism from within modernist traditions and from the critiques that developed alongside them. Thus cosmopolitans of all political hues have disputed that the state is the appropriate limit of human community and democratic relationships. Anarchists have rejected the elevation of the state as the focus of political activity and aspirations. Romantics and freudian psychologists have clouded the transparent rational actor with elemental passions and subconscious desires. Feminists have criticized the tendency to replicate the long-standing assumption that the more uncontrollable and irrational aspects of personhood are distinctive to women, who are thus incapable of rational thought, and they have also argued against the exclusion of the domestic sphere from the political. These dissident voices indicate that modernist assumptions have never had an unchallenged empire within modernity and that their social and philosophical bases are, in many ways, contradictory, unstable, incomplete, and continually contested. Nonetheless, modernist assumptions have generated frameworks for understanding democracy and social movements that continue to be influential today. Predominant among these frameworks is liberalism.

Liberalism, Individualism, and Civil Society

Liberalism is rooted partly in the assumption that the state is the major source of power in modernity. The capacity of the state to intervene in economic arrangements and to threaten the life and limb of individuals receives particular attention. At the same time, the state is seen as necessary for the mediation of social conflict. Historically, democratic principles and institutions were grafted onto liberalism in an effort to both increase state sensitivity to the will of the people and legitimize state authority over the people. Barry Holden expresses the relationship between liberalism and democracy thus:

> Democracy, then, refers to the location of a state's power, that is, in the hands of people, whereas "liberal" refers to the limitation of a state's power. From this viewpoint, a liberal democracy is a political system in which the people make the basic political decisions, but in which there are limitations on what decisions they make. (Holden 1993: 17)

Liberals continue to dispute exactly how much power the state should have and how much power the people should have over and through the state. This question is crucial for liberals not only because of their empirical recognition of state capacities but also because of their underlying commitment to an individualist ontology. Liberal individualism holds that the essence of the self is presocial, analytically separable from the society in which it is located, with ends formed pre-politically and liable to conflict with the ends of others (Warren 1992: 8–9). It is this belief in a conflictual sociality that gives rise to the demand for an adjudicating power—as Benjamin Barber puts it, rather caustically, this is "politics as zookeeping" (1984: 20). More positively, liberals emphasize the capacity of the individual for rational self-determination. This "involves seeking the maximum area of free choice and action compatible with an orderly society" (Carter 1973: 118) and justifies constraints on state and popular influence over the individual.

Thus individuals are accorded legal and political citizenship rights, which, "though they are guaranteed . . . by the state, . . . are also, in an important sense, guaranteed *against* the arbitrary exercise of state power" (Hall and Held 1989: 177). Citizenship rights carve out a realm of autonomy for each citizen in the private sphere, identified in liberal thought with civil society and understood to be composed of familial, social, and commercial interactions. Civil society should be as free as possible from public or state interference, although it still requires a stable regulative framework that only the state can provide (Kumar 1993: 376–377, 387).[3] Freedom in civil society also requires the maintenance of private ownership of the means of production and a competitive market economy. In the public realm, citizenship rights enable the individual to express his or her will to the state by voting for a representative from a political party in periodic elections and, according to most liberals, by participating in supplementary interest groups. These circumscribed modes of participation are intended to ensure that state elites remain responsive to the electorate, but also that majority blocs and mass uprisings able to manipulate the state cannot develop, and that civil society remains insulated from state influence. Change within this system is then implemented through government policy, negotiated by political elites competing for state power.

Beyond these core precepts, there are significant differences within liberalism. Indeed, there are several distinct forms of liberalism, with diverse and even contradictory beliefs and goals. For one thing, liberals disagree over the purpose of democracy besides limiting state power. For "developmental" liberals, the aim is also to enable the moral and social development of the citizen. "Protective" liberals want to protect individuals from arbitrary decisions by their governors, and "democratic elitists" or "competitive elitists" hope to protect the governors from the whims of the masses. For "neoliberals," the main point is to protect the market from state efforts to seize and redistribute property (Held, D. 1996: 100–118, 177–185; Pateman 1970: 14; Kymlicka 1990: 95–159).

Another source of disagreement is the appropriate role and structure of the state. Neoliberals insist on a minimal state with powers limited to the guarantee of property rights. They are reacting against the postwar efforts of "welfare" liberals to build a redistributive state in mitigation of the social divisions of capitalism. "Pluralists" break the state down into its constituent parts and focus on the interrelationships of these parts with nongovernmental organizations (NGOs). The state as a whole is conceived as a passive mirror of the dominant interests of society, as an active broker between those interests or, more idealistically, as a neutral referee of the conditions in which diverse groups and interests can flourish (Dunleavy and O'Leary 1987: 41–49).

Furthermore, liberals differ over the moral weight and political role granted to the individual. In the democratic elitist model, although "everyone is free to compete for political leadership"—in the rather vacuous, formal sense in which "everyone is free to start another textile mill"—the role of most individuals, prone to ignorance and irrationality, is expected to be limited to voting (Schumpeter 1976: 271–272; see also Held, D. 1996: 185–198). Developmental theorists hold to a richer notion of citizenship, exercised through a range of public activities and constituting the prime vehicle for personal development (Held, D. 1996: 100; Macpherson 1977: 46–48).

Finally, liberals differ over the concept of civil society. On the developmental account, civil society allows for a plurality of lifestyles. For pluralists, civil society is a sphere of diverse power centers in which numerous groups share and barter power to prevent any one faction gaining control of the state (Held, D. 1996: 199–208). Democratic elitists and neoliberals tolerate interest group activity as long as this does "not impede market efficiency or burden the fundamental liberties of non-members" (Cohen and Rogers 1995: 14). However, in many of their accounts, the relationship between the people and the state is mediated predominantly by parties, and civil society is little more than a sphere of market interaction (Held, D. 1996: 199).

Clearly, these varieties of liberal opinion carry conflicting implications for thinking about social movement activity. Most varieties can accommodate the formally organized, visible aspects of movements, in terms of political parties and interest groups. Parties can be defined, not without controversy, as "associations which participate in elections in liberal democracies with the aim of taking part in the process of government and which have a comprehensive platform, a definite philosophy and a permanent and extensive organization" (Graham 1993: 54). Such associations have been sanctioned by developmental and pluralist liberals on the grounds that they provide a conduit for individual participation in government and represent the interests of groups of individuals to the state. In contrast, democratic elitists have argued that parties are necessary to enable organized competition within ruling groups (Graham 1993: 3–16; Held, D. 1996: 169–170).[4] As this competitive function has gained in significance, parties have been increasingly attacked from within liberal democracy by those fearing the narrowing of political debate and the development of unresponsive bureaucratic hierarchies.

It is at this point that interest groups have received attention, particularly from pluralists. Some theorists prefer the term *pressure group, lobby group,* or even *nongovernmental organization* (NGO), but *interest group* seems most established among pluralists, particularly in the United States. It indicates a formal organization, independent of government, with a more issue-specific platform than a political party, reflecting the particular interests of its members. Interest groups lobby or pressure parties, governments, and intergovernmental organizations in accordance with these interests—some groups do so continually, others engage with the political system only episodically. They do not aspire to become part of government, like parties, but rather to influence public policy when necessary (Budge et al. 1998: 283–290; Richardson 1993: 1; Grant 1995: 3–5, 9–13; Willetts 1982a: 1). Pluralists have argued that interest groups are a necessary supplement to the party system, which by itself cannot secure an equilibrium of power in democratic states or ensure that all interests are represented within states or between them (Held, D. 1996: 201–208). As Ian Budge et al. put it:

> In theory, groups play an important part in democracy. They are an important means of political participation and influence, especially for minorities. They collect and sort out group opinions to produce an agreed position (interest aggregation), and defend these opinions in the political arena (interest articulation). Groups inform and educate their members about political issues, and act as channels of communication between citizens, and between

citizens and political elites. They mobilise citizens politically, and act as cen-
tres of influence outside government. . . . For their part, governments obvi-
ously have a democratic duty to consult with all interests affected, including
organised groups, and may depend upon them for policy information and
implementation. (Budge et al. 1998: 300)

There is an affinity here between pluralism and the resource mobilization approach in social movement theory. Both approaches share a focus
on the role of groups—whether defined as interest groups or social
movement organizations (SMOs)—in mobilizing resources and constituencies and pursuing interests in or against the state system (Mc-
Carthy and Zald 1977: 1218–1219). Resource mobilization theory developed partly in response to Mancur Olson's rational choice critique of the
pluralist assumption that groups would naturally and spontaneously
arise in society. Following Olson (1993), resource mobilization theorists
accept that participation in a collectivity may not necessarily be rational
for the self-interested individual, so they zoom in on the precise levels of
resources and leadership strategies required to encourage mobilization
and to gain political influence (Baumgartner and Leech 1998: 65, 67–68,
75–77; Scott 1990: 110). Nonetheless, the basic focus and the conclusions
reached are very similar to those of pluralism.

In my view, the shared focus on formal groups and their lobbying activities is a limited one that misrepresents movements. This is not to deny
the existence of significant organizational and ideological overlaps between movements and interest groups or parties. European social democratic parties originated in particular strands of the workers' movement;
Green efforts to organize a party along nontraditional lines suggest that
movements can still spawn parties; and interest groups in the United
States often "perform many of the functions of political parties such as
campaigning, providing political candidates with organization, funds,
and publicity" (Wilson 1981: 5). Movements can also give rise to interest
groups, one of countless examples being the links between the feminist
movement in the United States and the high-profile National Organization of Women (NOW). Nonetheless, movements are not reducible to
their more formal manifestations because they also have significant subterranean, cultural, extra-institutional dimensions. Pluralists and resource mobilization theorists are likely to neglect this side of movements
or to downplay its political significance.

This is in part because of their shared commitment to an empiricist
methodology that encourages a focus on the more visible and quantifi-
able aspects of movement activity (Smith, M. J. 1993: 3–4). Two underlying liberal assumptions are also significant. First, both approaches subscribe to an asocial individualist ontology that, among other things,

makes it difficult to conceive of the possibility of cooperative collective action unless defined in narrowly rational and instrumental terms. Although pluralists and resource mobilization theorists may disagree about the precise nature and difficulty of the mechanisms by which diverse individuals come together in a group, both approaches transfer the competitive pursuit of interests between individuals to the group level. The more identity-based dimensions of collective action and the solidaristic relationships that they may draw upon or generate are rendered invisible by this move, or are likely to be criticized as obscuring material interests, giving rise to totalizing demands, and hampering political effectiveness. Yet this is a one-sided picture of collective action. Critics have pointed out that even formal, institutionally oriented groups draw on forms of identity and modes of cooperation, including solidarity and friendship, to gain and sustain membership participation and political influence (Fireman and Gamson 1988: 21–32; see also Taylor 1995). Further, these elements of collective action may be of defining, and growing, centrality to the broader category of social movement activism, of which formal groups are but a part.

This brings me to the second liberal assumption at work: the acceptance of a division between state and civil society and the accompanying tendency to presume that real politics takes place within state institutions or is oriented toward them. As we shall see later, this move has been criticized by marxists for its separation of politics from economic realities and by feminists for the way it functions to exclude women from public life and to define their concerns as nonpolitical. The key point to note here is that pluralists and resource mobilization theorists tend to measure movement influence and success by the extent of inside track collaboration with state bodies and parties. Extra-institutional or cultural movement activities are consequently defined as nonpolitical and largely futile (Budge et al. 1998: 292–300; contrast with Grant 1995: 15–23, 141–143; Willetts 1982b: 181–182). Yet this is to buy into a narrow conception of politics and of the possibilities for social change that many movements would reject. It may also be a misinterpretation of the historical development of movements and the relationship of formal groups to them. As Warren Magnusson argues:

> We identify movements with the organizations that purport to embody them, and suppose that when the organizations are flourishing, so are the movements. The reality is that the death of an SMO may be an effect of the success of the movement itself. Once certain ways of acting are embedded in the culture, the organizations that called for them may seem superfluous. Of course, this is often an illusion, but it can take time for people to realize how much more change in the culture is required. Once this recognition spreads,

a new generation of SMOs is liable to emerge. . . . [T]he work of great social movements is never done . . . the organizations they create are bound to be temporary. (Magnusson 1993: 123)

Pluralists and resource mobilization theorists thus have a circumscribed conceptualization of the role of movements in democracy. Many pluralists also express strong reservations about that role. Although groups are acknowledged as necessary for democracy, they are also seen as potential threats because they "may help to stabilize injustices, deform civic consciousness, distort the public agenda, and alienate final control over the agenda" (Dahl 1982: 40). In part, this reservation about groups stems from the legitimate fear that group competition for influence may be unbalanced and unfair, enabling a minority to gain disproportionate power and influence. Consequently, pluralists emphasize the mechanisms by which power is dispersed, the necessity and inevitability of "countervailing" forces developing to balance every interest that organizes itself, and the need for the state to act on behalf of unorganized interests (Smith, M. J. 1993: 16–17; Dunleavy and O'Leary 1987: 32–37). These arguments have rightly been criticized as complacent, given the structural and cumulative power of business, which gains it privileged access to government and control over the political agenda (Dunleavy and O'Leary 1988: 292–299). Another dimension of pluralist unease about groups centers on their perceived partiality, emotiveness, and single-issue focus. This means that groups are seen as potential threats to the impartial, rational conduct required in the public realm of state and to efforts to cobble together broadly representative electoral platforms. Pluralists hope that the potentially atomizing effects of collective activity will be mitigated by all groups recognizing the rationality of adhering to the rules of the game. However, most movements have extra-institutional dimensions outside the remit of those rules, and many movement participants reject the rules altogether. At this point, pluralists turn to the state to set and enforce a constraining framework, although this move may be in tension with the desire of some pluralists to depict the state as just one group among many (Hirst 1990: 16–18).

Rather more problematically, democratic elitists insist that the state must actively preempt and prevent extra-institutional mobilization. Thus we finally uncover an open hostility toward movements within liberalism. Historical studies have demonstrated that this liberal hostility stems from deep-rooted fear of non-elite involvement in politics because of the supposed threat it poses to economic and political privilege (Macpherson 1972: 5; Wood 1995: 225–230). There are affinities here with the characterization by collective behavior theorists of movements as illegitimate, irrational mass responses to dysfunction in society. One example of an argument that bridges these theories is Samuel Huntington's analysis of the movement activism in the United States in the late 1960s and early 1970s widely known as the "New Left" (see below). Although Huntington recognized that this activism was rooted in American participatory traditions, he insisted that it was evidence of a "democratic distemper" that threatened to undermine the democratic institutions that already existed. He argued that those institutions required a period of realignment to adjust to changing demands—and a more apathetic citizenry (1975: 106–114). This argument severely curtails non-elite involvement in politics and the possibility of fundamental change in existing institutions. As David Held puts it:

> the only full participants are the members of political elites in parties and in public offices. The role of ordinary citizens is not only highly delimited, but it is frequently portrayed as an unwanted infringement on the smooth functioning of "public" decision making. All this places considerable strain on the claim of competitive elitism to be democratic. Little remains of the case for democracy except the sheer "protection-against-tyranny" argument. (Held, D. 1996: 198)

For neoliberals, on the other hand, little remains of the case for democracy except its role in protecting citizens against the supposed tyranny of state redistribution, thus guaranteeing the exercise of negative freedoms, particularly economic freedoms, in private life. In contrast to more interventionist forms of liberalism, neoliberalism positions the market economy as the *context* for democracy, not as an *issue* for democratic discussion. Although there are important differences between neoliberalism and democratic elitism, particularly in terms of the extent of the regulatory and redistributive role they would allow the state, there is also an unhappy convergence here in that attempts to challenge the limitations that have been imposed on participation and to subject the political and/or economic system to more extensive popular scrutiny are positioned as attacks on democracy itself. I would suggest that the fundamental problem with these two variants of liberalism may be less an antipathy to *collective* action than a desire to erase *oppositional* action. Democracy has been transformed from rule *by* the people into the elite enforcement of laws *for* the people, laws that are not open to popular contestation. The famously elastic concept is stretched to the breaking point.

This reconceptualization of the relationship between activism and democracy seems particularly misguided when we examine the historical role of movements in the constitution of liberal democracy. Political fictions about the origins of liberalism in the logically compelling nature of a social contract frequently obscure this role, but it is undeniable that liberal regimes in the United States and France were actually established through revolutions involving great swaths of the population, with the organization of the economically powerful and politically articulate proving crucial. The subsequent limitation of the franchise to propertied white men was then challenged by movements that frequently drew on the promise of liberal democratic discourse. As we have seen, debate still rages over whether the extension of liberal democratic rights to new constituencies and social and economic areas was granted by elites or won from below and whether this extension is evidence of movement victory or co-optation. David E. Apter takes a middle route. He insists on the impact of diverse struggles around liberal democracy: the extra-institutional protests of civil rights movements, trade unions, and women's suffrage struggles; the revolutionary insurrection of Jacobinism; and the activities of terrorist groups. He concludes that "emancipatory movements of all three types have been intrinsic to the evolution of democracy itself. Equally clearly . . . none of these movements ever fully succeeds on its own terms" (Apter 1992: 141). The "velvet revolutions" of 1989 in East Central Europe, for example, serve as a reminder that the struggle to implement and reconstruct liberal democratic norms still continues.

Marxism, Historical Materialism, and Class Struggle

Despite the collapse of marxist-influenced regimes in East Central Europe, the work of Karl Marx remains a potent source of criticism of the bourgeois limitations of liberal democracy. Marx attacked liberal democracy partly on ontological grounds. He was critical of abstract assumptions about human nature—insisting, according to Held, that "[i]ndividuals only exist in interaction with and relation to others; their nature can only be grasped as a social and historical product" (Held, D. 1996: 122). Further, Marx argued that individuals are not only social but also profoundly sociable, capable of a collective existence he called "species-being." This led him to insist that the political emancipation of the individual under liberalism was limited by the division between public political life, where the citizen is valued as a communal being, and the privatized vicissitudes of civil society, in which the individual is granted rights reifying the competitive egotism encouraged by capitalism (Marx 1977: 46–57; Schecter 1994: 6–7; Femia 1993: 16–28).

A second plank of Marx's critique was sociological (Femia 1993: 46–55). He developed an historical materialist explanatory framework, which begins from the assumption that civic, ethical, and political institutions "are not to be grasped from themselves nor from the so-called general development of the human mind, but rather have their roots in the material conditions of life" (Marx 1977: 389). Change in society is understood to be driven primarily by contradictions between the forces and relations of production, the latter organized into antagonistic social classes. On this view, the liberal democratic state is not an independent, impartial mediator of competing interests but either a direct instrument of the bourgeoisie or a superstructural expression of their underlying social power, perhaps capable of "relative autonomy" at moments of exceptional parity in class struggle (Dunleavy and O'Leary 1987: 209–211; Miliband 1989: 85–93). Civil society stands stripped down to its "anatomy . . . in political economy" (Marx 1977: 389). Its location outside the state and politics is revealed as ideological, leaving the coercions of capitalism untouched and rendering citizenship rights hollow (Wood 1995: 234).

It is sometimes presumed that Marx did not put forward an alternative conceptualization of democracy. This is partly a problem of his "overwhelming emphasis on economics," which "left the precise institutions of political power that were to shape the larger process of economic transformation unaddressed" (Boggs 1995: 32). It is also partly a problem of terminology. Marx argued that the revolutionary seizure of power should be followed by the abolition of socioeconomic inequality, private property, and the bourgeois state through the establishment of what he called "the dictatorship of the proletariat." C. B. Macpherson argues that this phrase can be interpreted as a return to the original sense of democracy as "rule *by* the people," in contrast to rule by a small elite of exploiters, given that Marx believed the proletariat to be a universal class (Macpherson 1972: 14–15). The concept of the dictatorship of the proletariat does, however, also seem to imply the extension of state power over social functions (Held, D. 1996: 141). From this starting point, three versions of marxist democracy can be distinguished (following Femia 1993: 68–142), each of which can draw legitimacy from different aspects of Marx's work. All share the view that democracy should be expanded over economic and social life but adopt quite divergent stances toward the state.

One variant is "participatory" marxism, which assumes that the extension of state power through the dictatorship of the proletariat will be temporary. Such an interpretation draws inspiration from Marx's argument that the end of the class struggle would mean the end of political conflict and the division between civil society and the state, the functions of government being reduced to matters of routine administration. To all intents and purposes, as Lenin insisted, this implies the "withering away of the state" (Held, D. 1996: 146–147). A model of decentralized and participatory administration along these lines is provided by Marx's analysis of the Paris Commune of 1871, in which he endorsed the communard system of a deliberative body fusing executive and legislative functions, constituted by mandated delegates paid workers' wages, and sending delegates to a larger regional body, which in turn nominates delegates to a national body, and so on (Marx 1977: 539–551; Held, D. 1996 144–147; Femia 1993: 69–76). This implies a pyramidal political structure in which authority flows from the bottom upward. Briefly manifested in the establishment of soviets in the early days of the Russian Revolution, this model of democracy continued to garner support from marxists like the "Council Communists," with their emphasis on the devolution of authority to workplace committees. It also resonated with the participatory schemes of anarchists and of nonmarxist socialists like G. D. H. Cole (Femia 1993: 77–79; Boggs 1995: 47–55; Schecter 1994: 11–15, 74–124; Cole 1920).

The victory of Lenin's Bolsheviks in the Russian Revolution instituted the dominance within marxism of what Femia calls "vanguard democracy" (1993: 118–141). Although Lenin apparently endorsed the "withering away of the state" and called for "all power to the soviets," he also advocated the seizure of the state by a centralized party vanguard. This, he argued, would gain democratic legitimacy from the soviets and would build a new, more democratic kind of state (Schecter 1994: 10–11; Boggs 1995: 42–47). It remains heavily disputed whether the anti-statist elements of Lenin's argument were a cynical ploy, or whether his argument was flawed or distorted in implementation by the exigencies of counter-revolution and war. The fact remains that, under Lenin's leadership, the institutions of party and state were fused, and centralized control was established over the soviets, effectively redirecting authority from the top of the pyramid down to the base.[5] Joseph Femia argues that such a move is rooted in the belief that the working class has objective interests, discernible through the application of a marxist framework, irrespective of the stated wishes of the workers themselves. From this it is a short step to the belief that a vanguard elite with knowledge of those objective interests can legitimately claim to rule on behalf of the working class, even without the overt consent of its members. This involves a transformation of the meaning of democracy from government *by* the people into government *for* the people (Femia 1993: 120–121). This is uncomfortably, and perhaps surprisingly, close to the position of elitist liberals described above, revealing a common antipathy to popular participation in political processes and indicating the authoritarian direction in which such antipathy can lead.

The third version of marxist democracy to which Femia draws attention is labeled "parliamentary." Proponents are state-centric, like vanguardists, but they draw heavily on notions of its relative autonomy to argue for the possibility of deploying extant liberal democratic state institutions against capital, thus justifying the organization of a party within the system to gain state power consensually (Hunt 1980: 16–18). Such a strategy was advocated early on by Eduard Bernstein and Karl Kautsky, who differed over whether it would lead to a revolutionary or gradual transition to a socialist society (Boggs 1995: 38–42; Femia 1993: 97–101; Hindess 1980: 23–26). Subsequently, Antonio Gramsci's arguments were influential. Gramsci identified the cultural and institutional dimensions of civil society as crucial sites of the construction of consensual class control, or hegemony. He argued that class struggle should be redirected to these dimensions of civil society with the aim of challenging the established order from within in a long term "war of position" (Hoare and Smith 1971: 210–276; Cox 1993: 50–58). Although Gramsci ultimately remained committed to vanguard politics, a gradualist road became dominant in major western communist parties. These submerged themselves, along with nonmarxist socialists and welfare liberals, in the social democratic consensus that emerged after World War II. The consensus hinged on the idea that social justice and substantive citizenship rights could be guaranteed by continued growth and redistribution by a welfare state, rather than by social ownership of the means of production. Participating "Eurocommunist" parties differed in their levels of commitment to more profound structural reforms of capitalism and in the degree to which they distanced themselves from leninist vanguard organizing (Boggs 1995: 95–138; Femia 1993: 104–115).

Despite their differences, these participatory, vanguard, and parliamentary strands of marxist democracy are all much more receptive than liberalism to notions of social movement. Their shared commitment to a view of individuals as socially embedded and sociable means that collective action is seen not only as possible, but as probable and desirable. Furthermore, the common underlying historical materialist framework identifies a primary social division from which collective action arises and provides a concrete basis for collective identification. Structuralist interpretations of marxism may undermine any notion of conscious political agency, but other readings assert that classes achieve political agency when their members become conscious of a shared interest and a class "for itself" emerges from a class "in itself." This class can then have a transformatory impact on society. Sidney Tarrow concludes that the marxist tradition has provided the skeleton of contemporary social movement theory:

Marx focused on the cleavages of capitalist society that created a mobilization potential (what students of social movements would later call "grievance theory"); Lenin created the movement organisations that were necessary to structure it and prevent its dispersion into narrow corporate claims (what would later be called "resource mobilization" by American scholars);

and Gramsci centred on the need to build consensus around the party's goals (what has come to be called "framing" and "collective identity" formation). (Tarrow 1998: 13)

However, marxism has limitations as a framework for understanding social movements. For Tarrow, the problem is that it provides no specification of the political conditions in which workers' mobilizations are likely to be effective. A more deep-rooted difficulty, I would argue, lies with the historical materialist framework. This can be interpreted in more or less rigid ways, but it tends to encourage readings of movement activity that are not simply monist but, more precisely, economistic: privileging and universalizing economic explanatory factors and elevating class as the primary source of social conflict and struggle. Indeed, collective action is understood to derive from and reflect class identity and interests. Transformatory potential is limited to workers' movements, burdening these with a weight of historical responsibility that they have rarely shouldered. Other movements, from feminism to environmentalism, are squeezed into constraining class categories, "annexed" to what is seen as the more fundamental, class-based, struggle against capitalism (Pieterse 1992: 19), or dismissed as mystifying, bourgeois distractions.

This brings me to a larger problem with marxist theory and practice, namely the restricted character of its reconstruction of democracy. Many of Marx's criticisms of liberal democracy remain trenchant, and his conclusion that democracy should be expanded into social life is particularly important. However, the economism of the historical materialist framework limits the scope of marxist democracy in other ways. To give one example, socialist feminists attempting to organize within and among marxist groups have struggled to expose the ways in which economism militates against an acknowledgment of the autonomy or seriousness of gendered dimensions of power, leading to a failure to expose these to scrutiny. This has functioned to stifle the construction of both more inclusive organizational forms within marxism and possible links with autonomous feminist groups. It has also encouraged the complacent presumption that the collapse of capitalism will automatically usher in a world free of gendered hierarchies and exclusions (see, e.g., Rowbotham 1979; Segal 1979; Molyneux 1985). Such problems may be particularly acute where leninist models of organization prevail but are typical of marxist praxis more generally. Gramsci's reformulation of civil society broadened rather than pluralized marxist notions of power and contexts of struggle, and even participatory marxist aspirations have remained largely limited to the industrial workplace.

Marxism also faces the more serious charge that it carries *anti-demo-cratic* ramifications. Some have argued that the problem here is Marx's underlying social ontology and its potentially authoritarian implications. Marx is accused of "yearning for organic unity" (Keane 1988: 52) and of asserting "the priority of the 'whole' over the individual parts" (Femia 1993: 65). It can reasonably be countered that he retained a dialectical understanding of the relationship between the individual and the social that allows space for agency. The crucial problem, I would argue, is rather the meshing of a social ontology with historical materialism. This leads to an emphasis on identities and interests stemming from productive work, to the neglect or misrepresentation of other dimensions of personhood, such as the intimate relationships and reproductive work emphasized by feminists as central to many women's roles and identities (Held, V. 1993: 130–131; Jaggar 1988: 51–82). The blending of social ontology with historical materialism also encourages the reduction of conflict to class struggle and encourages the conclusion that conflict will disappear once class is abolished. The expression of other desires, interests, and identifications is thus delegitimized, and no protection is provided from noneconomic forms of domination, notably in the form of the state, the masses, and the party. This opens the way for extremes of state and party control. The oppressive nature of marxist-influenced regimes that have developed is therefore not entirely attributable to the pressures of circumstances or to unscrupulous misappropriations of Marx, but has roots in marxism itself (Keane 1988: 56–64; Boggs 1995: 33–36; Held, D. 1992b: 29–31; 1993: 297–300). The rise of the opposition movements within East Central European marxist-leninist regimes demonstrates that social movements, and the individuals within them, continue to resist the imposition of one causal logic to social life, one social divide, and one political goal.

Republicanism, Citizenship, and the Public Sphere

According to Paul Hirst (1990: 1), the western left has become "almost exclusively parliamentary-democratic" in recent years. It now aims to deepen the democratic nature of existing institutions rather than to abolish them. A variety of strategies have been adopted to this end. Here I want to focus on what Hirst identifies as a "new republican" tendency (1990: 3; see also Rengger 1994: 63). Republicans draw on a long-standing heritage, stemming from the ancient Greeks and Romans and filtered through the Renaissance civic humanists and Italian city-states, Jean-Jacques Rousseau, and Hannah Arendt. Although proponents of contemporary republicanism claim to be "distinctively modern" (Barber 1984:

117), they refuse to accept that the delegation of authority to large-scale bureaucratic systems is the necessary tragedy of modernity. Instead, they insist that face-to-face, participatory modes of politics, characteristic of ancient democracy, can and should be revitalized.

There are three major components of the contemporary republican approach. The first is the reformulation of citizenship. Whereas liberals construct citizens "as *strangers* to each other" (Yuval-Davis 1997a: 6), republicanism, like marxism, is predicated on a social and sociable ontology. Citizenship is conceptualized positively as enabling participation in the public processes of the community and is seen as the most important aspect of personhood (Barber 1984: 217–229; Habermas 1996: 22; Warren 1992: 11–13). The second feature is a stress on processes of collective deliberation, which are seen as enabling citizens to create common goods. For republicans, this is the moment of "the political," as opposed to the pursuit of disparate interests or conflictual class struggle. This moment will be *democratic* if all citizens have the opportunity to participate in debate, if their concerns are taken seriously, and if they are prepared to revise their initial positions in the collective interest (Wolin 1996: 31, 42–43; Phillips 1996: 143–144). The third republican move is the relocation of democracy to the public sphere. This should not be confused with the liberal sphere of civil society because it is sharply differentiated from both economic and family life (Phillips 1991: 16–17). It is more equivalent to the concept of the polity and it is manifested wherever citizens gather together to deliberate on matters of common concern. Processes of deliberation can be facilitated through traditional methods such as neighborhood meetings and civic education, as well as through new techniques like deliberative opinion polls and communications technologies that enable debate and voting by people in disparate locations (Barber 1984: 261–311; Fishkin 1991: 1–13; Budge 1996: 24–33, 181–188).

Some commentators treat republicanism as a form of liberalism. Certainly, many republicans do accept elements of a liberal representative framework, including parties, voting, and a developmental view of the empowering and "educative" nature of individual participation in political life (Pateman 1970: 22–35). Yet it should be noted that there are striking differences within republicanism that mean that some versions are closer to liberalism than others. A distinction should be drawn between procedural formulations and those concerned with politics as a "mode of being," between direct deliberative versions and those focusing on increasing voting opportunities, between unitary and pluralist views of the relationship of the individual to society, and between those emphasizing social duties and those keen to retain an emphasis on individual rights (Benhabib 1996a: 7–8; Habermas 1996: 23–26; Rengger 1994: 64–65; Rourke et al. 1992: 3–6; Barber 1984: 145–155, 220–225). Clearly, procedural, voting-based, pluralist, and rights-oriented interpretations of republicanism are closest to liberalism. I would add, however, that all republicans share an understanding of the individual as profoundly sociable and socialized along with an aspiration to consensus, however temporary, which distinguishes republicanism per se from liberalism.

Republicans also have a distinctive view of power, discriminating between productive and coercive forms (Mansbridge 1996: 46–51). The former is located in the collective capacity of the people to act and, in a fundamentally nonliberal move, is seen as a positive force. Coercive power is most often located in the state, in an echo of liberalism, although there are also some parallelist formulations, influenced by leftist critiques, which insist too on the coercive potential of the capitalist economy. Coercive power is seen as largely unnecessary given people's capacity for reconciliation through debate. It is also feared for its capacity to distort that debate. It thus needs to be restrained. State power can be curtailed by expanding rather than limiting the scope of the political. This is achieved by increasing collective capacity to achieve a notion of the common good and to ensure that the state enforces it, and by devolving state functions to make civic control easier (Rengger 1994: 65; Kymlicka 1990: 206–207). Economic power demands a combination of state-enforced reform of its antisocial tendencies and local initiatives to "push back" capitalist influence on civic life (Frazer 1997; Barber 1984: 251–257).

At first glance, with its emphasis on participatory forms of democracy and the central role granted to collective, cooperative political action, republicanism appears friendly to social movements. Indeed, collective actors are granted some role in the transition to a republican ideal in terms of providing information to citizens, representing interests, channeling support, and acting as "schools of democracy." However, republicans have little faith in the capacity of contemporary groups to undertake such tasks (Cohen and Rogers 1995: 22–23). To some extent, this is a legitimate response to the combative realities of contemporary interest group politics. It is also rooted in an antipathy to collective action except in highly circumscribed forms. A key problem here is the elevation of citizenship as the *only* political identity, sovereign over others. Thus Benjamin Barber dissects the complex identities of a "long-time family man living on Mulberry Street in New York whose grandfather came from Bologna and who is a shop steward in the sheet-metal workers' union." Barber asks, "how can such a fractured soul exhibit anything but cognitive dissonance and political schizophrenia?" (1984: 208). He suggests that people with such complex identities should subordinate these to citizenship, a move with uncomfortably assimilationist implications and one that is reliant on an idealized view of the inclusivity of citizenship. More fundamentally, Barber reveals an underlying modernist belief in the unified, coherent political subject that has been under attack since Freud. It is by no means self-evident that people with multiple identifications are not capable of multiple kinds of political action. I suggest that republicans are making a further claim here that only *one* type of collective action is socially desirable: that of citizens acting together in the polity. Thus they call for the "insulation" of processes of deliberation in the public sphere from other kinds of activism to ensure "orderly political deliberation and efficient achievement of publicly declared ends" (Cohen and Rogers 1995: 22–23). Clearly, activism that does not fit under the rubric of citizenship is assumed to be partial, irrational, and intransigent, with associated collective identities and interests not considered to be amenable to modification through discussion.

This is not an accurate reflection of complex movement realities. Alberto Melucci's "constructivist" approach demonstrates that a movement is "always a composite action system, in which widely differing means, ends and forms of solidarity and organization converge in a more or less stable manner" (1989: 28). One element in the construction of such an action system, or one result of it (Melucci is elusive on this point), is the formation of a collective identity through which participants establish relationships to each other, locate themselves in their environment, differentiate themselves from others, and gain recognition as a collectivity. There is always a tendency for the "we" that emerges to become reified, given movement aspirations for permanence and continuity and the modernist tendency of commentators to presume that movements are coherent, unified subjects. But collective identity should actually be understood as a process, one involving ongoing communication, negotiation, and decision making among movement participants (Melucci 1989: 34–35; 1996a: 68–86). Furthermore, as Giddens argues, it should be recognized that movements can deepen and extend communication processes in society more generally:

> The democratic qualities of social movements and self-help groups come in large part from the fact that they open up spaces for public dialogue in respect of the issues with which they are concerned. They can force into the discursive domain aspects of social conduct that previously went undiscussed, or were "settled" by traditional practices. (Giddens 1994: 17)

Thus, for example, movements of workers, women, and ethnic minorities have unsettled the established discourse of citizenship, bringing a new language of rights and duties within its compass and extending it to a wider cross-section of the community (Hall and Held 1989: 176; Barbalet 1988: 97–107; Lister 1997: 4–5). It is precisely movements such as these, which have struggled to deepen liberal democracy instead of accepting its reified parameters, that have given impetus to academic republican aspirations.

The erasure of the activist history behind the extension of citizenship brings me to problems with the republican theorization of democracy. Republican complacency about the inclusivity of the identity of citizenship seems misplaced. It constitutes citizenship as a prepolitical category into which people must fit, rather than recognizing that "issues around membership—who does and who does not belong—is where the *politics* of citizenship begins" (Hall and Held 1989: 175). Further, the close historical relationship between citizenship and national identity is either not questioned or is explicitly endorsed by contemporary republicans. This is because of an unreflective adherence to methodological nationalism or an overt commitment to national community as the basis of democracy (Miller 1998). Both of these positions need to be opened to critical scrutiny given the association of nationalism with homogenization and imperialist expansion, as well as self-government, and in the context of the challenges posed by globalization, discussed in Chapter 5. Somewhat anachronistically, republicanism "re-emphasizes the idea of a single effectively self-governing political community at the very moment when the nation state is being undermined and a complex multi-focal politics is developing" (Hirst 1994: 13).

A closely connected problem here is the republican emphasis on an autonomous public sphere. As with the national character of citizenship, the territorial boundaries of this sphere are removed from democratic scrutiny as the prepolitical condition of politics. The same applies for the boundary between the public sphere and private life. There is an extensive feminist literature on the exclusionary implications for women of the public/private divide, characteristic of both liberalism and republicanism, which will be discussed at more length in the next chapter. The narrow republican formulation of the public has been particularly criticized for being "itself a political act . . . for when that-which-has-to-be-excluded overlaps so closely with women's lives, it begins to figure as one of the mechanisms for keeping women in their place" (Phillips 2000: 12). Further, there is little sensitivity to the fact that what is deemed suitable for discussion in the public sphere changes over time and in different contexts. The republican insistence on the need to *insulate* the public from the private is thus a deeply conservative move, rendering it illegitimate, even anti-democratic, to organize collectively against privatized sources of power and to debate them publicly. Further, the republican *elevation* of the pursuit of politics in the public sphere as the most quintessentially human activity has been attacked for downgrading the importance of other domains of existence. Feminists have emphasized that the elevation of politics in this way has been founded historically on the exclusion of women to ensure that domestic, bodily, reproductive, and affective needs are catered to. Most contemporary reformulations of republican democracy have as yet failed to show how it can be more than the activity of an elite few, whose transcendence of everyday life is dependent on the fact that others remain embedded within it.[6]

Anarchism, Power, and Movement

Like republicanism, anarchism is rooted in the aspirations of modernity, yet its proponents often trawl the premodern past for alternative models of political life. Unlike republicanism, anarchism has largely fallen out of favor in contemporary political thought. This may be because it challenges deeply rooted methodologically national and statist assumptions. Efforts to identify a core doctrine frequently emphasize a shared "hostility to the state" (Miller 1984: 5).[7] The state, anarchists agree, was established by force and deception and its continued appropriation of power and political activity is based on a monopoly of violence. This encourages military rivalry and social hierarchy, enables the promulgation of universalizing laws, and coercively enforces obedience to them (Miller 1984: 5–8; Marshall 1993: 17–35; Bourne 1977; Spooner 1977; Tolstoy 1977; Thoreau 1977). The dominant "social" tradition within anarchism, which is rooted in European socialist debates, insists also on the significance and illegitimacy of capitalist power. Many proponents prioritize economic struggle, albeit in broader terms than their marxist counterparts. The labels commonly used to distinguish different strands within social anarchism—mutualist, collectivist, communist, syndicalist—indicate divisions over the best way to socialize the production, distribution, and exchange of goods (see summaries in Marshall 1993: 6–10; Schecter 1994: 24–62). This has led some commentators to characterize anarchism in parallelist terms as opposition to both state power and the capitalist order (Rocker 1969: 43). However, other institutions have also attracted anarchist criticism, particularly organized religion, marriage, and the family (e.g., Miller 1984: 8–9; Goldman 1970: 37–46). Thus it is possible to justify a more expansive definition of anarchism as opposition to relations and structures of hierarchical and coercive power, wherever they may occur.

More positively, anarchism is rooted in a belief in the possibility of individual self-determination and the likelihood of voluntary cooperation. This belief takes a variety of forms. "Individualist" anarchists work with a liberal ontology, occasionally in an acutely egoistic version, albeit with the twist that self-interest will induce cooperation. "Social" anarchists share Marx's view that egoist man is a product of specific conditions and insist that individuals have the capacity to be profoundly sociable. Although some social anarchists also share Marx's emphasis on the productive dimension of personhood, most have agreed that this is only one aspect of the multidimensional human potential that could be released in a noncoercive society (Marshall 1989; 1993: 36–42; Miller 1984: 62–75, 131–132). Strategies for achieving such a society are correspondingly diverse. Individualists are left reliant on the force of rational argument to persuade others to withdraw cooperation from the state (Miller 1984: 43). In contrast, many social anarchists, particularly syndicalists, have emphasized class struggle in workers' organizations (Miller 1984: 124–130; Woodcock 1977). However, even the most economistic have rejected the more rigid elements of historical materialism, including the notion of laws of history, the reduction of politics and culture to superstructural effects, and the restriction of revolutionary capacity to urban, industrial factory workers. Anarchists have tended instead to stress historical indeterminacy, the role of political will and ideas, and the agency of all of those marginalized by the operations of capitalism and the state, from the peasantry to the unemployed (Miller 1984: 79–86). Thus agitation within workers' internationals and trade unions has frequently been combined with, or displaced by, "propaganda by the deed" in the form of armed insurrection, terrorist acts, or nonviolent direct action. The intention has been to inspire the self-organization of a wide cross-section of the disadvantaged (Malatesta 1977; Miller 1984: 94–140; Guérin 1989: 112–116).

A further point to note is that these diverse strategies for change share a common rejection of state-centric politics and hierarchical, coercive organizational forms. This is because of the declared need to match means with ends—to pursue the goal of a noncoercive, voluntaristic society through forms of organization that embody and encourage these principles. At its most rigorous, this can lead to a rejection of violent tactics, as in the pacifist strand of anarchism. The other side of this coin is the attempt to "prefigure" a revolutionary future. Thus, for example, self-governing collectives are established before wholesale social transformation has been achieved, to enable individual self-determination in the here and now and to demonstrate the workings of a new society within the ruins of the old (Marshall 1993: 625–638; Miller 1984: 121–123).

The effort to synthesize individual freedom and participation in the collectivity, as part of the process of struggle as well as its goal, means that democracy is crucial to social anarchism (individualists rely on market forces to regulate the relations between individuals and are thus of no further concern to us here). Although some anarchists reject the language of democracy entirely, I suggest that it is the liberal and republican kinds they have in mind. Liberal democracy is criticized for resting ultimately on coercion rather than genuine consent, for generating self-perpetuating

elites, and for preventing individuals from participating actively in all
the decisions that affect their lives (Martin 1989; Marshall 1993: 22–24;
Tolstoy 1977; Bakunin 1977; Proudhon 1977). Republican-style democracy is rejected for encouraging nationalism and reinforcing the power of
the state (Marshall 1993: 32–35; Bourne 1977). In their stead, anarchists
develop a vision of democracy that is very close to that of participatory
marxists, albeit extended beyond the workplace: a system of self-governing workers' councils and communes in which all members participate
and which sends recallable delegates to coordinating bodies. In contrast
to marxists, anarchists insist that participation in such a system must be
entirely voluntary. All agreements should allow secession, and dissent
should be freely expressed (Miller 1984: 50–57; Statement of Principles
1989: 133, 158–159). Finally, a number of anarchists have rejected the institution of marriage, striving instead to reconstruct personal relationships according to principles of self-government, voluntarism, and consent (Goldman 1970: 37–46; Wexler 1986; Hewitt 1986). Arguably, this
move expands anarchist democracy into the most intimate areas of social
life.

Anarchism offers a radical and thoroughgoing framework for thinking
about the possibilities of participatory and voluntaristic democracy beyond the state. However, it has been criticized on several grounds, perhaps most particularly for its rejection of the state. David Miller, for one,
has drawn attention to the close relationship between the state and national identity. He argues that the latter provides the most resonant form
of collective identity in modernity and is the necessary foundation of
democracy (1984: 179–181; 1998). However, this is to ignore an extensive
literature on the social construction of nationality, its fraught relationship
to the state, and the exclusions it can generate. More convincingly, Miller
highlights the democratic role of the state in providing a stable and impartial framework of law that can pass judgment on antisocial behavior
and provide continuity and constraint for decision-making processes
(1984: 173–179). Although anarchists could legitimately respond that current law is *not* impartial but reflects entrenched interests, Miller is surely
right that to reject any kind of institutionalized decision-making framework, and to rely instead on moral self-regulation and collective deliberation, is a practice more suited to small, cohesive communities. It is also
open to possible abuses caused by moral conservatism and the vicissitudes of the general will. The question remains as to whether a system of
law providing continuity and constraint for public policy and judicial decision-making processes could be devised in a more participatory manner, subjected to regular scrutiny and implemented without the centralized coercive machinery of the state.

Another criticism of anarchist democracy centers on the tendency to idealize human relationships within anarchist organization. Some might suggest that this idealization arises from underlying ontological assumptions. The anarchist belief in an intrinsic cooperative capacity is frequently accused of being naive and of neglecting the more unsavory aspects of human character. John P. Clark (1978: 16–17) insists that this is not the case and that anarchists are rather all too aware of the capacity of power to corrupt individuals and their relationships. This is precisely why they are hostile to the idea that hierarchically organized groups can create a more egalitarian society. Further, Clark suggests that the anarchist belief in the possibility of cooperation is rooted in the relatively uncontroversial notion that human interactions are environmentally determined. Anarchists recognize that society needs to change for a cooperative capacity to flourish.

I would argue that a more fundamental problem here is the anarchist analysis of power. Abstractly, anarchists have recognized that there are multiple forms of power and that power is thus pervasive in society. Concretely, however, most have focused their energies on its manifestations in the state and/or capitalist economy. These may have been particularly brutal and naked forms of power in nineteenth-century European contexts, but an emphasis upon them also reflects the social locations of major anarchist thinkers who were not attuned to their own relatively privileged position in, say, racial and gender hierarchies. After all, patriarchal power was also particularly brutal and naked in its operations at this time. Women had few economic and civil rights and were legally constituted as male property. Racialized hierarchies of power were being reconfigured and retrenched with the rise of eugenicist ideology and increasing competitiveness over imperial acquisitions. The neglect of forms of power such as these encourages the belief that anarchist organizations free of state and capitalist intervention will be free of power and conflict altogether. This is likely to obscure other processes of power and privilege and to lead to the marginalization or suppression of efforts to organize against them. The problem of selective blindness is exacerbated by the tendency, shared with versions of marxism, to fetishize spontaneity of struggle during revolutionary change and to presume that revolution will abolish power per se, revealing more authentic social relations in which the individual and collective will be in natural harmony (Marshall 1993: 14–17). If these arguments are rejected, and sensitivity to the multiple forms that power can take is increased, then anarchists would have to pay attention to the way in which their associations are likely to be continually shaped and stratified by power and to devise modes of decision making and implementation that take this into account.

These inadequacies in the anarchist approach to power have ramifications for thinking about the role of social movements. As with marxism, the insistence that the sources of power and conflict will be abolished in a postrevolutionary society carries the implication that significant movement activity will disappear. I have argued above that this assumption has dangerously anti-democratic consequences and has been constantly challenged by movements. More positively, anarchism, like marxism, does grant a significant role to movements in the transition to a more democratic society. Unlike marxists, anarchists have defended and participated in a variety of forms of activism. Nineteenth- and early twentieth-century European workers' movements were at times anarchist in outlook, particularly between 1880 and the First World War (Miller 1984: 4). Anarchists have been involved in mass uprisings from the Ukrainian Makhnovist struggle to the Spanish Civil War (Marshall 1993: 453–478), and from the nonviolent Gandhian Sarvodhayan movement in India (Ostergaard 1989) to the students and anti–Vietnam War activists of the New Left, discussed below. This plurality of movement forms and strategies finds explicit justification in anarchist thought. A rejection of the more rigid elements of historical determinism in favor of an emphasis on political will and ideas encourages skepticism toward the claims of a single movement that it is the vanguard of history and instead supports experimentation in strategy. What is more, the anarchist aspiration to match means with ends and prefigure the future in the here and now strongly suggests that movement struggles should be participatory, nonhierarchical, and voluntaristic—in other words, anarchism points toward a model of democratic movement organization even if the general insensitivity to multiple forms of power means that this model remains incomplete.

Two other aspects of the anarchist approach to movements, rather less developed in the literature, should be mentioned here. First, the idea of prefiguration involves an assumption that participation in anarchist struggle can generate new ways of being, knowing and identification. This points to some awareness of the cultural dimensions and influence of movements and the potential role of cultural innovation in social change. Second, anarchist recognition of the need for change in intimate relationships hints at the idea that movements can straddle private and public spheres of life. However, most anarchists have failed to acknowledge this point. For example, Emma Goldman's pioneering work on women and marriage effectively separated the psychological struggle of the individual from collective, political organization. For Goldman herself, the emotional and social costs of such a separation were great (Wexler 1986).

These hints about movement practice in anarchism were developed more fully in the New Left movement of the 1960s. The New Left was a "diffuse movement of protests and radical thought . . . which swept through most of the countries of the West in the late 1960s" (Miller 1984: 141), encompassing student activism, shifts in left theorizing, and strong linkages with the widespread, youth-based countercultural phenomenon of the period (Lerner 1970: 431–444; Bookchin 1989: 259–262).[8] Participants in this movement were frequently not self-declared anarchists. They were attempting to break out of old left orthodoxies and forge a new politics beyond social democracy and marxist-leninism by drawing, more or less reflexively, on anarchist and participatory marxist traditions.

An anarchist sensibility was particularly noticeable in New Left attitudes to movement organization. Participatory, voluntaristic, small-group democracy was cultivated as the means and ends of struggle and because it was understood to prefigure a new relationship between the individual and collectivity (Breines 1989: 46–66). Anarchism was also echoed in the rejection of an exclusive reliance on the revolutionary potential of the working class (although efforts were made to forge connections with associated organizations). However, the anarchist emphasis on the revolutionary potential of all the *materially* marginalized was replaced by an emphasis on relatively affluent but *culturally* disaffected groups (Woodcock 1968: 57; Miller 1984: 143). The New Left also went beyond anarchism in the importance accorded to culture as a terrain of power and politics. The struggle against commodification and consumerism was emphasized, alongside efforts to create new values and reinvigorate "the everyday." This brought with it an overt recognition of the importance of the subterranean and symbolic aspects of movement activity in inducing long-term social change (Miller 1984: 143–151; Apter 1970; Woodcock 1968: 59–60; Marshall 1993: 542–546; Sakolsky 1989: 36–40). Finally, the New Left attempted to integrate changes in intimate relationships into movement struggle and accorded these changes broader subversive potential, encapsulated in slogans like "make love not war." As we see in Chapter 3, analysis on this point remained limited because of a continuing failure to recognize that the personal could be systematically shaped by relations and structures of power other than those of capitalism and the state.

The New Left as a mass movement had dissipated by the early 1970s, with the violence of state responses, the escalation of the Vietnam War, and the development of conflicts elsewhere in the third world encouraging a shift among many participants toward distinctly Old Left models of organization and terrains of struggle (Stafford 1970: 483–484; Lerner 1970: 434–436). However, it is also from this radicalizing milieu that many so-called new social movements emerged, including second-wave feminism. These movements carried both long-standing and new anarchistic ideas about democracy and movements into contemporary theory and activism.

TABLE 1 Modernist Traditions

	Ideal-type Democracy	Operations of Power	Terrain of Politics	The Political Actor	Strategies for Change	Role of Movements
Liberalism	representative, constrained state government via party competition for votes in elections	the state as source of power over and guarantor of civil society	limited to the institutions of state and political society	the individual as rights-bearing citizen pursuing prepolitical interests in the state and civil society	state policy, generated by political elites competing for votes and by pressure group activity	reduced to formal, public aspects as pressure group or party, or censured as de-stabilizing
Marxism	worker control over social life via self-governing workplaces or party control of state institutions	control of the forces of production; currently wielded by or manifested in the bourgeoisie	expanded to class struggle in the workplace, civil society, and the institutions of state	classes acting for themselves or parties acting for them	economic contradictions generate class conflict and crisis; workers' struggle can precipitate revolution	workers' movements are the universal emancipatory vehicle; on their victory, mobilization will end

Republicanism	collective will-formation in the public sphere through inclusive deliberation	productive capacity of the citizenry, distinct from coercive power of state and economy	limited to the public sphere, differentiated from the private, bounded by the nation-state	the individual as active citizen pursuing social goals through participation in the public	civic activism can build the republican ideal; change then negotiated through public deliberation	"good" groups welcomed as schools of citizenship; most seen as destructive of cohesion
Social Anarchism	participatory, voluntaristic communal self-government coordinated by mandated delegates	pervasive, structuring all areas of life, most obviously in the form of the state and capitalism	expanded to encompass social self-organization bypassing the state	the individual as sociable and cooperative, pursuing self-determination through the collective	diverse revolutionary strategies aimed at broad constituency; means should match and prefigure ends	multiple movements, democratically organized, agitating for change; no activism likely after transition

Conclusion

The four major modernist traditions of social and political thought are compared and contrasted in Table 1.

To sum up, liberalism, marxism, and republicanism are limited in their understanding of social movements and generally (although not entirely) hostile to movement activity. Liberal thought can encompass cooperative collective action only in narrowly instrumental and visibly institutional terms. Marxist economism privileges class as the source of social conflict and the vehicle of history, thus downplaying or suppressing other kinds of activism. Republican nostalgia for a unitary identity and unified public sphere disallows most collective contestation, unless well-behaved and oriented toward the general public good. Diverse movements are thus marginalized and misinterpreted, despite the fact that they have played a central role in the constitution and implementation of all three traditions. This points to limitations in accompanying democratic frameworks. Liberal democracy is confined to the institutions of state and predicated on the removal of the capitalist context from political scrutiny. Marxist democracy can be put on hold until after the revolution and is then based on the assumption that the end of class conflict will mean the end of all social conflict. This opens the way for suppression of dissent. Republican democracy aspires to public homogeneity, colluding with nationalist reifications and removing private concerns from political scrutiny.

All of these problems share a common root in underlying modernist assumptions. The traditions of social and political thought discussed here share a monist or parallelist approach to power and oppression. They tend to limit the location and scope of democratic politics, either to the institutions of state, to economic relationships, or to the public sphere. They view the political actor as unitary and elevate certain aspects of personhood over others. Possibilities for change are polarized between a reformism that removes the boundaries of the political from scrutiny and a consequentialist revolutionism in which democratic principles are easily sacrificed.

The neglected tradition of anarchism contests the parameters accepted by other modernist approaches. Emphasizing the power of the capitalist economy and liberal state, it also points toward the fact that power takes multiple forms and is pervasive in society. It challenges the boundaries imposed on democratic politics, bypassing the state altogether and extending democracy to the self-organization of society, including economic and, in some cases, intimate relationships. Anarchism emphasizes the social and complex nature of individuals. It undermines the reform/revolutionary dichotomy by insisting on the need for means to match the ends of struggle and for the prefiguration of future possibilities in the here and now. This encourages a participatory and expansive notion of democracy, a tolerance of diverse movement struggles in the transition to a more democratic society, and an emphasis on the importance of their constitution according to democratic principles. Although anarchism itself has not always put these principles into practice, tending to emphasize state and economic power to the neglect of other forms and lapsing into a faith in revolutionary spontaneity, its key ideas were revitalized and reconfigured in the New Left movement of the 1960s. This movement introduced a new emphasis on culture as a terrain of politics and a stress on the cultural impact of movement activism. Participants also recognized the political importance of intimate relationships. These old and new anarchistic influences have fed into a range of contemporary movements and have surfaced in a frequently unacknowledged form in recent developments in social and political thought. It is to these developments that I now turn.

Notes

1. This is a controversial use of the term *modernism*, which is more usually applied to a shift in aesthetics. In the conventional sense, it involves the abandonment of the realist assumption that art can mirror nature and society, a preoccupation with form rather than content, and an attempt to wrest cultural production free from the dead weight of tradition and to subject it to the "pitiless rigour" of functionalism. Proponents of this kind of modernism were often allied to "forces of dynamism already at work in society," including revolutionary social movements (Outhwaite and Bottomore 1994: 389). This use of the term reflects many of the contextual factors highlighted in the first section of this chapter. However, I am using *modernism* more specifically here to indicate developments in social and political thought that reflect upon and reify aspects of the modern context. *The Enlightenment,* the more usual phrase for these developments, seems to me to refer primarily to epistemological assumptions and to neglect other dimensions of modernity reflected in contemporaneous thought.

2. Alberto Melucci (1996b) has argued that use of the term *social movement* in itself indicates a meta-theoretical commitment to the desirability of social change and the possibility of emancipation, and that this is a peculiarly modernist commitment. It is interesting to note that those who are wary of change and movement participation in it tend to talk rather of collective behavior, crowds, or even mobs.

3. As Krishan Kumar notes, liberals did not originally use the term *civil society* in this way. "Up to the end of the eighteenth century, the term 'civil society' was synonymous with the state or 'political society.' . . . [T]he contrast is with the 'uncivilized' condition of humanity—whether in a hypothesized state of nature or, more particularly, under an 'un-natural' system of government that rules by despotic decree rather than by laws" (1993: 376–377).

4. The exact sense in which parties are supposed to be representative is difficult to pin down. Hannah Pitkin's classic discussion of representation (1967) barely mentions parties. Bruce Graham asserts that "it is now generally accepted that party competition does serve to regulate the underlying conflicts between social groups and to represent the different sectors of the community in legislatures" (1993: 16). In other words, their representative function derives from acting on behalf of, or mirroring, conflictual social interests that cut across territorial constituencies, namely those of class. We are in murky waters here. Would many liberals want to argue that the representation of classes is possible or desirable? It seems to me that most focus rather on the functional role of parties as conduits for individual participation in parliamentary politics or as mechanisms of elite competition, as emphasized above.

5. The pyramidal structure of authority is thus common to both participatory and vanguard democracy. It is this common feature that is the focus of commentators who lump marxist reconstructions of democracy together under the heading of *direct democracy* (e.g., Held, D. 1996: 121–154; Potter 1997: 6). The problem with such a categorization is that valid critiques of the hierarchical authority structure of the vanguard system, and its association with one-party rule, are likely to be overextended to the notion of a pyramidal democratic structure per se. However, the participatory formulation of the pyramid structure seeks to avoid the centralizing and elitist tendencies of vanguardism by insisting that authority should be decentralized, flowing from the bottom upward.

6. The efforts of sympathetic feminist theorists to make republicanism more "woman-friendly" are examined in Chapter 3.

7. Another common definition of *anarchism* as opposition to government or to authority stems in part from the common conflation of these terms with the state and in part from the association of anarchy by critics with disorder and lack of authority and government. In fact, some forms of authority are acceptable to many anarchists and implicit in their schemes for a nonstatist future. The term *governance* may be useful here. *Government* in the strict sense of the executive of the state would clearly arouse anarchist hostility, but *governance* may be more acceptable. This distinction is explored in subsequent chapters.

8. Some commentators use the term *New Left* more narrowly to describe a small group of marxist intellectuals in the United Kingdom in the 1950s and 1960s associated with a libertarian reinterpretation of marxism (Miller et al. 1991: 355; cf. Stafford 1970: 480–483). Others mean the student-based movement that emerged in the United States in the early 1960s from roots in the Civil Rights movement and in the context of anti–Vietnam War protests (Breines 1989; Evans 1979). My more inclusive definition is intended to encompass both these phenomena, related mobilizations in Europe, and broader cultural developments.

2

New Times, New Social
Movements, New Democracy

We suffer, in the face of our era's manifold crises, not from too much but from too little democracy.

(Barber 1984: xix)

Our future now depends almost entirely on our own choices and decisions. Social life has never been so risky. That is why social movements are unlikely to disappear. They are a sign of this awesome power we have over ourselves—and of our enormous obligation to exercise this power responsibly.

(Melucci 1989: 232)

Introduction

In recent decades, there has been a convergence in social and political thought around the assumption that modernity is undergoing major structural change or that it is, at the very least, in some form of crisis. Social movements that were dominant in modernity appear to be fading or are being reshaped in dramatic ways, while institutionalized forms of democracy are seen to be under severe strain and new kinds of democratic ideas and practices are emerging. This chapter examines approaches in social and political thought that focus on such developments. These approaches all advocate an expansive, participatory democratic ideal and emphasize the role of movements in turning this ideal into a reality. In different ways, they all also limit the scope of democracy and either idealize movement activity or discipline it in ways frequently rejected by movements themselves.

The chapter begins by exploring debates about an epochal shift in modernity toward "new times." I examine claims that these changes are inducing a crisis in institutionalized democracy, encouraging innovations in movement activity and giving rise to new trends in social and political thought in terms of the emergence of postmarxism and postmodernism. The chapter then looks more specifically at reconstructive approaches to democracy and movements under the headings of associative democracy, civil society, radical democracy, and a postmodern politics of difference. As in the previous chapter, these are assessed according to their underlying analyses of power, the location and scope of politics, the nature and role of the political actor, and the possibility of social change. The conclusion remarks upon the limited concrete connections between these new theories and movement activism, their relationship to modernist approaches, and their continuing neglect of feminist and global concerns.

Epochal Change (2)

New Times

Claims about an epochal shift in modernity are varied and difficult to summarize. The umbrella term *new times* was developed within the British context in an attempt to encompass diverse concepts, describing changes in a variety of social structures. As Stuart Hall argues:

> If we take the "new times" idea apart, we find that it is an attempt to capture, within the confines of a single metaphor, a number of different facets of social change, none of which has any necessary connection with the other. In the current debates, a variety of different terms jostle with one another for pride of place, in the attempt to describe those different dimensions of change. They include "post-industrial," "post-Fordist," "revolution of the subject," "postmodernism." None of these is wholly satisfactory. . . . Each, however, signifies something important about the "new times" debate. (Hall, S. 1989: 117)

Key aspects of new times shifts in modernity can be mapped onto the framework laid out in the previous chapter.

i. The Economy.   Postindustrial economies are characterized by the dynamism of information technology and the service sector. The workforce is fragmented and managerial hierarchies flattened by the "post-Fordist" reorganization of production into decentralized decision-making, production, and delivery systems. A major cleavage emerges between those with access to knowledge and those without. Employment is casualized and "feminized," with women increasingly incorporated into sectors of the workforce that are playing a more dominant economic role and in which work is frequently part-time and precarious. High levels of male unemployment are normalized. Discourses of skepticism, risk, and crisis proliferate (e.g., Allen 1992b; Touraine 1974; Beck 1992; Peterson and Runyan 1999: 142–146).

ii. The State.   Rising expectations, increased spending burdens, and enmeshment in liberalized global markets have encouraged the collapse of the postwar social democratic consensus. States retreat from substantial economic intervention and from large-scale centralized planning. Administrative, infrastructure, and welfare responsibilities are fragmented and sloughed off to local authorities, interstate institutions, businesses, the voluntary sector, and the household. Businesses and substate governing institutions provide increasingly important centers of authority and loci of cultural identification (e.g., Offe 1985: 817–821; Held, D. 1996: 233–273; Balbo 1987; McCarthy 1989).

iii. The Household and Family.   Family forms diversify as people do not marry or do so more than once. The divorce rate rises, as does the number of families with only one parent and those headed by women. Few households are solely provided for by a male breadwinner. Women remain largely responsible for family life notwithstanding their incorporation into the formal economy. The family is increasingly commodified and subjected to media scrutiny and state regulation. Ideologies of gender hierarchy, domesticity, sanctuary, heterosexuality, and romance become sites of social struggle (e.g., Greer 1971: 171–189, 198–238; Friedan 1965: 13–29; Elliot 1986: 82–176; Walby 1990b: 147–157; Crowley 1992).

iv. Culture.   Populism, nostalgia, fragmentation, spectacle, and juxtaposition spread through art, design, and the media. Divisions between high art and mass consumption, masculine and feminine modes of expression, western and non-western culture, form and content, are undermined or reconfigured in new ways. Lifestyles are pluralized and hybridized, within constraints imposed by intensified processes of commodification and consumption and the contestations of traditionalist and countercultural social movements (e.g., Thompson, K. 1992; Hebdige 1989; Harvey 1989: 39–65; McRobbie 1994: 13–43).

v. Ontology and Epistemology.   The self is seen as fragmented, plural, and discursively mediated in relation to multiple social worlds. Aspirations toward equality are displaced by expressions of difference. Instrumental rationality, the distinction between subject and object, and the status of absolute truth are all undermined. Self-conscious reflexivity becomes increasingly significant (e.g., McLennan 1992; Giddens 1994: 6–7; Pieterse 1992: 23–30; Hall, S. 1997; Flax 1990b; Young 1990: 156–191).

Only some of the theorists who are arguing for a shift in modernity would concur with all or even most of the features listed here. The extent, meaning, and causes of change are highly disputed. Indeed, there has been substantial resistance to the idea that modernity has undergone *any* kind of significant structural shift, focusing either on continuity in economic and political institutions (Rustin 1989) or on the desirability of maintaining the "project of modernity" (Habermas 1985). Many of the processes described remain geographically and temporally uneven, and their cultural, ontological, and epistemological aspects have long roots, interwoven with modernist traditions of being and knowing. Nonetheless, more limited arguments for some kind of structural change in modernity are convincing, not least because of the dynamic nature and instability of modernity itself. I would suggest, following Anthony Giddens (1990: 149–150) and Ulrich Beck (1992: 10), that we have moved into a new stage of modernity rather than moving beyond it into a qualitatively new epoch. Finally, it should be noted that claims about *globalization* could be seen as part of the range of new times arguments. Several theorists referred to here have become increasingly preoccupied with the impact of globalization, and I discuss their claims in Chapter 5. However, most new times theorists still ignore globalization and limit their focus to structural shifts and political solutions in Western Europe, North America, and modernized parts of Asia and Australasia.

Democratic Crisis?

Democratic institutions in the West and elsewhere have been put under significant strain by the reconfigurations of modernity. Manuel Castells identifies several interlinked crises in democracy (1997: 342–349). The first is a crisis of the liberal nation-state, no longer able to fulfill its welfare commitments in current global economic conditions and losing the loyalty of its citizens as they develop multiple identities. The second is a crisis in the credibility of the party political system, which has been "[c]aptured into the media arena, reduced to personalized leadership, dependent on technologically sophisticated manipulation, pushed into unlawful financing, driven by and toward scandal politics" (Castells 1997: 343). Such phenomena have encouraged declining citizen confidence in professional politicians, mainstream parties, and the efficacy of government. This is revealed in opinion polls, the rise of third parties, and voter volatility. Castells also identifies a crisis in governing institutions, involving the replacement of stable one-party rule by unstable coalitions and regionalization. Alain Touraine summarizes all this as "a crisis of political representation" whereby people no longer feel represented by a failing state and political system, a self-interested political elite, or a singular national identity (1997: 7–8). Benjamin Barber argues rather for "a crisis of governability," in that leaders are unable to control the runaway train of modernity and the people refuse to be led (1984: xx–xxii).

New Social Movements?

Mobilization in innovative forms of movement politics could be seen as one form of citizen response to these developments. Since the advent of the New Left, many analysts have detected a shift in the forms and goals of movement activism. New social movement (NSM) theorists emphasize two structural changes in modernity: the shift to an economy centered around the production and control of information and knowledge (Touraine 1974; Melucci 1989) and the increasing legitimization crisis of the modern state given bureaucratic stagnation and the expansion of techno-bureaucratic rationality into everyday life (Habermas 1981; Offe 1985). These changes mean that the workers' movement that dominated the nineteenth and early twentieth centuries can no longer play a central role in the constitution and contestation of social structures. It is also no longer an appropriate model for understanding contemporary activism. The workers' movement was rooted in class identity and was hierarchically organized, statist in orientation, and aimed at socioeconomic transformation. In contrast, "new" movements are understood to be constituted by the information-rich but disaffected middle classes and marginalized underclasses. They are organized in devolved, participatory grassroots networks within civil society and pursue "self-limiting" strategies aimed at constraining or "pushing back" state and economic power rather than gaining control over it. Finally, they are preoccupied with the reconstruction of identity, values, lifestyles, cultural symbols, and knowledge (Melucci 1989; Touraine 1985; Habermas 1981; Cohen and Arato 1992: 510–532; Scott 1992: 12–35).

This account has been subjected to substantial criticism within social movement theory. It is frequently argued that there is more diversity within and between contemporary movements than NSM theory allows for, including reactionary or fundamentalist elements (Martell and Stammers 1996: 140–141) and very different kinds of activity in non-European contexts (Foweraker 1995: 24–25). Further, the sharp distinction between old and new movements has not withstood empirical scrutiny. Cultural innovation, symbolic intervention, and fluid organizational forms have been documented in religious and workers' movements of the last century (D'Anieri et al. 1990; Tucker 1991). A working-class basis, statist orientation, and concern with material redistribution can be seen, for example, in contemporary toxic waste activism (Brown and Ferguson 1995). However, to paraphrase Alberto Melucci (1989: 41–43), none of this should lead to the assumption that nothing under the sun is new, thus attributing a spurious continuity and coherence to movement activity and reifying diverse contexts. I would suggest that the "newness" of contemporary western movements lies in the *political importance* now accorded both to the cultural dimension of activism and to organization in devolved and democratic ways. Movements have also diversified into new arenas of social conflict, thus challenging monist and parallelist frameworks in social and political thought.

New Theoretical Frameworks?

The above developments have encouraged two distinctive theoretical frameworks to gain prominence. One has been labeled *postmarxism*. The "post" suffix is contestable here: Stuart Sim notes that "post-Marxist tendencies can be traced back more or less to the origins of Marxism itself," although he adds that "it is only really in the last few decades that it takes shape as a specific [intellectual] movement in its own right" (1998: 10). Postmarxists are so called because they originate in the marxist tradition or have been influenced by it. They accept the veracity of aspects of Marx's critique of capitalism and his commitment to collective action and economic change. However, they reject those elements of historical materialist analysis that reduce oppression to economic exploitation, social struggle to class struggle, radical change to the transformation of the mode of production, and civil society to market relations (Cohen and Arato 1992: 70–80). In other words, they attempt to move beyond marxist monism. Postmarxism is also closely connected to the republican revival, with advocates frequently sharing the desire to develop a more substantive notion of citizenship and to expand the sphere of the political. Further, postmarxists follow the trend of actual social struggle, as evident in East Central European revolutions, the South African transition, and many Asian mobilizations, to replace socialism with democracy as the primary emancipatory goal.

From this shared starting point, analyses diverge dramatically. "Post-Marxists can variously want to reject, revitalise, or renegotiate the terms of their intellectual contract with Marxism" (Sim 1998: 1). Many approach marxist arguments from a liberal or social democratic political perspective. They stress the inevitability of the market economy, the importance of a plural political culture, the necessity of a state that can constrain civil society and that is itself constrained, and the need to reconceptualize the state's interventionist role (Held, D. 1992b: 43). Other post-marxists—and this appears to be the sense in which Sim uses the term—write from a postmodern or poststructuralist philosophical perspective. They may also reach liberal political conclusions, but this is not the primary impulse at work.

There is an overlap here with the other development in social and political thought associated with new times: *postmodernism.* This is a more general category than postmarxism, indicating ontological and epistemological commitments rather than a relationship to a particular political tradition. Again, the label is not unproblematic. Like "post" marxists and "new" movements, "post" modernists gain their identification through a contrast with something that went before, this time modernism—despite the fact that modernism has never been a unified body of thought and has had postmodern thinking intertwined within it since its inception. Further, much postmodern writing "involves defamiliarisation—an attempt to turn the familiar into the unfamiliar and vice versa—and this feature is annulled rather than explicated by a narrative that clarifies and familiarises" (Brown, C. 1994: 223). Nevertheless, the label serves to indicate the emergence of a body of work concerned with "the role of reason, knowledge and power" and "the exclusions of modernity, the dark side of the Enlightenment" (Pieterse 1992: 23).

Following Jane Flax (1990b: 32–37), Seyla Benhabib characterizes the postmodern moment in terms of "the deaths of Man, History, and Metaphysics." For Benhabib (1992: 211), this indicates a shared rejection of the essential, transcendent, or "spectator" self; skepticism about the imposition of unity and patterns of progress on the past; and a revolt against claims that transcendent reason and transparent language can provide a grounding for truth and moral certainty. Benhabib argues that this shared critique has given rise to both "weak" and "strong" versions of postmodernism (1992: 211–225). I understand the latter to be rooted in a relational analysis of language in which words gain their meaning from their shifting relationships to other words rather than mirroring external realities, with meaning pinned down only temporarily in shifting discursive fields. Proponents may also adopt Michel Foucault's extension of the notion of discourse from utterances to "a system of representation" encompassing a range of social practices (Hall, S. 1997: 44; Benhabib 1992: 208–209). Strong postmodernists argue that "Man" is a fragmented, fluctuating product of discourse, "caught in the web of fictive meaning, in chains of signification, in which the subject is merely another position in language" (Flax 1990b: 32). Analysis is limited to historical disjunctures and microlevel processes and all grounding for truth is refused, given "the irreconcilability and incommensurability of language games" (Benhabib 1992: 209, 219–220). In contrast, Benhabib argues, weak postmodernists "*situate* the subject in the context of various social, linguistic and discursive practices" and insist that it retains "a certain autonomy and ability to rearrange the significations of language" (1992: 214, 216). Weak postmodernists also retain a focus on macrolevel patterns and historical continuities and argue for "a more limited investigation of the conditions under which a community of inquirers can make warranted assertions about truth and the real" (Benhabib 1992: 212, 219, 224–225). I would add that strong postmodernists remain primarily deconstructive in technique, whereas weak postmodernists strive ultimately for analytical and political reconstruction.[1]

Variants of postmarxism and postmodernism are likely to yield very different conclusions about the changing nature of movements and democracy. However, I want to draw attention here to four commonalities that distinguish them *in general* from the modernist approaches outlined in the last chapter.

First, postmarxist and postmodernist theorists tend to reject the monist assumption that power emanates from only one or two major sources, namely the state and/or economy. Instead, in an echo of anarchism, power is seen as emerging from two or more sources and as having pervasive and dispersed effects. This does not mean that state and economic power are ignored but rather that they are considered to have transmogrified into less concentrated and brutal, more diffuse and insidious, forms and that they are increasingly recognized to be interconnected with new, or newly significant, forms of power stemming from ethnicity and gender. Beyond this shared starting point, the precise operations of power are theorized in very different ways. Second, postmarxist and postmodernist theorists share the belief, in another echo of anarchism, that democratic politics must be expanded beyond the state, class struggle, or the public sphere, to challenge relations of power wherever they are manifested. Third, both postmarxists and postmodernists are wary of unitary conceptions of the person and the privileging of one aspect of personhood, although their approaches to agency differ sharply. Fourth, the modernist faith in progressive change is undermined. Revolutionary and reformist strategies are regarded with equal skepticism. Some follow anarchists in rejecting a focus on state-led change and in emphasizing a necessary plurality of struggle. Most now reject the possibility of abolishing power entirely. Postmodernists and postmarxists then disagree over whether and how significant change can be achieved.

These theoretical shifts are likely to have been encouraged by the fact that social and political theorists are now drawn from a somewhat broader cross-section of society and thus have more diverse experiences of the exclusions of modernity. Further, the impact on the academy of new forms of movement activism should not be underestimated. I would suggest that the influence of the feminist movement has been crucial. Particularly since the late 1960s, feminism has generated a rich and reflexive literature on the limitations of modernist ontology, epistemology, and politics. We see in the next two chapters that feminists have theorized the operations of power, developed expansive and participatory reformulations of politics and democracy, offered thoroughgoing critiques of modernist models of subjectivity and agency, and put forward strategies for change that bypass both revolution and reformism. Their arguments are often interpreted as symptomatic or reflective of the more general move toward new times preoccupations. However, some commentators have insisted that many feminist innovations emerged prior to this move and had great influence on it. New times theorists, particularly postmodernists, have been charged with failing to acknowledge feminist trailblazers and with absorbing their insights without proper acknowledgment or recognition of their full implications (on the contested relationship between postmodernism and feminism see Flax 1990a and 1990b: 209–221; Bordo 1990; Fraser and Nicholson 1990; Benhabib 1992; Butler 1992; Sylvester 1994: 143–168; Parpart and Marchand 1995: 4–11). The result is that new times theory may problematize key tenets of modernist frameworks, but the gendered marginalizations of modernism are frequently allowed to continue or to resurface in different guises. This problem is evident in the postmarxist- and postmodernist-influenced approaches to the changing relationship between democracy and social movements that are the focus of the rest of this chapter.

Associations, States, and Markets

One example of a postmarxist approach to the relationship between democracy and social movements is the scheme for "associative democracy" developed by Paul Hirst, Joshua Cohen, and Joel Rogers. Drawing on corporatist and guild socialist ideas about functional representation and the liberal pluralist emphasis on groups, this scheme is offered as a solution to the problems of social democracy (Hirst 1990: 12–18; 1994: 15–21). One major plank of the scheme is the decentralization and democratization of the economy. As well as the establishment of "in-plant organizations for workers," in the participatory socialist tradition (Cohen and Rogers 1995: 59), associative democrats envisage the devolution of economic control to regions and localities, the slimming down of companies to their core services, and the encouragement of a range of forms of ownership. It is argued that companies should be restructured so that all stakeholders are accorded rights and given the opportunity to participate in company decision-making processes. Other suggestions include the establishment of a minimum wage and guaranteed income, the decentralization of trade unions, and the setting up of an "international corporate senate" to oversee the restructuring of transnational businesses (Hirst 1994: 128–157, 167–189).

Additionally, associative democrats argue that state functions should be devolved to territorial and functional fora, from the local to the global. This amounts to the creation of multilevel governance. "Like globalisation, 'governance' is a recent buzzword in social and political thought. Its increased currency since the 1980s reflects a growing awareness that questions of regulation, public order and authority are not reducible to [state] government" (Scholte 1995b: 3). For associative democrats, the state is not robbed of all authority but is instead reconstituted as the mediator and even creator of associations (Hirst 1990: 7–8, 70–82; 1994: 26–34; Cohen and Rogers 1995: 40).

Finally, and perhaps most importantly, associative democracy is predicated on an enhanced role for civic groups or "associations," particularly those with an economic dimension. Here the corporatist strategy of institutionalizing cooperation among the state, business, and trade unions, cultivated to differing extents in several European countries as part of the postwar social democratic consensus, is revived and expanded. Associate democrats envisage that a variety of groups should become participants in multilevel decision-making processes, including within the state and within other regulatory bodies. Groups should also become primary mechanisms of welfare provision, which would involve them competing for funding from the state and being monitored by it (Hirst 1990: 70–82; 1994: 21–26, 167–189; Cohen and Rogers 1995: 42–46, 55–63). This emphasis on groups would enhance opportunities for the involvement of individuals in democratic politics by enabling the election of a variety of representatives in different fora and participation in a range of group activities. Cohen and Rogers seem to take this positive emphasis on groups from liberal pluralism (1995: 27–33). Hirst argues against their specifically American pluralist characterization of groups as "secondary associations," guaranteeing the democratic nature of the "primary association" of the state. Hirst favors the British pluralist and participatory socialist tradition, which sees "self-governing voluntary bodies . . . as the primary means of both democratic governance and organising social life" (Hirst 1994: 26). A related distinction is apparent in strategies for encouraging group activity and implementing associative democracy. Cohen and Rogers point toward the need for state intervention in the patterns of division and distribution in society to enable groups to develop. Hirst limits the proactive role of the state to setting regulatory frameworks. He also emphasizes "a process of rebuilding associations from below, by political campaigning and voluntary action in civil society" (Hirst 1995: 111).

Associative democracy is in many ways an imaginative and pragmatic response to the failings of social democracy. It emphasizes the need to decentralize state power, grant a role to collective agency, and expand democracy into economic and civic life. Yet perhaps this view of democracy is not expansive enough. The main focus of democratizing efforts is the globalizing economy and accompanying reconfigurations of state power. This is evidence of a postmarxist move to combine a marxian monist focus on the economy with a liberal monist focus on the state, resulting in a parallelist focus on both. I am not disputing the importance of either for a theory of democracy, but I am concerned about the neglect of other forms of power and the consequent limitation of the scope of democracy.[2] Further, it should be noted that the economic democratization suggested has certain limits. Although Hirst's proposals are more thoroughgoing and radical than those put forward by Cohen and Rogers, the point is still to subject capitalist accumulation and exchange to social controls, not to challenge its raison d'être. Hirst is justifiably anxious to keep his proposals realistic and widely acceptable, but it seems to me that a genuinely pluralist vision would have to allow for the possibility of the generation of alternatives to the capitalist system.

The parallelist focus on the economy and state also limits the theorization of movements. Associative democrats focus primarily on activism around economic issues and interests, thus betraying a continuation of social democratic, corporatist, and marxist priorities. Other groups are included only insofar as they too can also play a role in economic governance—in the formulation of environmental regulation and nondiscriminatory work practices, for example, or in the provision of social welfare (Cohen and Rogers 1995: 55–60). Again, this problem is exacerbated rather than solved by combining it with liberal preoccupations, this time in the shape of a focus on formally constituted organizations, rationally pursuing collective interests in the public and civil spheres. As feminist theorist Iris Marion Young points out (1995: 210–211), this neglects the question of other kinds of groups in society, including those that emerge from imposed identifications or deep-rooted social cleavages. Groups in this sense are not conjured into being overnight and often do not have formal, organizational dimensions. They include classes but are not reducible to these. The focus on formal groups also ignores a whole range of collective action, including so-called new movements stemming from social groups based on ethnicity, gender, and sexual orientations, and concerned with issues of identity and cultural expression (Offe 1995: 128–129; Young 1995: 208–210). Associative democrats do not deal with the ways in which groups in their sense or Young's are connected to movement activity. The more subterranean and cultural aspects of collective action drop out of the picture.

Finally, the neo-corporatist emphasis on collaboration with state decision-making and policy implementation effectively squeezes out the *oppositional* dimension of collective action. As Andrew Szasz asks:

> If government busied itself deliberately crafting secondary associations that
> are well-behaved, not mischievous, and if secondary associations thence-
> forth knew their place, stayed in their place, dutifully played their assigned
> role and contributed responsibly to democratic governance, would we not
> lose some of the oppositional space from which the pressures for real change
> have always come? (Szasz 1995: 148)

Szasz invokes the example of toxic waste activism to demonstrate that
a movement that rejects collaboration and lobbying in favor of direct action can still have a significant and positive impact on society, in terms of
broadening the political agenda and encouraging progressive legislation.
He suggests, furthermore, that "the *process* of the movement has itself
produced important results" (Szasz 1995: 154, emphasis added). Given
widespread citizen apathy and alienation, "the hazardous waste movement's capacity to mobilize and radicalize thousands of previously inac-
tive people is to be praised and cherished. Day-to-day-life in the movement *is* the stuff of popular, truly participatory democracy" (Szasz 1995:
155).

Radicalizing Civil Society

Whereas the oppositional dimension of movement activity is downplayed in associative democracy, other postmarxist approaches attempt
to take it on board. This is the case with recent reformulations of "civil society." The notion of civil society has been popularized in part by the influence of social movements, particularly Eastern Bloc oppositional
movements. Prominent participants in these extensively invoked the
concept of civil society as an anti-totalitarian strategy. Debates about new
social movements in the West have also emphasized their location in and
orientation toward civil society (Scott 1992: 17; Cohen 1982: 35–37; Cohen
and Arato 1992: 31–69). This is the context from which a distinctively
postmarxist, radical version of civil society has emerged, theorized most
exhaustively by Jean Cohen and Andrew Arato.

In contrast to the two-part model of civil society found in liberalism
and marxism, which conflates the civil sphere with the market and juxta-
poses it to the state, Cohen and Arato draw on Gramsci's reformulation
to advocate a tripartite model. Civil society is seen as "a sphere of social
interaction between economy and state" constituted by the self-conscious
activity of social movements as well as by families and civil associations

(1992: ix–xi). However, Cohen and Arato reject Gramsci's residual attachment to marxist economism and his consequent privileging of class as the basis of hegemony within civil society, his aspiration to absorb the state into civil society, and his instrumental approach to civil society politics as a means to a revolutionary end. Rather, they insist that distinctions among state, economy, and civil society must be preserved and deepened, with civil society recognized as an autonomous sphere of social agency, capable of generating genuinely plural cultural and political forms (1992: 142–159; cf. Wood 1990: 62–67).[3]

Most crucially, civil society is characterized as a site and source of democracy. Jürgen Habermas's (1990) formulation of discourse ethics is important here in enabling a theoretical reworking of the context and precepts of democracy. The "ideal speech situation" developed by Habermas specifies the conditions necessary for arriving at a legitimate and rational consensus, namely that all participants must recognize that the dialogue should be widely accessible and characterized by the principles of "symmetry, reciprocity, and reflexivity" (Cohen and Arato 1992: 348). For Cohen and Arato, this specification of the way in which inclusive agreement should be reached provides norms of democratic legitimacy. Further, Cohen and Arato argue that there are built-in assumptions here about the possible content of such an agreement, because the ideal speech situation is predicated on a recognition of the autonomy of political actors, the plurality of ways of life, and the differentiation of social spheres. It is thus likely to generate agreements that preserve and extend basic rights, "those that secure the integrity, autonomy and personality of the person and those having to do with free communication" (Cohen and Arato 1992: 403; see, more generally, 345–405). Although such rights are ultimately stabilized and guaranteed by the rule of law through the state, and although they require the maintenance of existing formal democratic systems, Cohen and Arato emphasize that they are generated within and driven by "chances to assemble, associate, and articulate positions publicly on the terrain of civil society" (1992: 395). Activities like these supplement and deepen formal democratic systems and extend a plurality of democratic forms into social life, most notably into the institutions and publics of civil society but also into political society and economic relationships (Cohen and Arato 1992: 15–17, 410–420). In effect, democracy is redefined here as both the process and the result of inclusive public deliberation that respects, guarantees, and extends basic rights and is rooted in civil society.

As does associative democracy, this framework draws on a complex understanding of agency. Both representative and participatory elements are featured, with the mechanisms of the liberal state left intact but bolstered by increased opportunities for individual participation in a vigorous civil society. Further, agency is granted to both individual and collective actors. Distinctively, the role of social movements is seen as key. On this point, Cohen and Arato are concerned to rebut the conclusions of Habermas (1981), otherwise so influential in their schema, that NSMs other than feminism are essentially defensive, preoccupied with the preservation of cultural forms in what Habermas calls the "lifeworld." For Cohen and Arato, movements remain progressive forces. They are located in civil society, which bridges the lifeworld and the political realm, and movement-instigated cultural change and discursive innovation is a necessary part of the expansion and institutionalization of democracy (1992: 405–406, 527–532). Using the example of feminism, Cohen and Arato distinguish a "dual logic" of movement activism, directed inward to civil society and the lifeworld and outward to state and economic institutions, via interrelated strategies of identity, influence, inclusion, and reform (1992: 548–563). They characterize contemporary movements as "self-limiting": rather than being oriented toward the seizure of economic and political power and the erasure of differentiation between social spheres, movements are now concerned to democratize the existing framework and to maintain social differentiation (1992: 15–16, 493).[4]

In many ways, radical civil society theory offers a valuable corrective to associative democracy. It highlights the role of social movements in establishing and deepening democratic institutions, extending this role beyond class-based and economically oriented movements and emphasizing the significance of their cultural and oppositional dimensions. However, there is some validity in the charge that radical civil society theory idealizes movements. Cohen and Arato insist at the outset that "movements are not always internally democratic, and they often engage in action that violates the democratic procedures or laws generated by a nonetheless legitimate political order" (1992: xviii). However, they do not pay systematic attention to the internal constitution of movements. Further, their framework draws on the activities of "new" movements organized around peace, environmental, and feminist issues. Although they recognize the need to modify NSM theory—insisting, for example, on the dual logic of new movements—they neglect movements that do not share NSM traits and that are not engaged in efforts to deepen democracy. The activities of contemporary nationalist or religious fundamentalist movements, for example, are ignored.

The radical civil society framework itself encourages inaccuracies in the theorization of movements, for two interrelated reasons: It is predicated on the differentiation of different realms of social life, and it underplays the operations of power in the realm of civil society. Critics of varying perspectives have long argued that analytical differentiation can obscure the reach of capitalist and state power into social life. Marxist and gramscian frameworks have drawn attention to this penetration but at the cost of a monolithic interpretation of civil society. The postmarxist reformulation runs the converse danger of presenting an idealized interpretation, in which civil society is a source of democratization of power relations that exist outside its borders. Further, the postmarxist view fails to face up to power relations that are not reducible to state or economic forces, such as the hierarchically organized gender identities that "run like pink and blue threads" through "all arenas of life . . . a basic element of the social glue that binds them to one another" (Fraser, N. 1987: 45). All this militates against recognition of the ways in which social movement activity can be penetrated and co-opted by the state and stratified by other forms of power. It may also misrepresent the complex politics of movements. As their name suggests, movements are dynamic entities that transgress boundaries and operate simultaneously in several social spheres, in ways that "cannot be grasped through categories of containment" (Walker, R. B. J. 1994: 700).

These criticisms point toward the limits of democracy as envisaged by radical civil society theorists. I do not mean here to be insensitive to the achievements of the civil society strategy in many parts of the world, particularly in Eastern and Central Europe in the 1980s, nor to underestimate the democratic importance of the postmarxist goal of creating forms of social interaction resistant to marketization and government intervention, and influential over them. Nonetheless, it seems to me that the failure to recognize the systematic nature of the penetration of different spheres by diverse forms of power is likely to function to reify those forms and remove them from democratic scrutiny. For example, it will become clear in Chapter 6 that the civil society strategy pursued in East Central Europe failed to tackle hierarchies stemming from ethnic and gender identity that have since served to stymie democratization. Further, a democratization strategy aimed at expanding civil society and gaining influence over the state and market may imply that the latter two ultimately cannot and should not be transformed or transcended. Indeed, I would suggest this is precisely what is entailed in Cohen and Arato's reinterpretation of the concept of *self-limitation*. This concept was developed originally by the strategists of the Eastern and Central European movements, who insisted on the need to avoid direct confrontation with the state because this risked provoking Soviet military retaliation. Nonetheless, there was still a belief that the self-organization of society could transform the authoritarian state and centrally organized economy, albeit indirectly (Stammers 1996). Cohen and Arato argue rather that the liberal state and market economy constitute the necessary framework for a flourishing civil society–based democracy and that these are locked into a symbiotic relationship that movements should not jeopardize. As

with the associative project, change can only go so far and democratization must stay largely within its modern liberal limits.

Radical Democracy and Hegemony

It is the civil society theorists' acceptance of a capitalist framework to
which Ernesto Laclau and Chantal Mouffe take exception and which represents one point of departure for their model of "radical democracy." In
this sense, their approach is closest to the marxist roots of postmarxism,
albeit with an insistence that there have been significant "structural
transformations of capitalism" that, paradoxically, make an orthodox
marxist monism untenable. These transformations include:

> the decline of the classical working class in the post-industrial countries; the
> increasingly profound penetration of capitalist relations of production in ar-
> eas of social life, whose dislocatory effects . . . have generated new forms of
> social protest; the emergence of mass mobilisations in Third World countries
> which do not follow the classical pattern of class struggle . . . [as well as] the
> exposure of new forms of domination established in the name of the dicta-
> torship of the proletariat. (Laclau and Mouffe 1998: 57)

Laclau and Mouffe argue that these developments have enabled and
require what amounts to a strong postmodernist approach to power, social life, and politics (1998: 58). More specifically, Laclau and Mouffe
draw on Foucault's work on power and Lacan's on identity formation.
Power is depicted as discursively produced and as pervasive, productive, circulatory, and fluid. There is a corresponding insistence on the
"unfixity" of identity and of social relationships; these can be given only
temporary meaning through competing discourses, in relation to other
discourses, and they can never be completely determined. This leads to a
characterization of politics as *agonistic,* or as an unendingly conflictual
process whereby no resolution of social conflict, stable consensus, secure
identity, or total change can be achieved (Foucault 1986; Hall, S. 1997:
48–51; Sawicki 1991: 20–24; Rengger 1994: 64). Laclau and Mouffe argue
that these structural and theoretical developments have "exploded . . .
the idea and the reality itself of a unique space of constitution of the political" (Laclau and Mouffe 1985: 181). Rather, the political is constituted
wherever a hierarchical relationship of power is discursively rearticulated as one of oppression (1985: 153). On this account, democracy is
reconceived as a radically pluralistic and egalitarian discourse, expanding throughout society to contest power relations rearticulated as oppressive. Because power is immanent in all discursive relationships, and because no final closure or resolution of social difference is possible,

democracy is seen as an ongoing process rather than a stable framework or an end-state aspiration. It is a journey without a destination. Indeed, Laclau and Mouffe argue that a "democratic revolution" is still occurring, with democratic discourse continuing to filter outward from its original location in the public sphere. This process has been aided by the dislocations of capitalism reaching farther into society; by the internal "logic of equivalence" of democratic claims to equality and rights; and by the activities of social movements, from the workers' movement to feminism (1985: 152–159; 1998: 65).

As in other new times arguments about democracy, the activities of movements are brought to center stage. This time, however, they are given a distinctive interpretation, combining elements of marxist and postmodernist frameworks. Mobilization is understood as a product of the intertwined effects of the dislocations of capital and the logic of the democratic revolution. The displacement of class struggle by new movements is explained in terms of "the double perspective of the transformation of social relations characteristic of the new hegemonic formation of the post-war period, and of the effects of the displacement into new areas of social life of the egalitarian imaginary constituted around the liberal-democratic discourse" (Laclau and Mouffe 1985: 165). The increasing plurality of movements is stressed, along with their internal diversity. The logic of the democratic revolution is understood to have displaced social struggle into more and more fields of conflict, constituting new political subjects. Further, it is argued that constituent parts of movements gain their meaning and purpose from their discursively constructed relationship with other movements in specific contexts. There is thus no progressive "essence" to movement struggles and no predetermined unity is possible within or between them (Sandilands 1995: 82–86; Laclau and Mouffe 1985: 87, 168–171). The continuing marxist prioritization of the workers' movement is seen to be predicated on a mistaken view of how that movement has been constituted as well as of what its role might be in society. It is revealed as unrealistic and fundamentally anti-democratic (Laclau and Mouffe 1985: 167, 176–179).

Having said that, the democratic impulse taken to its logical extent implies the "unraveling of the social fabric," "the disappearance of the political," and the denial of the possibility of any common meanings and struggles. This radically relativist prospect is itself totalizing, as Laclau and Mouffe recognize (1985: 188). This brings me to another dimension of their approach to movements, which is an insistence on the continuing need to construct a shared anti-capitalist struggle. A complex reworking of the gramscian concept of hegemony is critical here. Laclau and Mouffe retain the notion of the consensual construction of alliances in opposition to capitalism but reject Gramsci's privileging of the sphere of civil society, class struggle, and the associated role of the party. Instead, they argue for the possibility and necessity of articulating an anti-capitalist hegemony and a shared reconstructive project with no foundations, no boundaries, and no privileged subject. Diverse movements, in forging discursive connections with each other, transform themselves (Laclau and Mouffe 1985: 134–145, 168–171, 188–193).

The effort to carve out a democratic path between solidarity and difference, reform and revolution is broadly to be welcomed. However, this form of it has serious drawbacks. These derive partly from the fact that Laclau and Mouffe are primarily concerned to locate themselves on postmarxist terrain, situating their work as both critique and adaptation of marxist theory. This encourages a continued emphasis on capitalism as a source of social change and a privileging of the struggle against capitalism, which has, historically, encouraged an anti-democratic approach to political organization. It is not clear whether Laclau and Mouffe entirely shake off these associations with their reworking of the concept of hegemony. They still prioritize the contestation of capitalism and this would seem, by definition, to require the subordination of other movement goals. As Sim concludes, "monism and pluralism remain incommensurable, for all the ingenious efforts of theorists such as Laclau and Mouffe" (1998: 8). Further, it remains opaque exactly how and why diverse movements should come together in an anti-capitalist struggle when there is no a priori reason why they should do so and no structure of authority to maintain cohesion. The reasoning here is perhaps rooted in what Sim identifies as an emotional or nostalgic commitment to marxist politics even though the theoretical basis of that politics has been cut away (1998: 7). An additional problem is that Laclau and Mouffe remain overwhelmingly concerned with detailed conceptual debates within marxist theory. This is perhaps exacerbated by an acceptance of the postmodern shift to the discursive that slips too easily into a privileging of textual analysis. It means that Laclau and Mouffe are more concerned with the discursive production of movements in marxist and postmarxist theory than with examining how movement practices could affect those discourses or broader social developments.

Another set of problems haunting radical democracy stems from the strong postmodern formulation of the relationship between power and discourse. I would suggest that the material dimension of power is displaced, even downplayed, by the focus on the discursive. For example, although the restriction of access to economic resources has important linguistic dimensions (i.e., the meaning of the term *poverty* shifts in different contexts), to focus on this exclusively is to marginalize more viscerally material effects of deprivation (including, in its most brute form, starvation).[5] Further, the effort to evade what might seem an apolitical focus on textual representations by expanding the category of discourse to encompass all kinds of representative mechanisms ends up lumping together linguistic formations, institutions, and social practices. This does not enable distinctions to be drawn between different dimensions of the social, or the identification of causal relationships. Critics have concluded that the postmodern move in Laclau and Mouffe "has the ironic effect of replacing one form of reductionism (namely, economic) with a 'discourse reductionism'" (Carroll and Ratner 1994: 14). I would argue rather that Laclau and Mouffe retain a form of economic reductionism, by which I mean that they still privilege the causal role of capitalism, alongside a form of discourse reductionism, according to which they explain the effects of capitalism in primarily discursive terms. Either way, a form of monism has been smuggled back into their analysis—except that although power is reduced to capitalism and its discursive effects, those effects are seen as highly dispersed.

Here another difficulty arises: the denial of regularity and sedimentation in the way power operates. This makes it doubly unclear how Laclau and Mouffe can justify their commitment to an anti-capitalist struggle. Why is such a struggle important if not because of the systematically hierarchical relationships to which capitalism gives rise? Furthermore, the notion of transformatory struggle as conventionally understood in marxist approaches is seen as impossible according to both strong and weak postmodern perspectives. Strong postmodernists insist that power cannot be abolished because it is continually reproduced even in efforts to contest it. This has led to the development of a model of politics as subversion, resistance, and resignification. Such a politics involves drawing on residual meanings and the unpredictable effects of discourse to exacerbate discursive dissonance, to expose the unfixity of identity and the social, and to open up space for alternative ways of being and knowing. One problem here is the fact that Laclau and Mouffe seem to aspire to more fundamental change in the social relationships of capitalism, involving a role for collective organization, than a postmodern politics of resistance can allow. Further, critics of strong postmodernism have questioned how a politics of resistance is possible at all when the subject is produced by, and subjected to, power as manifested in discourse. Debate over this issue has raged particularly strongly in feminist quarters, where there is concern that efforts to recover female subjectivity and agency are being undermined just as they begin to bear fruit (e.g., Flax 1990b: 219–221). To paraphrase Benhabib (1992: 218), how can a subject be produced by discourse and yet not fully determined by it? Where do the resources come from for the contestation of discursive production? To respond, as does Susan Hekman, that "discursive subjectivities other than the one that is scripted for the subject provide the possibility of resistance" (1995: 111) is to imply that discourses remain causal. This still does not tell us where discourses come from or how and by whom new ones can be created.

It is becoming clear that it is not only monism that is reinstated by marxist nostalgia and discourse theory but also the marxist tendency to structuralism and the erasure of agency. This is neatly illustrated by Laclau and Mouffe's analysis of the relationship between movements and democracy. Movements are understood to be mobilized by the discursive logic of the democratic revolution and the disruptive impact of capitalism; they are thus effects rather than instigators of democratic discourse, capable of extending democratic logic but not, apparently, of generating alternatives.[6] Democracy originates in the contradictions of capitalism and is dispersed by continuing developments in capitalism and its own internal logic, as much as by movement activity. A more adequate understanding of the relationship among democracy, movements, and the social context needs to allow for the possibility that each plays a role in the constitution of the others.

A Postmodern Politics of Difference

Whereas Laclau and Mouffe cannot explain why irreducibly plural movements should come together in anti-capitalist struggle, advocates of a postmodern politics of difference abandon the idea of striving for such a commonality altogether. They share Laclau and Mouffe's analysis of power as immanent in all social relations, discursively mediated, productive, and diffuse but add an insistence that no source or site of power can be privileged as a target for political struggle appropriate in all contexts. Marxism is entirely discarded for strong postmodern terrain. This has significant implications for thinking about democracy and social movements, as is evident in work by William Connolly and Judith Butler. As in other new times approaches, democracy is expanded beyond the institutions of state. Distinctively, it is seen as a cultural medium enabling the continual contestation of attempts to fix the scope and character of the political:

> Democracy . . . is a form of *rule or governance,* but it is much more than that as well. It is an egalitarian constitution of cultural life that encourages people to participate in defining their own troubles and possibilities, regardless of where these troubles originate and how narrow or broad they are in scope. It is, moreover . . . a social process through which fixed identities and naturalised conventions are pressed periodically to come to terms with their constructed characters, as newly emergent social identities disturb settled conventions and denaturalise social networks of identity and difference.

> ... Democracy is, amongst other things, an affirmative cultural/political re-
> sponse to the problematisation of final markers that marks the late-modern
> condition. (Connolly 1991: 476–477)

As with Laclau and Mouffe's formulation, this is democracy reconceived as an ongoing activity rather than a stable framework or an
achievable state of being. This view of democracy entails a characteristi-
cally liberal political commitment to individuality and pluralism, although on the very different ontological grounds that individuals are discursively produced subjects with fluid and fractured identities and
interests that democracy enables to flourish. Again, the role of NSMs in
this process is emphasized (Connolly 1991: 478–479; Butler 1998: 36–39).

As Jan Nederveen Pieterse has noted, "The themes and sensibilities of
the NSM overlap with those of poststructuralism and postmodernism"
(1992: 23). There is a shared emphasis on power as socially diffuse and
generating plural forms of resistance to the meta-narratives of modernist
politics. There is also a common identification of culture as a crucial terrain of politics. Butler stresses that the cultural character of new movements should not be taken to mean that they are disconnected from questions of political economy, demonstrating this point with an account of
the implications of "queer politics" for thinking about the normalizing,
heterosexist operations of late modern capitalism (1998: 38–43). Connolly
emphasizes that new movements challenge the territorial and bounded
character of modern democracy. This is partly because of their plurality
and partly because of their transnational character, which mean that
movements can "challenge a state's monopoly over the allegiances, identifications and energies of its members" (Connolly 1991: 479). Further, social movements are interpreted as irreducibly diverse. This diversity is
seen as a product of the underlying unfixity of the social and is emphasized as a democratic value in and of itself. It undermines modernist and
nostalgic efforts to fix identity to singular, national conceptions of the citizen, to unify the individual with the social, or to domesticate and subordinate a range of mobilizations to left politics (Butler 1992: 36–38).

Of course, the postmodern turn is not without its own "silences and
exclusions" (Pieterse 1992: 27). Three problems are especially pertinent
with regard to the theorization of social movements. First, there are the
difficulties produced by the strong postmodern, foucaultian approach to
power and discourse. As explored above, these include the monist tendency to reduce power to discourse; the neglect of continuity in the effects of power; an emphasis on small-scale, linguistic resistances; and the
problematization of agency. How movements can actually effect discursive and cultural change, and to what extent, remains unclear. Second,
the postmodern elevation of difference as a value in itself does not offer

any normative criteria for evaluating differences between movements. This may reflect a tendency, as with other new times approaches, to universalize NSM assumptions and see all movements as intrinsically critical of concentrations of power, cultural intolerance, and epistemological reifications. This ignores the more problematic aspects of movement activity. There is a deeper problem here, though, to do with the possibility of normative judgments. It has been argued that the "turn away from the referent and toward the free play of significatory difference ... eventuates in a political 'hyper-voluntarism'" yielding "no rational grounds for adjudicating competing assertions and social interests" (Carroll and Ratner 1994: 14). As Laclau and Mouffe argue, the play of difference without limits leads ultimately to the atomization of the social and is itself totalizing. It is also logically unsustainable, given that some expressions of difference, from the ethnic cleansing of Kosovo to the killing fields of Rwanda, are antithetical to others, producing new violences and closures.

Third, the notion that movements are irreducibly diverse is in danger of reifying the differences between them, rendering them unbridgeable and thus paradoxically constructing movements in modernist fashion as unitary wholes. Butler would deny this last charge. Movements, she insists, are not entirely "discrete and differentiated entities" but "overlapping, mutually determining, and convergent fields of politicization" (1998: 37). She argues that difference is "the condition of possibility of identity": in other words, it is only through the discursive possibility of being not-A that the identity of movement A becomes possible, thus A and not-A can never be entirely distinct nor merged but must always remain in some kind of relationship to each other. Efforts can then be made to construct "*a mode of sustaining conflict in politically productive ways*" (emphasis in orginal) (Butler 1998: 37). Although this formulation is useful in drawing our attention to the relational mechanisms by which identities are formed, it still seems to assume that a coherent movement is constituted in relationship to another coherent movement. Because of the underlying agonistic ontology of a strong postmodern approach, this formulation also posits an intrinsically conflictual mode of identity construction and thus of interaction between movements.

Laclau and Mouffe insisted that this kind of discursive process of identity construction characterizes relations *within* movements as well as between them. Melucci's constructivist social movement theory complicates the picture even further. Melucci depicts movements as ongoing processes, systems of action through which participants negotiate shared meanings, identities, and interests. *One* of the ways participants do this is literally through discourse, in the form of discussion between participants. According to Melucci, movements are constructed by their participants largely through "submerged" or "subterranean" networks of meaning in everyday life, only occasionally surfacing as visible, public actors (1989: 70–73; 1996a: 113–116). To this account of movement construction, we can add the description of movement *structure* alluded to by Melucci (1996a: 113), and originally put forward by Luther Gerlach and Virginia Hine (1970). Contemporary movements are depicted as "decentralised, segmentary and reticulate," without central leadership or control, "composed of a great variety of localised groups or cells which . . . constantly split, combine, and proliferate" and interconnected by "crossing and intercrossing lines" of communication that are "weblike" (Gerlach and Hine 1970: 33–55). The boundaries between movements are thus extremely unclear. Individuals may participate in more than one process of collective identity construction, and subterranean networks may overlap or "blend" together so extensively that they are not separable for the participant or observer (West 1992). In other words, movements are embedded in each other to a greater extent, and are capable of a more substantive and sustained politics of solidarity, than the agonistic and discursive ontology of Butler or Laclau and Mouffe can allow.

These three problems with the strong postmodern approach to movements—the conflation of power and discourse, the lack of evaluative criteria, and the reification of differences—raise corresponding difficulties with the depiction of democracy. On the first point, the concern with the cultural dimension of democracy is a welcome corrective to what remains the overwhelmingly economistic and statist focus of both modernist and new times approaches. However, the postmodern turn is in danger of sloughing off the material and substantive aspects of democracy entirely. Butler rightly warns us to be wary of caricaturing postmodern politics as "merely cultural" when culture is constitutive of so much of social life, but this does not tackle the tendency identified above whereby all realms are seen as fundamentally discursive in nature, with discourse defined in an all-encompassing way that does not enable us to distinguish between the material and symbolic aspects of a phenomenon. The converse tendency to narrow the meaning of discourse to a focus on texts makes it all too easy to lose sight of the ways in which democracy has been a vital social struggle.

This brings us to the second problem. How is it possible for strong postmodernists to justify their adherence to democratic discourse? John Keane (1988: 235) argues that relativists must defend democratic procedures that can guarantee tolerance for difference. The postmodern commitment to democracy thus establishes grounds on which movement differences can be judged and those antithetical to the expression of others can be deemed anti-democratic and censured. However, it remains unclear on what grounds democracy can be privileged in the first place. Andrew Linklater's discussion of Foucault concludes that no philosophical defense for the political advocacy of certain values is provided (1990: 215). In other words, there may be a gap between theory construction and other kinds of political practices.

Finally, it is not enough to emphasize the democratizing impulse of the expression of difference manifested by a plurality of movements. It is surely also necessary to scrutinize the possibility of the democratic construction of commonalities between them. Strong postmodern antipathy to this stems from an underlying agonistic ontology that posits the immanence of power in all discursive relationships and the impossibility of imposing closure and fixity on identity. Any effort to build commonalities across differences is thus positioned as totalizing. However, an agonistic conception of society and politics is challenged both by the constructivist conceptualization of how movements operate and by concrete movement efforts to forge solidarities. These demand an account of democracy that is open to the need for the continual contestation of power relations while also providing tools to construct solidarities on a democratic basis. In effect, the strong postmodernist approach to democracy replaces the subordinating dynamic of models of unity with a politics of particularism and conflict. The possibility of a politics of democratic solidarity threading between the two remains unexplored.

Conclusion

The central themes of the four new times approaches to the relationship between social movements and democracy are compared and contrasted in Table 2.

Despite their differences, new times approaches share an underlying commitment to the broadening and deepening of democracy in response to the diversification and diffusion of power in late modernity. Social movements are emphasized as playing a central role in democracy thus reconceived, precisely because of the qualities that encouraged the hostility of modernist approaches: their embeddedness in social life, concern with culture, reluctance to capture state power, and diversity of struggle. Yet new times approaches also share a tendency to misrepresent movements. They uncritically universalize the characteristics of NSMs or ignore movements that do not share those characteristics. They privilege certain kinds of activism in particular spheres or reduce movements to effects of discourses. The theories of democracy that result are consequently less expansive and holistic than might have been expected. Either democracy is reconfined to the civil sphere and economic interrelationships, or exclusive emphasis is given to its cultural and discursive dimensions.

Another limitation is the lack of attention paid by new times approaches to the twin contextual concerns of this book: the exclusions and mobilizations generated by gender hierarchies and the impact of globalization. There is some analysis of the activities of the feminist movement, as one of a range of NSMs. Cohen and Arato rightly draw attention to the diversity of feminist strategy, including the coexistence of cultural and institutional strategies (1992: 548–563). Mouffe has sustained an interest in feminist activism, as we see in the next chapter. Yet, this interest is not fully integrated into the radical democracy framework, where feminism is referred to fleetingly as one manifestation of the democratic revolution. Associative democrats would presumably only be interested in feminist groups organizing around economic demands. In contrast, strong postmodernists would presumably include feminism as one of a range of movements manifesting difference in ways that challenge state-centric politics and the hegemony of the left on radical politics. Like Mouffe, Butler has written extensively elsewhere on feminism (1990; 1992; 1993). However, the point remains that none of the frameworks for understanding democracy and social movements discussed in this chapter integrates feminist concerns about the marginalization of women in democracy or pays significant attention to feminist movement debates. The long-standing gender biases evident in modernist approaches are thus likely to be replicated.

Even less attention is paid to the burgeoning literature on globalization and its impact on democracy and movements. An exception here is Hirst's formulation of the associative democracy scheme, which shows awareness of the political and economic dimensions of globalization. Hirst argues for multilevel forms of territorial and functional governance, ranging from local authorities to regionwide regulation in the European Union as well as the creation of global-level bodies to regulate transnational corporations. Most of the other approaches discussed here were developed before the concept of globalization was popularized. Cohen and Arato are aware that the theory and practice of civil society has crossed state boundaries "in the crucial sense that similar things occur elsewhere," but their analysis is limited to a comparative study of movement activity and to concepts of civil society that remain inscribed within national boundaries (Walker 1994: 682–683; see Cohen and Arato 1992: 31–69). We see in Chapter 5 that theorists concerned with globalization have recently adapted the radical reformulation of civil society for their own ends. Laclau and Mouffe reject the notion of relocating democracy within civil society at any level. They remain preoccupied with the associated gramscian notion of hegemony, which, at least in its initial formulation, is a profoundly methodologically nationalist notion of oppositional politics, advocating the stitching together of a class-dominated

TABLE 2 New Times Approaches

	Ideal-type Democracy	Operations of Power	Terrain of Politics	The Political Actor	Strategies for Change	Role of Movements
Associative Democracy	representative, participatory, devolved state governance with groups involved in policy debate and delivery	the state and economy as equally significant sources of power	expanded to economic relationships	the individual as active, rights-bearing citizen and group member; groups as key actors	groups spread associative ideal, perhaps with state support; governance then requires stability	formal, public organizations pursuing economic interests can be democratic actors; others marginalized
Radical Civil Society	participatory deliberation, grounded in and enabling the collective generation of rights in civil society	the state and economy as equally significant sources of power	expanded to civil society	the individual as active, rights-bearing citizen and movement participant; movements as key actors	immanent in activism that extends rights; self-limiting refusal to gain state or economic power	NSMs as key sources of democracy, located in civil society, pursuing diverse strategies

Radical Democracy	pluralistic discourse expanding into society to contest power relations rearticulated as oppressive	pervasive, discursively produced in a plurality of sites; economic structures still seen as key	expanded to areas of life discursively reconstituted as political	individuals and movements as discursively produced subjects	immanent in discursive expansion and dissonance; stress on need to contest capitalist hegemony	NSMs as manifestations of democratic discourse and capitalism, can construct anti-capitalist solidarities
Politics of Difference	cultural medium for unsettling the parameters of politics	pervasive, discursively produced in a plurality of sites	expanded to areas of life discursively reconstituted as political	individuals and movements as discursively produced subjects	discursive expansion and dissonance; stress on movement contestation of political and cultural fixity	NSMs as manifestations of democratic discourse, their diversity challenging attempts at closure

civil society and state into an "historic bloc" (Cox 1993: 55–58). Laclau and Mouffe's reformulation, emphasizing the construction of alliances among diverse movements, could encompass the transgression of state boundaries in anti-capitalist struggle, but this point is not developed. It is, however, taken up by advocates of a postmodern politics of difference. Connolly explicitly argues that the transnational dimension of new movement activity expands democracy beyond the state. He is not writing in response to globalization but out of an ongoing interest in IR theory and its constitution as a separate realm of inquiry. In my view, his argument can only be taken farther if the theoretical universe of IR is forsaken for a more direct and detailed study of transnational movement activity.

The relative detachment from movement activity is one reason for the shared limitations of new times approaches to democracy and movements. Although the influence of the New Left, of NSMs, and of Eastern Bloc dissident movements is clearly visible in new times theory, their impact has been relatively attenuated and mediated through secondary texts. This contrasts sharply with modernist traditions, formulated by theorists who were frequently also participants in movement activity, from the French Revolution to the Spanish Civil War. It is possible that the increasing institutionalization and professionalization of social and political thought has encouraged the disconnection of theory from practice. It may militate against the recognition of the more complex dimensions of contemporary movements, including those aspects that do not chime with NSM categories or their transnational activities.

Another reason for the problems with new times approaches lies in their inadequate responses to the limitations of modernist frameworks. In particular, neither postmarxists nor postmodernists offer convincing reconceptualizations of power, politics, agency, and change. Postmarxists make the parallelist move of privileging two sources and sites of power in society, excluding others, such as gender, from democratic scrutiny. The strong postmodern response that power is pervasive, productive, and discursive provides a view of social relations that is undifferentiated, one-dimensional, and unrelentingly agonistic. Democratic politics has been expanded beyond the state, but postmarxists have removed the division between state, economy, and civil society from political scrutiny. Strong postmodernists either allow no boundaries at all or their boundaries are unclear. What is more, the reification of divisions between inside and outside the state and between the public realm and private life, receives only fleeting attention. A more complex, multidimensional view of the political actor has begun to emerge, but postmarxists tend to privilege political, civic, and economic dimensions of agency, and postmodernists cast doubt on the notion of agency altogether. Finally, strategies for change remain limited. Most postmarxists complacently accept the reconfigured liberal state and capitalist economy of late modernity as preconditions of democracy. Radical democrats privilege the transformation of capitalism while adopting a strong postmodern ontology that undermines the possibility of such transformation. Advocates of a postmodern politics of difference argue that transformation as conventionally understood is not possible. They focus rather on movement plurality, resistances, and transgressions. Efforts to forge alliances or to pursue a more radical program of change are deemed intrinsically totalizing.

I suggest that a weak postmodernist approach, which does not fall into the reductivisms of either the liberal turn in postmarxism or strong postmodernist ontology, could offer a fruitful way forward. The anarchist insights uncovered in the last chapter also need to be rehabilitated. I am not arguing here for a wholesale revival of anarchism but for a selective recovery of certain arguments, including the notion that power takes multiple forms (although this has often been inadequately thought through by anarchists themselves) and the accompanying aspiration to expand democratic politics throughout society in ways that undermine the modernist contention that the state is the primary site and source of political activity. Further, anarchists assert that individuals are social and multidimensional and have transformatory capacity, as do movements. They reconceive transformatory change as the construction of alternative kinds of relationship between the individual and the collective in the here and now, insisting that the struggle for a more democratic society should itself be democratic. These arguments were revived by the New Left, alongside an original emphasis on the cultural dimension of movement activity and its capacity to bridge the public/private divide. Although these innovative aspects of the New Left have been highly influential on new times analytical frameworks, anarchism as such has been allowed to drop from theoretical sight. As we see in the next two chapters, it continues to inform dimensions of feminism, feeding into efforts to uncover the gendered dimension of power, politics, agency, and change and to construct a more radical kind of movement democracy.

Finally, an adequate theorization of the relationship between democracy and social movements necessitates more attention to movements themselves and to the "direct theory" they generate. There is a need to move beyond a generalized discussion of the movement form to the detail of the goals pursued by different movements. "One needs to know about specific emancipatory movements, examine their internal system tendencies, their discourses and symbolic power . . . before assessing whether the result will . . . broaden the scope of democracy itself" (Apter 1992: 167). It is also important to examine the construction of relationships within and across movements. Above, we saw a dichotomy emerging between arguments for the imposition of a consensus between movements and the idealization of the differences between them. Constructivist social movement theory indicates that this is a false dichotomy, undermined by the actual heterogeneity within movements and the overlaps between them. What has yet to be established is whether the fragile connections within and among movements are themselves a site of democratic struggle. It is on this basis that I now turn to feminism.

Notes

1. This terminology and categorization are controversial. Many theorists who fit the weak postmodern tag—including self-labeled critical theorists, communitarians, and some liberals, according to Benhabib—would probably not think of themselves as postmodernists at all. Interestingly, Benhabib at no point calls herself a weak postmodernist, although the thrust of her argument is clearly to endorse that position as more compatible with feminist politics. The pejorative overtones of the term *weak* are also inappropriate. However, the categorization remains useful because it points to both a shared rejection of modernist ontological and epistemological assumptions and the very different theoretical agendas that have been constructed on this basis. It helps to situate the projects of some feminist theorists, such as Iris Marion Young and Sandra Harding, who are clearly not postmodernist in the strong sense of the term. In later chapters of this book, the disctinction is crucial in enabling me to make sense of the metatheoretical assumptions and disputes of black and third world feminism. It also allows me to distinguish different threads in the work of IR theorist R. B. J. Walker and to uncover affinities between this work and that of black and third world feminists.

2. This parallelist focus on economy and state is in marked contrast to the schemes of G. D. H. Cole, otherwise so influential on Hirst's formulation of associative democracy. Cole included a role for citizens' collectives organized around education, health, and cultural issues (1920: 96–116).

3. Other postmarxists have adopted more conventionally liberal or gramscian versions of civil society that include economic actors and influences (e.g., Keane 1988: 14).

4. These conclusions resonate with the work of NSM theorists Alberto Melucci and Alain Touraine. Both see movements as engaged in the creation and expansion of independent public spaces throughout society, such as schools, committees, and institutes, and in rendering new issues visible in public debate. As a result, movements encourage the dual democratization of everyday life and established political institutions (Melucci 1989: 165–179; see commentary in Keane and Mier 1989: 8; for this interpretation of Touraine's work on democracy, see Pécault 1996: 167–168).

5. This is a wearyingly familiar point to postmodernist theorists. The feminist Judith Butler has responded to similar criticisms of her work on sex and gender by insisting on a more thoroughgoing constructionism whereby any residual dualism between the material and the realm of the symbolic and discursive is abandoned in favor of a recognition that the material is an effect of discursive prac-

tices. More specifically, her work examines how the body is "sexed," given concrete, material shape and cultural meaning, through discourses of heterosexuality (Butler 1993). This is extremely important and influential work, but it strives, ultimately, to overcome the dualism between the material and symbolic/discursive by locating causality entirely in the latter. There is still no possibility here of theorizing a more *dialectical* relationship between the material and discursive dimensions of embodiment.

6. In later work, Mouffe leans toward a republican concern with the individual subject, as discussed in the next chapter, and then toward approval of associative democracy, in which "associations" replace movements (1995). Neither of these strategies answers the questions raised here. Furthermore both, I think, are deradicalizing.

3

Constructing a Woman-Friendly Polity[1]

Democracy without women is no democracy!

(Declaration . . . of Independent Women's Democratic Initiative 1991: 127)

Women have tried to change the contours of a male-defined concept of democracy and assert the struggles for democracy which have been present within women's movements as integral to a democratic body politic.

(Rowbotham 1986: 106–107)

Introduction

Feminist theory and practice occupies an illuminating position in debates about the relationship between social movements and democracy. As both a social movement *and* an academic body of thought, feminism is frequently invoked as an object of analysis by the theorists discussed in Chapter 2. It also offers a distinctive, if marginalized, theoretical contribution. Although feminists are not the only movement participants to have been both objects of and subjects in academic debates, they are arguably unique in emphasizing issues of democratic exclusion and inclusion. As I argued in the introductory chapter, this emphasis stems from the historical experience of women's marginalization in the polity, their subordination within radical movements, and the difficulties that feminists have faced in their attempt to create an autonomous, inclusive movement of women.

From these experiences, two distinct trajectories of analysis have emerged. The first, feminist democratic theory, focuses on the incorporation of women in the polity. The second, emerging from debates about feminist organizing, focuses on the democratization of relationships within the movement itself. Both are rooted in a critique of the masculinist limits of liberal, republican, and leftist democratic theory and practices and are committed to constructing expansive, inclusive, and participatory alternatives. However, their reconstructive strategies are very different from each other. Debates about feminist organizing are the subject of Chapter 4; the arguments of feminist democratic theory are the focus here.

The chapter opens with a brief survey of the evidence regarding the marginalization of women in "malestream" democratic theory and practices. Then feminist explanations of this phenomenon are explored, under the headings of the nature of power, the scope of politics, the political actor, and approaches to social change. These explanations, and reservations about them, have given rise to constructive proposals from feminist democratic theorists aimed at including women in the polity. Reformist, maternalist, democratic cultural pluralist, and feminist republican proposals are discussed and their limitations mapped onto the four headings used above. I argue that feminist democratic theory is an important and imaginative effort to apply a feminist agenda to existing democratic theory and institutions. However, it has become deradicalized by a shared commitment to reinscribe power and democracy within the public realm. It is caught between essentialist, individualist, and elitist conceptions of political agency and it is timid in its approach to change. Paradoxically, feminist democratic theory allows scant role for the movement activity from which it originally arose.

Gendered Exclusions and Feminist Explanations

Women's marginalization within liberal democratic institutions was starkly evident at the end of the nineteenth century and the beginning of the twentieth. The vote was gradually extended, at least nominally, to all adult men decades before it was to women. Full female suffrage was not won in Great Britain, for example, until 1928. In France it was not granted until after the Second World War and in Switzerland not until the 1970s. Early feminists felt that the exclusion of women from the vote and other rights and privileges liberals accorded to "mankind" was inconsistent and ignorant, a hangover of pre-Enlightenment prejudice and custom that needed only to be brought to public attention to be remedied.[2] However, it "turned out to be the merest tip of the iceberg: a discouraging hint at deeper structures that keep women politically unequal" (Phillips 1993: 103).

This is not to say that women do not exercise their vote as often or as independently as men. This has been the conclusion of some nonfeminist studies of female voting behavior, which have argued that women are apolitical and prepared to delegate decision making to the male head of household. Subsequent feminist studies have concluded that gender differences in voting behavior are highly context specific, stratified by social and geographic location, and likely to diminish as women gain access to education and formal employment (Randall 1987: 50–53; Conway et al. 1997: 77–80; Baxter and Lansing 1983: 17–39). However, once we move beyond the vote, the involvement of women of all backgrounds in those institutions central to the functioning of liberal democracies, from parties to lobbying groups, remains significantly less than that of comparable men, although the proportion still varies over time and space (Randall 1987: 53–58; Conway et al. 1997: 80–128). At the highest levels of government, the numbers of women shrink dramatically, with little difference between democratic and nondemocratic regimes. A sweeping empirical survey of both reveals:

> a bleak picture of women's participation as national leaders, cabinet ministers, members of national legislatures and incumbents in the high civil service. At the end of 1990, only 6 of the 159 countries represented in the United Nations had women as chief executives. In nearly 100 countries men held *all* the senior and deputy ministerial positions in 1987–89. Worldwide, only 10 percent of national legislative seats were held by women in 1987. (Chowdhury et al. 1994: 15)

There are variations in the extent of women's participation, even at this level. Most notably, Nordic countries have long outpaced other liberal democracies in the proportion of women in their legislatures because of facilitating welfare reforms, an egalitarian culture, and the introduction of political quotas. For example, women made up 37.5 percent of the legislature in Norway in 1994 (Nelson and Chowdhury 1994: 775) and 47.4 percent of the cabinet in 1991 (Bowker-Sauer 1991: 277). Jane Jaquette has argued that there were noticeable increases in indicators of women's representation in many regions during the 1990s. Yet the figures she cites underline the overwhelming reality of continuing female marginalization: "In the United States, women now make up 11.2 per cent of Congress"; more than double the figure of 1987, to be sure, but the fact remains that men still constitute 88.8 percent (1997: 26–27). To take another example, women gained around 20 percent of the seats in the British Parliament in the 1997 elections. This was a dramatic rise, but one leaving around 80 percent of representatives male. What is more, these advances remain fragile. In the British case, they were the result of the victorious Labour Party having ensured that a proportion of its candidate shortlists was composed of women, a move that subsequently was ruled illegal. Finally, any advances have been counterbalanced by the sharp *drop* in female levels of participation during the East Central European transitions to liberal democracy. The important point to recognize is that Nordic distinctiveness and recent incremental advances in some countries do not fundamentally alter the stark and relatively static discrepancy between male and female levels of participation in liberal democratic institutions worldwide.

Women have also not been integrated as equals into alternative visions of democracy. The formerly marxist-leninist regimes in East Central Europe made an explicit effort to establish a substantial women's presence within their policy-making institutions, achieving an average proportion of between 25 and 35 percent. However, this was again much lower than women's presence in the general population and it was achieved through quotas. Although they are not necessarily undemocratic in themselves, quotas meshed with male-dominated, one-party rule to impose a female presence lacking in legitimacy, autonomy, and real power. Furthermore, efforts to democratize relations of production remained circumscribed by the top-down imposition of decisions by the party and by continuing gender hierarchies within the party, workplace, and home. Women were incorporated in large numbers into the workforce but in lower paid, lower status work. They remained burdened with domestic responsibilities, and their capacity for self-determination at work and in the home was thus not effectively increased (Jaquette 1997: 27; Janova and Sineau 1992: 119–123; Mezei 1994; see Chapter 6). Anti-colonial revolutionary movements that arose elsewhere during the twentieth century, from Vietnam to Nicaragua, were ostensibly more popular-democratic in nature and frequently succeeded in mobilizing large numbers of women in a wide variety of roles. However, they have also shown a tendency to revert to more traditional divisions of labor on achieving state power, excluding women from positions of authority (Molyneux 1985; Jayawaradena 1986). The record is not much better for radical movements that are not primarily oriented toward gaining state power. The New Left, for example, mobilized many women and was characterized by an egalitarian, participatory democratic ethic, but it generated predominantly male spokespeople and privileged masculinist modes of behavior. It also failed to challenge the sexual objectification of women and channeled them into community-oriented activism and supportive, administrative tasks (Evans 1979: 108–155, 177–179). Similar stories of women's subordination and the trivialization of their concerns have emerged from more recent radical nonstatist movements' organizations, from the Israeli peace group "The 21st Year" (Rapoport and Sasson-Levy 1997: 8) to the ecological activists "Earth First!" (Sturgeon 1997: 49–57).

Feminist explanations of the reasons why women are excluded from full and equal participation in both liberal and leftist visions of democracy are complex and diverse. Below I focus on arguments from the so-called second wave of autonomous feminist mobilization. This arose across western societies in the 1960s and 1970s, subsequently becoming more diffuse, subterranean, and institutionalized. I discuss arguments by predominantly white feminists that became orthodoxies over the first two decades of the second wave—hegemonic articulations of competing liberal, radical, marxist, socialist, and anarchist strands of feminism. These draw attention to the gendered operations of power; the implications of confining democratic politics to the spheres of state and economy; the masculinist character of political agency; and the limits of reformist, revolutionary, and statist strategies for change.

Uncovering Patriarchy

A major insight of early second-wave feminist thought was the identification of gender itself as a site and source of hierarchical power, functioning to privilege masculine traits, roles, and values over feminine equivalents. This brought with it an emphasis on the pervasiveness of power and a focus on its operations at the microlevel of everyday interactions, or what Nira Yuval-Davis calls "primary social relations" (1997a: 13). This contrasted with the focus of most modernist approaches on power in "more impersonal secondary social relations" (Yuval-Davis 1997a: 13), namely the state and/or economy.

Early second-wave feminists explained the causes and operations of gendered power under the rubric of *patriarchy*. The literal meaning of patriarchy as rule of the father, "the principle of the domination of senior males over juniors, male as well as female" (Uberoi 1995: 196), was stretched in very different directions. It was conceptualized by "radical" feminists as the primary and most fundamental form of power, exercised by all men over all women throughout the world and originating in either male biological capacities and psychological alienation or women's vulnerability to physical attack and pregnancy. Patriarchy in this sense was understood to be maintained through male aggression, the ideology of heterosexuality, and the institutionalization of both in marriage and the family. In contrast, feminists working within marxist and socialist theoretical traditions concentrated on the operations of patriarchy in capitalist modernity. Some argued that capitalism was intrinsically patriarchal, with varying emphasis given to the gendered division of labor, the reproductive role of women, or the function of the household within the economy. Others insisted that patriarchy and capitalism were distinct if interrelated systems of power, although they disagreed on the precise nature of that interrelationship. All accepted that neither patriarchy nor capitalism should be analytically or politically privileged, both being equally significant forms of power. In addition, socialist feminists agreed that patriarchy was a property of structures that positioned both women *and* men in patterned roles within society (see summaries in Beechey 1979: 66–77; Connell 1987: 41–46, 54–61; Walby 1990a: 2–7; Tong 1989: 71–194). Most socialist and radical feminists held to the view that it was both possible and necessary to abolish patriarchal and capitalist power relations and thus create a power-free world.

A third strand in second-wave feminist thinking about gender and power should be mentioned here, one drawing a distinction between *power over* as domination and control and *power to* as creative capacity, exercised in association with others rather than at their expense. The latter form of power also featured as an important strand in republican thinking (see Chapter 1). Feminists have argued that it reflects specifically feminine, relational modes of being and acting, of the kind typically exercised in intimate realms of life and in local communities (French 1985: 504–512; Elshtain 1990: 139–142; Mansbridge 1998: 147–150). Such arguments have generally not been intended as a rejection of theories of patriarchal power over but do modify them by insisting that women's experiences are not entirely negative and that their capacity for agency should be recognized alongside the constraints imposed upon it. This implies that patriarchal power has not entirely prevented women from making a contribution to democracy although it has ensured that their contribution has not been fully valued.

The Public/Private Divide and the Scope of Politics

Second-wave feminist criticisms of the limited scope of most formulations of democracy focus particularly on the distinction between public and private life. Many feminists have recognized the force of Marx's critique of the liberal divide between public life and the private world of civil society. However, they have added that both liberalism and marxism, and other approaches to democracy, rely on and reify a different public/private distinction, that between the *domestic* realm and the rest of social life (Elshtain 1993; Pateman 1989: 118–140). The gendered character of the domestic sphere was explicitly recognized and defended in early liberal and republican work, and criticized in some marxist and anarchist tracts, but it has since been subsumed within the amorphous mass of civil society. Women's continued association with the domestic, and the positioning of the domestic as doubly private and outside of the public, has served to naturalize the relations of inequality between the genders that structure all realms of life and to ensure that most women remain politically invisible.

Whereas some second-wave feminists have produced ahistorical and transcultural theories of this phenomenon, others have stressed that its precise formulation and the ramifications for women have varied over time and place. Carole Pateman's influential analysis of the recasting of this relationship in modernity (1988, 1989) describes a transition from a monolithic public patriarchal order, in which paternal control of the household was subordinated to a masculine hierarchy descending downwards from God and the King, to a system of private patriarchy whereby male heads of households were reconstituted as free and equal agents in the public sphere through the maintenance of hierarchical gender relations in the home. This meant that the state and the supposedly private civil sphere were constructed as fraternal associations of specifically masculine equals. This argument is reinforced by feminist critiques of the masculinist and Eurocentric character of public modes of behavior and language, such as rational speech and impartial judgment. Feminists have argued that the dominance of these modes is predicated on the relegation to the private sphere of bodily, affective, and irrational ways of being and those people, including women, who are considered to manifest them (Young 1987).

Perhaps most feminist analyses of the public/private divide in modernity, particularly those influenced by marxism, have focused on the gendered division of labor under capitalism: the systematic allocation of responsibility for "public," paid work to men and "private," unpaid labor to women. This is *not* an argument that women have been entirely absent from the public economy. Total confinement to the home should be understood as a bourgeois aspiration rather than a reality for most women. It was officially rejected in ostensibly socialist regimes and is increasingly being rejected by women of all classes in most locations. However, women still take on the overwhelming responsibility for family and domestic chores and this, combined with associated ideologies of domesticity, romance, and sexuality, channels them into marginalized, subordinated, and often sexualized roles in the formal economy. Exactly where the causal mechanism in this process has been located by feminists has depended on their precise analysis of the way patriarchy operates and its relationship with capitalism. There has, however, been general agreement on the effects. In the West, women are concentrated in public welfare provision and service sectors, clerical and nonunionized manufacturing occupations, and part-time and lower paid rungs of the workforce. Women in developing economies carry out the bulk of textile and electronics production, usually in nonunionized conditions that are often appalling. Those on the fringes of the world economy eke out a living from marginal agriculture, the informal economy, and sexual and domestic work (Mackintosh 1981; Boserup 1989; Peterson and Runyan 1999: 130–147). The double burden of insecure and low-paid work in the formal economy and domestic chores in the private sphere operates as what feminist political scientists call a "situational constraint," limiting the participation of women, particularly those from certain classes, races, and locations, in public, political activities (Randall 1987: 127–129).

All the above arguments focus on the gendered exclusions arising from the restriction of politics to the public sphere. Feminist analysis also implies that the gendered hierarchies of the private sphere need to be recognized as political. This was the reasoning behind one of the most well-known second-wave slogans, "the personal is political." The slogan insisted that apparently personal issues usually faced by isolated individuals behind closed doors—such as whether to have sex, whether to have children, or how to organize caring roles and responsibilities—were systematically shaped by structures and relations of power that disadvantaged women relative to men. These power relations also limited women's access to participation in those areas of life more typically understood as political—and they required collective contestation (Morgen and Bookman 1988: 8–9; Randall 1987: 12–13). In effect, this necessitated a rejection of restricted notions of politics as a distinctive activity separated out from social life, or as limited to a specific realm or social struggle. Politics was expanded to encompass the maintenance or contestation of coercive power relations wherever they were manifested. This is an essentially agonistic formulation of politics as intrinsically conflictual. It brought with it an expansive notion of *democratic* politics as the contestation of coercive power relations, and the inequalities and marginalizations they produce, in even the most intimate areas of life (Rowbotham 1986: 85–86; Phillips 1991: 102–103; Jones 1990: 788).[3]

It could be argued that this too is an agonistic formulation, one that preempts the postmodern reconfiguration of democracy as an ongoing process of conflict and contestation rather than an achievable end state. However, there is another dimension to the expansive feminist formulation of democracy, and that is the aspiration to construct more cooperative, inclusive, and participatory relationships between individual women and the community. Of course, second-wave feminists have had vastly different visions of possible "utopias" to which they aspired and they have advocated very different routes to get there. Moreover, their arguments have rarely been articulated using the language of democracy per se. But the general point remains that much of early second-wave feminism sought to facilitate the self-determination and creative flowering of individual women and the development of more egalitarian and genuinely consensual relationships between women and/or between women and men. This resonates strongly with anarchist arguments about democracy, as explored in Chapter 1. One important difference is that early second-wave feminists were frequently preoccupied less with the reconfiguration of economic relations necessary to achieve a new interrelationship between the individual and collective than with the reconstruction of sexual and family relationships. However, like anarchists, many feminists insisted that the task of constructing new relationships could not be deferred until after a convulsive social change but had to begin in the here and now, within the movement itself. As we see in the next chapter, an emphasis on participatory, nonhierarchical, egalitarian democratic forms emerged early in the second wave and structured much movement activity.

Political Man

One reason for the second-wave emphasis on participatory modes of democracy was a concern with women's political agency and its historical erasure. "Malestream" approaches to democracy were criticized for universalizing masculinist ideas about who can act in democracy and how they do and should act, in ways that function to exclude women or marginalize their activities. One focus of criticism was the liberal notion of the political subject as an asocial individual engaged in the rational pursuit of pregiven ends. Drawing on histories of the social and cultural impact of gender roles, psychoanalytic theories of gender constitution, and the experience of giving birth and living in families, feminists have argued that women rarely have the opportunity or the desire to live as completely separate and distinct persons to the degree presumed by liberal ontology. Men can do so only if they distance themselves from feminine traits and roles, relying on women to undertake the major responsibility for domestic labor and emotional interrelationships in the domestic sphere (Gilligan 1982: 1–23; Tong 1989: 149–168; Benhabib and Cornell 1987: 10–13; Held, V. 1993: 171–173, 182–185).

The more social conceptualization of citizenship put forward by republicans, whereby individual self-determination is achieved through public deliberation, has been seen as little better because it shares with liberalism the insistence that all bodily differences and particularist emotional attachments must be transcended in the public sphere. In early liberal and republican formulations, the gendered implications of this move was made explicit. The bodily differences of women from men and their association with sexuality, childbirth, and childrearing earned them a subordinate service role in the private (Jones 1990: 790–792). Furthermore, second-wave feminists have noted that the historical connection between citizenship and military service, particularly evident in republican formulations, has reinforced women's confinement to the private by positioning them as vulnerable and in need of protection (Stiehm 1981, 1983). The fact that women eventually won formal inclusion as citizens (and, to some extent, as soldiers) has not, many feminists have argued, altered the underlying masculinist model. Women's participation is likely to remain partial and riven with contradictions. This is supported by the findings of feminist political scientists with regard to the situational constraints faced by women with childcare responsibilities and the socialization of young girls into domestic roles and passive traits, both of which limit women's capacity to become political actors as conventionally understood (Randall 1987: 123–126).

Leftist versions of the political actor have also not escaped feminist criticism. For example, the marxist emphasis on involvement in production and the transformatory potential of class struggle has been shown to marginalize women's lives and agendas. Although many marxists have recognized that production has a gendered dimension, structured by a division of reproductive labor, productive labor remains the key site of revolutionary struggle and postrevolutionary concern. The priority is still to integrate women into production rather than to reallocate parenting and domestic responsibilities, and women are urged to submerge their specific interests and autonomy of action within class identifications (Molyneux 1985: 250–251; Benhabib and Cornell 1987: 2–4; Thompson, J. 1986: 105–109). Other nonfeminist challenges to the economistic emphasis on the left have also downplayed or reified the gendered dimension of agency. For example, feminists have argued that the New Left movement imported the masculinist and individualist biases of the liberal democracy, privileging intellectualism and verbal aggression (Evans 1979: 108–115).

Despite these problems, feminists have clung to aspects of both liberal and leftist notions of political agency. The developmental belief that political participation is a value in itself for individuals, enabling them to flourish in all aspects of their lives, has been strongly restated by many second-wave feminists who have struggled to extend opportunities for participation to women. Also, the leftist argument that extensive and meaningful participation requires attention to the material contexts of people's lives has been widely adopted. Feminists add that it demands efforts to tackle the specific economic constraints faced by women.

Second-wave feminists have not only been concerned to find ways of integrating women into preexisting models of political agency. They have also drawn attention to the ways in which women already act, on issues and in spheres of life normally considered nonpolitical. Second-wave historical, sociological, and political science research into women's activism of the past and present has revealed that women have participated extensively in different kinds of social movement activity. Guida West and Rhoda Lois Blumberg have identified four main types of issues around which women have mobilized and women-dominated or even women-led movements have developed: "(1) those directly linked to economic survival; (2) those related to nationalistic and racial/ethnic struggles; (3) those addressing broad humanistic/nurturing problems; and (4) those identified in different eras as 'women's rights' issues" (1990: 67–68). Other commentators add workplace struggles, ad hoc community organizing, and women's civic associations to this list, with women's participation in "fundamentalist" movements gaining attention more recently (Randall 1987: 58–68; Morgen and Bookman 1988: 8–19; Bystydzienski 1992: 2–3; Jones 1990: 797–804; Molyneux 1998: 65–69; see also Carroll 1989 for a survey of women's involvement in "direct action"). With the exception of struggles for women's rights, these diverse political activities share an orientation toward pragmatic, quality of life concerns or the defense of family, friends, community, and tradition. Feminist analysts have suggested that this is a reflection of gender-specific interests and traits, "variously explained as some essential feminine attribute or derivative of the specific social positioning of women as carers and those responsible in the domestic sphere for the work of social reproduction" (Molyneux 1998: 66).[4] It would seem plausible that this second-wave feminist recovery of women's modes and spheres of agency also helped to legitimize the attempt of many second-wave feminists to create feminine modes of protest and alternative cultural forms, as well as encouraging the expansion of feminist activism into intimate relationships and community life.

Reformist and Revolutionary Strategies for Change

A final area of second-wave feminist criticism has drawn attention to the limits of strategies for change in "malestream" democratic frameworks. This is not to deny that many feminists have accepted conventional strategies. Reformism has been and remains advocated by those working within liberal and social democratic frameworks, who insist that women have to seize the opportunity to lobby for incremental change by exercising their vote and organizing collectively as an interest group to put more direct pressure on states, parties, and legislatures. The state is seen here as a neutral arbiter of conflicting interests that women have an equal chance to shape to their purposes if they mobilize collectively. Their capacity to do so, welfare liberal and social democratic feminists add, can be facilitated through economic redistribution. Such an approach has long been criticized by other feminists for its lack of radicalism, its search for compromise, and its emphasis on the activities of relatively educated and economically privileged women. A conventionally marxist model of revolutionary change through seizure of the state has frequently been pursued by more left wing feminists, often from within existing leftist organizations. The argument here is that gendered relations of power will collapse with capitalism and the liberal state, and a state controlled in the interests of the working classes will enable a more substantive democracy for both women and men to develop. This view has been criticized by those who refuse to subordinate feminist demands to anti-capitalist struggle. As the experience of so-called socialist states demonstrated, such subordination is likely to continue after the revolution. Gendered inequalities, although they may be substantially reconfigured, are unlikely to be decisively overturned.

I want to suggest that a third and distinctive approach to change emerged early in second-wave feminism, associated with elements of anarchist, socialist, and radical feminism. This approach offered an alternative to both reformism and revolution and had four main components. The first was the centrality accorded to ongoing, autonomous, feminist mobilization. The second was an emphasis on the role of small-scale consciousness-raising groups of women within the movement. These groups were intended to link personal transformation to broader struggle, to enable each woman to speak for herself, and to facilitate the construction of collective goals. The third component of this approach was an emphasis on cultural production, in terms of women-centered music, for example, or nonstereotypical imagery of women. This was intended to provide alternative psychic and social resources for feminist women and/or generate long-term changes in attitudes in the wider society (e.g., Levine 1984: 18–22; Melucci 1989: 63–68; Eduards 1994: 185). All of these strategies were predicated on the anarchistic notion that the means and ends of struggle are interrelated: that feminist women must strive to create in the here and now the kinds of relationships and resources that they wish to see generated in society as a whole in the future.

The fourth component of this distinctive feminist approach to change was a rejection of the state centrism that is characteristic of both reformism and revolution. This echoes anarchism, but I suggest that the impetus for it emerged more directly from feminist theories of patriarchy. These theories threw doubt on feminist capacity to secure the state for their own ends, by whatever means this was achieved. Although the state was rarely seen as the cause or crux of patriarchal power, radical feminists characterized it as coterminous with the male viewpoint and male interests. Marxist and socialist feminists argued that the state reflected both capitalist and patriarchal power or was an instrument of bourgeois masculine interests capable, at best, of partial autonomy (see summaries in Mackinnon 1989: 157–160; Watson, S. 1990: 4–6; Allen 1990: 23–26). As we shall see, a suspicion of the state continues to resonate in feminism and other radical movements. As Jean Bethke Elshtain argues:

> To hope that one might use the state as a vast instrumentality to be turned unambiguously to our good ends and purposes is to be naive and, paradoxically, to find oneself supporting practices that subvert the democratic-egalitarian core of feminism. (Elshtain 1990: 145)

Feminist Reconstructions of the Polity

In recent years, these second-wave critiques of democracy and pointers toward alternatives have given rise to a generation of feminist democratic theorists working in the academy. These theorists are centrally concerned to incorporate women into democratic ideas and institutions on a more equal basis. Although they could not have begun their reconstructions without the groundwork on the gendered nature of power, politics, agency, and change undertaken by their feminist predecessors, they have abandoned or transformed many of the above arguments. This needs to be put into the context of a more general move in feminism, from the 1980s onward, to question earlier orthodoxies.

Perhaps the most important dimension of this move involves the rejection of theories of patriarchy. It is now frequently argued that patriarchy is a universalizing and monolithic concept, insensitive to historical and geographic differences. Radical feminism has been particularly attacked on these grounds, accused of biological reductionism and cultural essentialism (Tong 1989: 127–137). Further, patriarchy is seen as a singular and simplistic concept or theory, incapable of capturing social complexity *within* societies, let alone across them. Thus socialist feminist analysis has been criticized either for separating out capitalism and patriarchy or for blurring them together and neglecting sexual and cultural factors (Beechey 1979: 75–79; Connell 1987: 43–46; Tong 1989: 183–186; Walby 1990a: 6–7). Radical feminism has been criticized for downplaying the role of capitalism. Both approaches are accused of neglecting ethnic and racial hierarchies and the autonomy of state power. To put it another way, they are recognized to be either monist or parallelist. Finally, patriarchy is characterized as a totalizing, oppressive, and politically harmful concept that eradicates women's agency. In particular, the radical feminist catalog of male violence and atrocities against women is now widely rejected as reducing women to victims and as complicit in sexist and racist discourses of women's vulnerability and need for protection (e.g., Lorde

1983). For many contemporary feminists, this sits uneasily with efforts to reconstruct democracy and uncover women's political agency.

Questions have also been raised about the expansive formulation of politics and democracy. Elshtain has criticized the radical feminist aspiration to abolish a distinction between the personal and the political (1993: 217–221). She insists that feminists should rather be attempting to push back conflictual and invasive modes of politics, thus opening up space for genuine privacy and intimacy beyond politics and contributing toward a more ethical and restrained polity (1993: 317–353). Others have pointed out that there may be sexual and familial interactions, from sadomasochistic practices to childcare, in which coercive and hierarchical power relations and the inequalities that result are actually desirable, or at least very difficult to contest. Feminist achievements on these issues are certainly difficult to quantify (Rowbotham 1986: 89–92; Phillips 1991: 103). The second-wave emphasis on participatory modes of democracy has been criticized for its undifferentiated application in widely different contexts and despite conflicting strategic demands. It has also been accused of generating new exclusions, as discussed at more length in Chapter 4.

Finally, wariness of the state as a source of change and the consequent turn toward movement and cultural activity has been rejected by many contemporary feminists. Such an approach to change is now seen to rely on a simplistic, monolithic view of the state (Watson, S. 1990: 7–8) and to be politically naive and unrealistic. It appears to lead ultimately into the cul-de-sac of cultural feminism and withdrawal from engagement with the mainstream issues that affect most women's lives (cf. Taylor and Rupp 1993).

Anne Phillips argues that feminist democratic theorists have begun to offer an alternative to the expansive and participatory second-wave democratic agenda in recent years. Feminist democratic theorists insist on the need to redraw the public/private divide in social life, in such a way as to facilitate the self-determination of women in both realms. Their attention has shifted from "the micro-level of democracy inside a movement and democracy in everyday life" to "the macro-level of women's membership in the political community"—and from participation to representation and citizenship (Phillips 1993: 104). From this shared starting point, four main approaches have emerged: *reformism* (with political and social strands), *democratic cultural pluralism, maternalism,* and *feminist republicanism.*

Reformist pressure for full incorporation into the existing public institutions of liberal democracy has remained a constant feature of feminist organizing. Reformist strategies often have far-reaching implications. As one historian argues, "the vote was far from an end in itself for [first-wave] feminists. It was the tool with which they would restructure society, extend rights and protection to women and children. . . . [T]hey aimed at the end of patriarchy" (Gullickson 1989: 599). However, given the gap between formal and substantive equality that has emerged since the vote was won, many contemporary reformist feminists are less sanguine about the radical possibilities of equal access and demand institutional changes to expand women's public presence. Several analysts have focused on the need for prior *social* reforms, such as educational policies aimed at altering the socialization of girls or policies to alleviate women's domestic burden, from the provision of childcare facilities to regulations allowing paternity leave. These reforms are aimed at giving women the time and skills to participate as equals in the public realm (e.g., Lister 1995: 14–32). The preoccupation with the substantive conditions of participation locates this approach in the welfare liberal or social democratic tradition.

Phillips, on the other hand, focuses on *political* reforms, advocating quotas of women representatives on party lists and in Parliament. She justifies these on the grounds that a representative body should mirror the make-up of society, the physical presence of different categories of people ensuring the symbolic recognition of diverse ways of life. On the occasions when representatives, even in a tightly controlled party system, get to exercise their own discretion, it is hoped that experiential diversity will encourage a more genuinely representative decision and enable more vigorous advocacy on behalf of the less advantaged (Phillips 1993: 90–101; 1995: 1–83; 1996: 146–151).

In what has become known as the equality/difference debate, many feminists have questioned the desirability of striving for equality within liberal democratic institutions when this leaves unquestioned a masculinist model of the individual and of politics and accepts the patriarchal devaluation of women's experiences and roles. "This not only means that, for many women, it will be difficult, if not impossible, to 'win the game,' it also means accepting the rules of the game—where those rules dictate that pregnancy is an illness and child care a disadvantage" (Mendus 1992: 215). Instead, critics argue, feminists should question and reformulate the rules of the game on the basis of the specifics of women's modes of being and acting. Two strategies to transform the democratic polity on this basis have been developed.

The first is Iris Marion Young's democratic cultural pluralism. Young claims that a participatory and inclusive polity cannot be achieved through the traditional liberal and republican standards of a homogeneous public sphere, impartial rationality, formal modes of communication, and abstract equality between individuals. These standards function to devalue and exclude from the public those social groups, like women, who are different from the culturally dominant norm of the white European male (Young 1987: 57–73; 1996: 120–126). Instead of suppressing difference, a democratic polity should encourage it, by facilitating culturally diverse forms of political communication and adopting "group conscious" policies. Examples of the latter include paid leave from work for women having babies, bilingual-bicultural education provision for linguistic minorities, and dual rights for American Indians as both tribe members and citizens (Young 1990: 168–183; 1996: 126–133). Most crucially, Young argues for the institutionalization of mechanisms of group representation in policy-making processes. This would give subordinated groups institutional visibility, enable them to generate policy suggestions, and grant them the power of veto on issues that particularly concern them. For example, women as a group would be granted veto power over decisions on reproductive rights (Young 1990: 183–191).

The second "difference" strategy, chiefly associated with Jean Bethke Elshtain and Sara Ruddick, has been labeled *maternalism* (in Dietz 1992; DiQuinzio 1995). Instead of the institutional inclusion of women as a group, proponents call for the diffusion of the values traditionally associated with women, particularly the nurturing and relational modes of being that stem from mothering. Elshtain criticizes the feminist neglect and even denigration of motherhood and argues that women should not renounce the traits and responsibilities of motherhood but should rather struggle to elevate their moral and social status and to nurture the nuclear family environment in which they emerge (Elshtain 1993: 325–337; 1982; 1990: 45–49). Ruddick, in contrast, insists that motherhood and feminism enrich each other and argues for a more radical, reflexive, and feminist maternal practice in which men can and should also participate (Ruddick 1990: 40–57, 236–244). Both theorists believe that the values and tasks associated with motherhood could form the basis of a new mode of ethical political discourse and active citizenship in the public. This is exemplified by the activities of the Mothers of the Plaza de Mayo in Argentina, who held vigils to bear witness to their missing children, believed kidnapped and murdered by the military regime (Elshtain 1981: 348–351; 1990: 146–147; Ruddick 1990: 79–81, 176–184, 225–234).

These two "difference" approaches have provoked substantial criticism from other feminists. They are accused of being essentialist, a point discussed in more detail below. In addition, the emphasis on women's particularity is criticized as incompatible with democracy. Young's insistence on the need to enable and support different modes of expression in the public sphere worries Seyla Benhabib, who insists that democracy demands the privileging of critical, impartial modes of communication in the public (1996b: 82–83). Chantal Mouffe, following Mary Dietz, argues that maternal values are an expression of a relationship that is unequal, "intimate, exclusive and particular." "Democratic citizenship, on the contrary, should be collective, inclusive and generalised" and is predicated on the equality of individuals (Mouffe 1993: 80). These critics share with difference feminists the desire to transform the liberal public sphere, but they believe that this requires the revitalization of genuinely gender-neutral notions of citizenship and universalizing modes of political debate. Their position could thus be characterized as *feminist republicanism.*

My use of this label may be controversial. As Anne Phillips has emphasized, feminists have long had an ambiguous, even fraught relationship with republicanism, finding some aspects of it useful while being sharply critical of others (Phillips 2000). So it should be stressed that most feminist republicans identified here attempt to modify republicanism by expanding the category of citizenship and the domain of politics to make both more inclusive. Even if the label of *feminist republican* is declared acceptable, there is likely to be disagreement about which feminists it describes. Judith Squires accepts that Dietz fits this category but argues that Mouffe should be understood as a critic of the turn to the republican tradition (Squires 1999: 178–184). Certainly, Mouffe is perhaps the least comfortable fit with the feminist republican label, given her strong postmodern ontology and her criticisms of the homogenizing implications of the emphasis of some republicans on a common good and common values. However, as I argued in Chapter 1, the republican revival encompasses many theorists who are critical of the more unitary and unifying dimensions of republicanism and who combine a republican emphasis on participation and deliberation with a liberal insistence on individual rights and social pluralism. It seems to me that some of Mouffe's work fits neatly here, attempting as it does to bridge liberal and republican views of citizenship via a strong postmodern approach to the subject. Her shift from a concern with the collective subject in the form of social movements, as discussed in Chapter 2, to a republican focus on the individual subject as citizen is reflective of the more general trend in left theorizing in the last decades of the twentieth century.[5]

Just as there are significant differences within the republican revival more generally, proponents of feminist republicanism diverge on some key points. For example, Dietz holds to a conventional republican insistence on the developmental and transcendent qualities of citizenship as an identity that can elevate us all above our gendered roles in society (1992: 75). Mouffe, in contrast, insists that citizenship is not "the dominant identity that overrides all others" but "an articulating principle that affects the different subject positions of the social agent" by encouraging collective identification with the democratic community while "allowing for a plurality of specific allegiances" (1993: 84). Furthermore, whereas Dietz holds to a conventional republican insistence that democratic processes should be reinstated within a unitary public space, albeit one expressed at different levels from the neighborhood to the nation, Mouffe and Benhabib share the view that democratic processes should be encouraged to proliferate in the form of diverse and dispersed discourses and processes, including social movement activities. "The public" is thus reconceived as heterogeneous and multicentered, or even as pluralized into many "publics" (Benhabib 1996b: 73–74, 83–84). Despite their differences, these varieties of feminist republicanism agree that the revitalization of citizenship and its expression in more genuinely participatory, open-ended, democratic processes should facilitate the expression of the multiple differences of all individuals, both women and men, and encourage their reconciliation along nongendered lines.

These are diverse approaches to incorporating women into the polity, each with distinct strengths and weaknesses. I want now to map my reservations about them onto the four points of feminist criticism of "malestream" democratic theory and practice explored above: the pervasive and gendered nature of power, the public/private divide, the masculinist political actor, and the limits of reformist and revolutionary strategies for change. This mapping exercise indicates that, despite their differences, feminist theories of democracy share certain problematic assumptions and have largely failed to offer convincing alternatives to the limitations of "malestream" democracy.

Democratic Limitations

The Retreat from Patriarchy

Feminist democratic theorists accept that gender is a site and source of power that systematically disadvantages women. They also reject the more totalizing implications of theories of patriarchy. For example, those working within an equality frame do not accept that the state and categories of citizenship are irredeemably masculine, whereas those emphasizing women's difference insist on the existing impact and possible extension of women's political agency. Elshtain goes farther than this in rejecting the radical feminist characterization of patriarchal power as pervading both public and private spheres. Elshtain insists that the home is a source of women's strength, rather than of their oppression, with women exercising a distinctive, informal kind of power within it (1993: 212–218, 332–337; 1990: 139–142). This is a useful corrective to tendencies in feminist analysis to deny women's agency, eradicate privacy, and deny the more pleasurable aspects of family life. However, Elshtain overstates her case by naturalizing and idealizing the nuclear heterosexual family and by denying that the imposition of this as the norm with its associated maternal duties has in any way impinged on women's self-determination. It is surely possible to reject the more totalizing aspects of theories of patriarchy without casting off the central feminist insight that hierarchically gendered power relationships affect even the most intimate spheres of life.

If the latter assertion is still valid, then a serious problem with feminist democratic theory emerges. Political reformist advocacy of quota mechanisms, the cultural pluralist insistence on modifying public debate and institutionalizing group representation, the feminist republican argument for pluralizing and expanding citizenship, and the maternalist effort to diffuse women's values all focus on modifying the operations of gendered power in the public sphere. Consequently, they tend to neglect the power relations that women face in the home. One notable exception here is Ruddick, who insists that the diffusion of maternal values requires the restructuring of domestic labor. However, she does not indicate how this is to be achieved. Of the approaches discussed above, only social reformism pays systematic attention to private power relations, advocating educational and economic reforms that are explicitly intended to have an impact on the structure of family life.

This connects with another problem: the neglect of forms of power other than those stemming directly from gender. Social reformism is distinctive in emphasizing the need for intervention in economic power relations. It also implicitly recognizes the power of the state, as does political reformism and cultural pluralism, given that all of these approaches rely on the state to intervene in society to mitigate the effects of gendered power. What is missing here is an awareness that the state itself might be stratified by other forms of power, and that these may limit its capacity to act in women's favor. I shall return to this point below. It should also be noted that Young draws attention to processes of cultural imperialism and marginalization and to more direct forms of violence affecting ethnic and sexual minority groups as well as women (1990: 53–63). However, the fact remains that none of these approaches to democracy is grounded in an analysis of the diverse sources of power, the various forms that it can take, and the ways in which these forms can interconnect.

Reconfining Democracy

In line with their focus on the public operations of power, feminist democratic theorists share a commitment to reinscribing democratic politics within the public sphere. This is, in part, a legitimate reaction to unresolved problems in the expansive second-wave feminist vision. Nonetheless, reconfining democracy in this way is a conservative move. Again, this is most explicit in Elshtain's writings:

> That is where the heart of "politics and the family" should lie—not in over-
> politicizing our most intimate relations and turning the family into the war
> of all against all to be negotiated by contract, but in fighting the pressures at
> work from the outside which erode, impoverish, or preclude the flourishing
> of our most basic human ties. (Elshtain 1993: 337)

In effect, Elshtain wants to protect the private from public scrutiny and
public modes of being while encouraging the diffusion of private values
into the public. There are two main problems with this argument. First, it
exempts the operations of coercive and hierarchical power in the domestic sphere from collective public challenges. Yet power relations may
erode and impoverish family life as well as functioning to limit women's
access to the public, thus constraining the possibility of women exporting
distinctive values into public life. Second, at the same time as Elshtain invokes the possibility of a republican-style ethical and involved form of
democracy in the polity through the expansion of private values and
modes of being, she characterizes the inverse feminist project to extend
democratic principles to the domestic sphere in liberal, agonistic terms.
This may indeed be the kind of language used by the radical feminists
who are the focus of Elshtain's critique, but many feminists who advocate expanding the political into the domestic insist rather on the need to
combat private power relations to produce more genuinely inclusive,
participatory, and cooperative modes of social organization in all spheres
of life. Certainly, feminist republicans Mouffe and Benhabib assert that
an engaged and deliberative democratic citizenship can be manifested in
a range of domains. Yet their formulation is also limited. It extends and
pluralizes the concept of the public rather than expanding democratic
politics to the home. Domestic relationships are thus still removed from
democratic scrutiny.

Further, reconfining democratic politics within the state or polity excludes the possibility of democratizing economic relations. It has long
been central to left thinking that such a move is essential to ensure that
democracy is more than a mere formality and that it can enable people to
have control over the material forces shaping their everyday lives. Marxist and socialist-influenced theories of patriarchy indicate that such control is as crucial for women as it is for men, although it cannot be
achieved without also challenging the domestic division of labor that is
tied up with production processes. In other words, democracy needs to
be expanded to both economic and domestic life if it is to be made substantive for women. These arguments are almost entirely bypassed by
feminist democratic theorists, influencing only social reformism. Even
here, the primary concern remains democracy in the state and polity.
State reforms of the private are seen as a means by which the public

sphere can be made more accessible to women and thus more fully democratized, rather than as a democratizing impulse in themselves. Indeed, the social reformist approach could be compatible with the restructuring of relationships of power and inequality in the private sphere rather than their abolition—as we shall see below, critics of state systems of welfare argue that they have not made women more independent but rather have functioned to replace women's dependency on men with dependency on the state (Brown, W. 1995). Expansive visions of democracy undoubtedly leave us with unanswered questions about how we protect intimate aspects of our lives. Nonetheless, the reification of the old modernist division between the public and the private, and the confinement of democracy to the latter, is clearly not an adequate solution.

Exclusion and Elitism in Reformulations of the Political Actor

I now turn to the concepts of political agency underpinning the schemes of feminist democratic theorists. All these theorists are concerned to recover women's political agency from the more totalizing implications of theories of patriarchy. They share the republican and liberal developmental commitment to the possibility and desirability of self-determination through participation as a citizen in the polity. For reformists, the challenge is to integrate women into existing categories of citizenship. For difference feminists and republicans, the challenge is rather to transform citizenship so that it can include women. Their diverse strategies for achieving this, however, are dogged by essentialist reifications, individualist abstractions, and elitism.

The charge of essentialism has been leveled most often at maternalists, for their reliance on notions of shared female attributes and subjectivities that "threaten to turn historically distinctive women into a-historical, universalized entities" (Dietz 1992: 74). Patrice DiQuinzio notes (1995: 25–35) that this charge is more applicable to Elshtain than to Ruddick because the latter insists that maternal identity is a variable form of social practice, only contingently associated with biological mothers and specific social backgrounds. Nonetheless, there is still a danger here of reinforcing the long-standing restriction of women's political role to their capacity to give birth, given that this is still necessarily prior to childrearing and a distinctively female act. There is also a danger of restricting agency to particular types of women, given that not all are mothers. Although the connection to biological capacities is loosened in Ruddick's formulation so that women and men who are not parents could adopt associated modes of behavior, she is still privileging a mode of being that is more accessible to some people than others. Young, on the other hand, rejects the idea that women share attributes or roles but argues for their representation as a "social group" on the basis of shared experiences of oppression (1990: 40–48; 1994). The fact remains that Young is "supposing that there are some experiences, interests and values that *all* women (in the US at least) have in common . . . when it is precisely this that has been brought into question under the name of anti-essentialism" (Nash, K. 1998: 47).

I propose that the nub of the problem with both of these approaches is not essentialism per se. The difficulty with maternalism is rather that it *universalizes* a specific mode of being as a political strategy appropriate to all contexts. Noël Sturgeon's discussion of North American ecofeminism reveals that some essentialist claims about women's roles can be more emancipatory than others. They can generate unity between women, opening up the possibility of collective struggle and the contestation of the essentialism that enabled that struggle in the first place (1997: 5–12). The crucial point is to be attentive to how and why essentialisms are constructed and to their context-specific effects. Thus maternalist rhetoric may well have been a powerful force for change in women's lives in the struggles against Latin American dictatorships, but it would severely limit women's capacities for self-determination in contemporary East Central Europe, as we see in Chapter 6. The difficulty with Young's framework, in contrast, is the aspiration to *institutionalize* a specific mode of being and identification. The granting of representation to groups on the basis of shared identity necessarily fixes and reifies that identity. Although Young does not pay significant attention to the implications of this, flexibility could possibly be introduced through mechanisms such as the frequent elections of representatives, periodic scrutiny of criteria for membership, and deliberative procedures for devising shared platforms. A more intractable difficulty surrounds the decision regarding which groups get representation in the first place and whether this would be open to change over time, given differences in the lobbying power of groups and the likelihood that groups would support the status quo that sustains them.

Reformist and republican efforts to avoid essentialism, on the other hand, end up accepting variants of individualism. These generate their own exclusions. As argued above, feminists have demonstrated that both the presocial self of the liberal citizen and the republican social citizen are intrinsically biased against women. It is unclear to me how feminist versions of republicanism, which either deny this gender bias or argue that it can be overcome by a recognition of the plurality, situatedness, and/or instability of the subject, can function in practical terms to aid the incorporation of women into citizenship. Indeed, Mouffe's strong postmodern reformulation of the subject may actually create new exclusions by reducing the complex, concrete, and patterned ways in which women are embodied to unstable discursive effects.[6] Without specifying strategies for changing citizenship, feminist republicanism is in danger of insisting that women should be squeezed into existing categories. Reformists who argue explicitly for this do at least offer concrete strategies for how it can be achieved. However, they do not challenge the masculinist individualism of liberal categories of citizenship into which women are supposed to fit. Moreover, both republicans and reformists focus on individual participation at the cost of collective activism. As we saw in Chapter 1, republican frameworks allow collective action only to the extent that it trains "good citizens," and liberalism acknowledges only formally organized interest groups and parties acting in the public sphere. Feminists working within these frameworks are thus potentially colluding with the exclusion of a whole spectrum of feminist activity.[7]

An additional problem emerges at this juncture: a focus on the agency of a very limited number of women. Reformists and cultural pluralists share an emphasis on getting women into legislatures and political elites. It might be presumed that these strategies are aimed at ensuring that the interests of women in general will thus be more effectively, more genuinely represented. However, this would be to ignore the fact, emphasized by Phillips, that elected women are not likely to represent the interests of the women who vote for them in any straightforward way. Arguably, women's interests may be distinct from men's but they are still extremely diverse. Phillips recognizes the additional problem of institutional elitism, highlighted by anarchists, whereby those elected are likely to gain an identification with each other and an interest in the maintenance of the system to which they are elected. Phillips also stresses that parties seriously restrict the extent to which representatives can pursue their own agendas. The implication is that women are only likely to be able to represent what they presume to be women's interests on issues where the party whip is removed, if there is some mechanism to keep them accountable to women in their constituency, and if there are enough women in the institution to constitute a critical mass capable of challenging masculine culture and agendas (Phillips 1995: 68–83). As Phillips rightly warns us, getting women into legislatures is a minimal condition of more radical change on behalf of women, not a guarantee. As we have seen, Young's framework is more radical because it directly attacks the composition of the political elite. Young advocates breaking the monopoly of parties on representation and institutionalizing participation for women as a group. Yet such a strategy requires more attention to in-group mechanisms of accountability than Young currently provides, given that representatives of the group would be likely to develop an interest in maintaining their own power. In any case, both theorists neglect the wider question of what can be done to ensure that ordinary women have more say in the processes that affect their everyday lives. They ignore the evidence that many women have attempted to do so through movement activism.

Reformism and Statism

Here we reach a final problem with feminist democratic theory: its focus on state-led change and the accompanying neglect of movement activity. Thus the political reformism of Phillips privileges access to parties and legislatures. Social reformists concentrate on the enabling effects of state welfare policies. Democratic cultural pluralism strives to develop mechanisms of group representation in state and other public institutions. Republican feminists focus on citizen participation in that nebulous entity, the polity, which has historically been all too easily conflated with the institutions of nation and state. To some extent, this state centrism is an understandable reaction to theories of the patriarchal state as straightforwardly representative of male and capitalist interest and to the separatist strategy this led many feminists to adopt. However, there have been other developments in feminism that should reinforce a wariness of state-led reform.

For example, there is now a considerable critical literature on the masculinist character of nationalist state-building processes. This draws attention to the symbolic association of women with birth and nurturing that lies at the root of the idea of the nation, "constructed through metaphors of human reproduction and its basic organisational form, the family" (Böröcz and Verdery 1994: 223). This underpinning of national identity is shown to have encouraged national and state elite manipulation of women's fertility and enforcement of their traditional reproductive role in both civic and ethnic forms of nationalism, from democratic France (Halliday 1994: 150) to Islamic Iran (Afshar 1989). Moreover, it may have been a factor in the rape of women in situations of ethnic conflict and interstate war. Rape in such contexts is frequently an attack not simply on women's bodily integrity but also on the honor and ethnic homogeneity of the entire community. A reinforcing factor here is the physicalization and eroticization of the nation as feminine in symbolic representation, particularly when threatened. This serves to bind men and women to the nation in distinct ways, men as active protectors and women as the violable protected (Verdery 1994: 249).

Such findings resonate with another feminist literature, on the military dimension of the nation and state. Militarism is shown to be still saturated with gendered codes and divisions of labor that elevate men as aggressors and protectors, and associated masculine traits, over women and associated feminine traits. Where women have been incorporated into militaries in recent years, critics argue that their incorporation remains partial and problematic, provoking crisis and backlash rather than a dismantling of masculinist values (Enloe 1988, especially 117–172, 207–220; Yuval-Davis 1997a: 20).

Wendy Brown takes the arguments even farther, insisting that gendered structures of dependency characterize women's relationship to the state in all domains in which the state is active, not just those such as national security and the military. Indeed, this dependent relationship is expanding, as is evident in the increasing numbers of women whose economic reliance on men has been transformed into dependency on state welfare. Brown argues that this characteristic of the state positions all women as vulnerable. It divides those "deserving" of protection from those "less deserving." It also extends the scope of disembodied rationality and will to power over women's lives and intensifies the disciplining of their behavior (Brown, W. 1995: 169–177, 185–193). The implication is that state-led policies aimed at improving women's status in society ultimately relocate female dependency rather than challenging it.

These arguments do not necessarily confirm the radical or socialist feminist depiction of the state as monolithic, all powerful, and entirely negative in its implications for women. On the contrary, their proponents emphasize that the relationship between gendered hierarchy and the state differs over time and space and that it produces contradictions and opportunities as well as threats. This is in tune with new times developments in social and political thought more generally. However, these feminists agree that the state remains a site and source of hierarchical, gendered effects. Feminists may not be able to avoid the state; more positively, they may be able to engage with some aspects of it for women's advantage in certain contexts. However, such an engagement will always be fraught with dangers of co-optation and coercion. This could be characterized as a *skeptical* and *strategic* attitude to the state (Peterson 1992b: 45–56; Waylen 1998: 3–9; Brown, W. 1995: 193–196).[8] The reliance of most feminist democratic theorists on the state as the primary source of democratization for women, and the lack of engagement with the potential ambiguities and pitfalls of such an approach, begins to look somewhat complacent.

Moreover, feminist democratic theorists play down the role of social struggle in democratic change, notwithstanding their own indebtedness to the feminist movement. Phillips argues that participation in early second-wave feminism was heavily circumscribed. Her arguments on this point are explored at more length in Chapter 4; the key point here is that her reformist turn to state-led, top-down change stems at least partly from an argument about the limits of movement-led change. However, following the logic of liberal and social democratic arguments, one could presume that a limited space is allowed in reformist schemes for formal social movement organizations in the public sphere, lobbying political elites to persuade them to institute quotas of women or to pursue women-friendly educational and economic policies. Young's democratic cultural pluralism, on the other hand, draws more directly on the activist legacies of feminism and other movements. Young has been inspired particularly by movement debates about difference and by activities offering "some beginning models for the development of a heterogeneous public" (Young 1990: 163). There is a recognition here of the capacity of movements to generate direct theory. However, Young is concerned to institutionalize such ideas and models rather than to provide an ongoing role for movements.

Feminist republicans also touch on the role of movements. We saw in Chapter 2 that Mouffe views feminism, along with other movements, as an expression of the logic of democratic discourse, functioning to extend that discourse deeper into society and constitute more sectors of society as democratic subjects. Dietz draws attention to the ways in which feminism and other movements have generated a variety of participatory forms of debate and decision making (1992: 78). Both, however, emphasize that their arguments apply only to the "right kind" of feminism. For Mouffe, this is one that avoids essentialist claims by and for women in favor of "a struggle against the multiple forms in which the category 'woman' is constructed in subordination" (1993: 88). For Dietz (1992: 78–79) it is one that rejects "womanism," "a position of gender opposition and women's superiority."[9] This meshes with the more general republican insistence that only "well-behaved" movements, acting as "schools for citizenship," are to be encouraged. Much feminist activism challenging the parameters and content of citizenship would thus be dismissed as essentialist, "womanist," and anti-democratic.

It is precisely those elements of feminism and women's activism of which republicans are most fearful that are stressed by maternalists as central to democratization. Maternalists are distinctive in retaining a bottom-up focus on women's lives and values as a force for democratic change. Their praise of the Argentinean Mothers of the Plaza de Mayo indicates that one way in which women's values and experiences can be brought into the public sphere is through movement politics:

> Preservative love, singularity in connection, the promise of birth and the resilience of hope, the irreplaceable treasure of vulnerable bodily being—these clichés of maternal work are enacted in public by women insisting that their governors name and take responsibility for their crimes. They speak a "women's language" of loyalty, love, and outrage; but they speak with a public anger in a public place in ways they were never meant to do. (Ruddick 1990: 229)

The Mothers, then, are an example of women articulating a public presence *through* their maternal responsibilities, not *despite* them. There is a strong resonance here with the arguments of historians, sociologists, and political scientists documented earlier in this chapter about women participating in large numbers in pragmatically oriented and community-based movements. Taken together, these claims point toward the possibility that the movement form enables women to act on issues affecting their everyday lives without removing themselves from their domestic responsibilities. It may allow women acting politically to draw on roles and skills learned within the family and domestic sphere, such as cooperative modes of organization, maternal authority, and the protection of children. In other words, movements can bridge public and private spheres and facilitate a form of agency that is rooted in the traditional domestic division of labor rather than requiring its transcendence.

The danger here, highlighted by feminist republicans, is that movements drawing on such notions of agency may entrench the domestic division of labor, the restrictive conception of womanhood upon which it relies, and the gendered insecurities and burdens that it entails. Yet, as I argued above, the crucial task for feminists is to distinguish between progressive and reactive essentialisms according to context, rather than universalizing one essentialist moment or dismissing essentialism altogether. In addition, Sturgeon emphasizes that movements mobilized by essentialist categories can also generate democratic structures, enabling essentialist categories to be subjected to scrutiny and contestation (1997: 11). This is a possibility to which feminists clearly need to be attuned. This brings me to the point that maternalists, as evident in the above quote, focus primarily on the *public* presence and impact of mobilization. Yet from anti–toxic waste activism at Love Canal in New York to the anti-nuclear camps at Greenham Common in the United Kingdom, maternalist-inspired mobilization has ultimately functioned to politicize the *private*. It has expanded women's understanding of their mothering role. It has encouraged the restructuring of domestic divisions of labor and enabled the expression of more public, diverse, and transgressive dimensions to women's identity (Brown and Ferguson 1995: 148–164; Roseneil 1995: 3–5, 34–37, 155–163). A feminist approach to change needs to take on board this impact of movement activism on intimate life, as well as its public political effects.

Conclusion

The main tenets of feminist approaches to reconstructing the polity are summarized in Table 3.

TABLE 3 Feminist Democratic Theory

	Ideal-type Democracy	Operations of Power	Terrain of Politics	The Political Actor	Strategies for Change	Role of Movements
Political Reformism	representative state government in which women make up half of the legislature	the state has power over society, which is also stratified by gender	limited to political society and the institutions of state	the individual as rights-bearing citizen, recognized as gendered	establishment of quotas of women in state legislatures and political parties	formal social movement organizations lobby parties and state institutions?
Social Reformism	representative state government in which women have capacity to participate at every level	the state has power over society, which is also stratified by gender and capitalism	limited to political society and the institutions of state	the individual as active and rights-bearing citizen, recognized as gendered	state policies of economic redistribution and gender resocialization	formal social movement organizations lobby parties and state institutions?
Democratic Cultural Pluralism	representative, participatory government with oppressed social groups involved in policy-making	hierarchies of cultural difference pervade society	expanded to political society, the institutions of state, and the domain of culture?	the individual as active and rights-bearing citizen and member of social groups; the latter also seen as actors	state policies recognizing, supporting, and modified by social groups	movements generate models of a heterogeneous public and of liberation through difference

Maternalism	collective will-formation in the public sphere, informed by women's maternal ethics	productive capacity of women can counter coercive economic and state power	limited to the public sphere, differentiated from private life but shaped by private modes of being	the individual as gendered, active citizen, shaped by or adopting traits associated with mothering role	immanent in maternalist activism by women	maternalist movements enable women to express private values in public realm
Feminist Republicanism	collective will-formation in multiple public spheres via genuinely inclusive deliberation	productive capacity of the citizenry can counter state, economic, and gendered power	expanded into plural public spheres, differentiated from the private	the active citizen, transcending gender, pursuing social goals through participation in politics	immanent in civic activism, including nonessentialist feminism	"good" groups welcomed as degendering citizenship; others feared as essentialist

Second-wave feminism has been extremely important in drawing attention to the gendered limits of modernist and new times frameworks of democracy. It has highlighted the importance of gender as a long-standing and pervasive source of power, the impact of the division between private and public life, the masculinist bias of notions of political agency, and the limits of both reformist and revolutionary strategies for change. Feminist democratic theory, which has developed out of these critiques, offers a range of imaginative reconstructive strategies aimed at creating a more genuinely democratic polity in which women's contribution is valued and their participation facilitated. Four main approaches have emerged: political and social versions of reformism, democratic cultural pluralism, maternalism, and feminist republicanism. However, these do not, ultimately, provide adequate alternatives to the limitations of "malestream" democracy. They neglect the operations of power in supposedly private domestic and economic relationships; reconfine politics and democracy within the polity; fall back on individualist, essentialist, or elitist versions of political agency; and rely, for the most part, on a statist and reformist model of change.

A more adequate feminist theorization of democracy needs to acknowledge and explain the continuing role of the feminist movement in challenging the limitations of "malestream" democratic frameworks and also in developing alternatives. As I argued with regard to new times theorists in Chapter 2, much contemporary social and political thought has been produced by a generation of theorists that has been highly influenced by movement activism, but disciplinary and professional pressures have ensured that movement links have become attenuated. This may be a particular problem for feminist-identified women, under pressure to establish their intellectual credentials given the masculinist character of academia and the openly political and emotionally involved character of feminism.

There may also be an issue here about stages of movement development. Some social movement theorists have argued that movements generally shift from "forms of noninstitutional, mass protest action to institutionalized, routine interest group or party politics" (Cohen and Arato 1992: 556). Increased integration within the academy could be one manifestation of such a process. This would go some way to accounting for the increasing presence of feminist democratic theorists in the academy and their preoccupation with formal institutional politics rather than social movement activity. However, critics of the stage model have pointed out that many movements, including feminism, maintain both formal and informal dimensions simultaneously and that a higher degree of institutionalization is not necessarily indicative of movement success (Cohen and Arato 1992: 556–562). The increasing institutionalization of feminist democratic theory in the academy should be seen to carry costs as well as benefits, one of which is the turn away from extra-institutional activism. Significant countervailing tendencies in feminist theory and practice also need to be recognized.

Feminist democratic theory responded to the undoubted problems with the early second-wave vision of expansive and participatory democracy by retreating from such a vision altogether. Other strands of feminism have continued to try to work out how such problems might be overcome. They deal primarily with the problems and possibilities of democracy *within the feminist movement* and are the subject of the next chapter.

Notes

1. The phrase *woman-friendly polity* is taken from Kathleen B. Jones (1990).

2. Many early liberal feminists also accepted that women had praiseworthy distinctive qualities, particularly of moral judgment, which stemmed from traditional feminine roles in the domestic sphere. It was argued that such roles should therefore be maintained but that the true value of their associated qualities should be acknowledged and allowed expression in the public sphere, as a complement or counterbalance to the attributes of men (Pateman 1992; Sarvasy 1992). As we shall see in the discussion below, a tension between demands for equality between men and women and recognition of the differences between them continues to structure contemporary debates.

3. Alternative formulations include Vicky Randall's argument (1987: 11–12) that radical feminists redefine politics as relationships of power. The radical feminists she has in mind are in danger of totally conflating power and politics so that there is little analytical distinction between them. In contrast, Sandra Morgen and Ann Bookman (1988: 4, 9) derive from feminist theories of power a more useful activity-based concept of politics as efforts to *challenge* power relations. However, this too is surely inadequate in ignoring efforts to *sustain* power relations. Confusions like this dog the literature. It is perhaps best to stress that the formulation above, distinguishing power, politics, and democracy, is my own.

4. Maxine Molyneux (1985) has drawn an influential distinction between two different types of women's mobilization: those stemming from *practical* gender interests, or from women's perception of their immediate needs arising from their location in the gendered division of labor, and those related to *strategic* gender interests, which are derived from an explicit analysis of women's subordination and aimed at overcoming that subordination. This distinction could perhaps be mapped onto the kinds of women's movements identified here, with most falling into the practical category and with women's rights movements distinctive in pursuing strategic interests. Critics of Molyneux's initial formulation have argued that it sets up a dichotomy that privileges feminist struggle over other kinds of women's activism and seems to presume an archimedean point from which women's real or objective strategic interests can be discerned. It may also be in

danger of replicating a reformist/revolutionary dichotomy when "[m]ovements arising out of practical gender interests can have revolutionary, or transformatory, consequences and movements arising out of strategic gender interests may result only in reform, and only for a few women" (Peterson and Runyan 1999: 178; see also Wieringa 1994: 835–841). Peterson and Runyan suggest that the multiplicity, context-specificity, and changeable character of women's practical and strategic interests is best conceptualized in terms of a continuum of struggle rather than a dichotomy (1999: 178; see also Molyneux 1998: 74–49). Whatever the nuances of this ongoing debate, the general point remains that women's political activism frequently reflects their locations in gendered divisions of labor, and it may draw on as well as contest the traits and roles to which these give rise.

5. It should also be noted that Jean Elshtain and Iris Young have feminist republican elements to their work, such as a joint commitment to the rejuvenation of a more inclusive form of public life, public discourse, and active citizenship. However, I would argue that their divergences from feminist republicanism are more significant than their affinities. For one thing, both retain a commitment to women's difference from men and insist that this gives rise to a distinctive form of political subjectivity, something rejected by feminist republicans as I have defined them here. Further, Elshtain argues explicitly against the "Aristotelian" idea of a "public space," entirely distinct from private life and modes of being (1993: 346), and Young's focus on group rights runs counter to the feminist republican emphasis on the individual citizen.

6. Kate Nash distinguishes between the abstract universalism of Mouffe's abstract conception of citizenship and its "concrete instanciations." She argues that the institutionalization of radical citizenship would require social struggle over the definition of social relations and that this necessarily brings with it the risk of essentialism. For example, movements for radical citizenship "might institute certain maternity rights specifically for women in the name of sexual equality." This would involve "freezing . . . identities in their current forms" (Nash, K. 1998: 55). It seems that a thoroughgoing anti-essentialism is possible only at an abstract theoretical level. In which case, one wonders about the point of abstract theory in the first place.

7. Another approach to citizenship, developed by Nira Yuval-Davis and Ruth Lister, seeks to foreground difference in terms of gendered and ethnic embodiment and social and geographic location. As this approach deals with exclusions caused by territorial boundaries as well as gender, it is discussed in Chapter Six.

8. In a strong postmodern move, Wendy Brown insists that neither the state nor male power is "unitary or systematic" (1995: 177). I would argue that the state can be conceptualized as multidimensional rather than unitary without denying its continuing capacity to centralize power and to produce systematic effects. This is an argument for a weak postmodern approach to the state of the kind developed in Chapter 4.

9. It should be noted that the term womanism has been adopted by some black and third world feminists to characterize a distinctive ethics and politics centered on black women (Walker, A. 1990). This does not entail a belief in the superiority of women, as Dietz's pejorative use of the term implies.

4

Reconstructing the Feminist Movement

Black feminist theory returns feminist theory to the discourse and *enactment of revitalized democratic values.*

(Caraway 1991: 70)

Introduction

Second-wave feminist critiques of the limits of "malestream" democracy did not only give rise to feminist democratic theory in the academy. They also generated an ongoing concern with the problems and possibilities of democracy within the feminist movement itself. Literature on this topic can be read as a kind of "direct theory," generated by activists and theorists who are reflecting on the movement in which they are participants. This direct theory also has relevance for social and political thought more generally.

This chapter begins with an analysis of why the democratization of the second-wave western feminist movement became such an important goal for many feminists. The limitations of early efforts, I suggest, do not mean that the entire enterprise was misguided but rather that democratic principles were inadequately implemented, in part because of assumptions about movement cohesion and the unity of sisterhood. The rest of the chapter focuses on black and third world feminist interventions. Their critiques of the feminist movement indicate that democracy was hampered more specifically by the operations of racism. This has led many black and third world feminists to organize autonomously, under the rubric of what has become known as identity politics. However, this strategy has generated its own instabilities and exclusions, giving rise to a more complex model of political engagement. The democratic implications of this move will be discussed under the now familiar headings of power, politics, agency, and change. Of profound importance for the future of feminism, black and third world feminist arguments also point toward an expansive, participatory, and complex democratic framework in which social movements play a crucial role.

Democratizing the Feminist Movement

The early second-wave approach to movement democracy can be seen as a logical extension of the arguments about power, politics, and democracy explored in Chapter 3. Recognition of the gendered and pervasive nature of power led to the expansion of the political into the personal and of democracy into intimate life. Broadening the *scope* of democracy in this way encouraged a critique of the liberal democratic *form*, because secret ballots and party competition were clearly not easily transferable to all spheres of life. A preference for participatory democratic forms was also drawn from marxist and anarchist traditions, feeding into more radical strands of feminism through their links with the New Left. The radical suspicion of representation as alienating and elitist was given a specifically feminist spin with the argument that it had functioned historically to delegate women's voice to men acting on their behalf in the public sphere. "In this context," as Luisa Passerini insists, feminist movement efforts at "direct democracy, refusing mediation and representation . . . [gave] many women for the first time, the sense of their right to exist [and] . . . the right to speak as *women*" (1994: 237). The expansive, participatory reformulation of democracy also encouraged an emphasis on movement politics as a vehicle through which women could participate directly in the contestation of diffuse, elusive power relations and develop their individual and collective voices.

Second-wave feminist movement democracy had the following significant features. It was manifested in small, leaderless, nonhierarchical groups holding face-to-face meetings. Every participant was given the right and opportunity to participate in the decision making of the group or meeting. Activities were divided out equally or rotated between participants so that "no one woman should be able to assume responsibility for the more interesting or influential tasks. Expertise and authority should be divided and shared: democracy was conceived not as a matter of representation or accountability but as a genuine equalization of power" (Phillips 1991: 122). Decisions had to be reached through open dialogue in which every woman could speak and be listened to. This was expected, ultimately, to generate consensus. This notion of the processes and outcomes of democracy characterized a wide variety of feminist activities, from consciousness-raising groups to community nurseries. It even spread into more formally organized, institutionalized groups such as the National Organization of Women in the United States (Phillips 1991: 121–124; see also Freeman 1984; Levine 1984).

The feminist movement, thus constructed as a *site* of democratic politics, was also perceived to be a *source* of democratization in society. It was to function as a kind of democratic laboratory, enabling women to act out their "democratic aspiration to embody new relationships" as well "the older democratic insistence on the need for a more equitable distribution of resources." This echoes the anarchist strategy of "prefiguring" wider social possibilities (Rowbotham 1986: 101). More originally, feminists argued that the movement enabled women's individual and collective agency in the context of pervasive patriarchal power:

> women's collective actions give women a wider range of experience, an identity as part of a group with common interests and *a sense of agency*. There are many testimonies from women in networks and organizations that they feel empowered and strengthened by coming together. This is an invisible change in the short run, but probably of great importance for altering sexual power relations in the long run. (Eduards 1994: 185)

In Chapter 3 I suggested that the movement form might be particularly hospitable to women's political agency because it could straddle the public and private boundary, thus enabling women to act in the public sphere in ways that draw on their private roles and responsibilities. The argument of early second-wave feminists was that the feminist movement *in particular* enabled women's political agency. This is because it did not simply bridge the public/private divide but politicized it, enabling women to challenge the stereotypes, inequalities, and silences that flowed from their association with the domestic sphere. A related democratizing function of the feminist movement resided in the way it operated to contest power relations in previously naturalized areas of social life. Efforts were made to expand democracy through feminist actions ranging from campaigns against differential wages for men and women to theatrical challenges to preconceived ideas of femininity, from lobbying for legislation against rape in marriage to the establishment of shelters for women suffering domestic violence. In all such actions, gendered structures and relations of power were exposed and challenged and efforts were made to construct more egalitarian relationships.

These democratic ideas and practices were the subject of criticism within feminism from the moment of their inception. Participatory democracy within the movement was attacked in an influential pamphlet by Jo Freeman (1984), originally published in the early 1970s, in which she argued that claims to "structurelessness" masked informal structures and that the lack of formal leaders did not prevent informal elites from arising. Anne Phillips adds that the equal distribution of tasks forced many women to deny their talents and abilities, that the emphasis on frequent meetings imposed too high a burden on most women, thus limiting participation, and that an unrealistic emphasis on consensus stifled debate (Phillips 1991: 127–145; see also Randall 1987: 254–257; Jones 1990: 808–809; Ford-Smith 1997: 235–253). Furthermore, Freeman cast doubt on the political effectiveness of organizing in small groups, implying that the strategy of encouraging democratization in society through the prefiguration of alternative social possibilities was unsustainable and indulgent, leading to political impotence:

> Unstructured groups may be very effective in getting women to talk about their lives; they aren't very good for getting things done. . . . So the movement generates much emotion and few results. . . . The women in the movement either turn in on themselves and their sisters or seek other alternatives of action. There are few alternatives available. (Freeman 1984: 10–11)

Freeman's argument, finally, implied that the expansion of democracy through movement activity into intimate areas of life was a misplaced priority when feminists should be challenging the "big structures" of the state, the media, or the economy.

However, it seems to me that the undoubted problems in early second-wave feminist organizing do not entirely invalidate the expansive, participatory, movement-centered view of democracy. Some of the criticisms are misjudged. Cathy Levine's (1984) impassioned retort to Freeman's pamphlet argued that there was an implicit alternative model of movement politics running through it, that of a mass organization with strong centralized control like that of a political party. Levine pointed out that such a mode of organization perpetuates the hierarchical, masculinist values that feminism is ostensibly supposed to challenge. The left, Levine insisted, should be more afraid of the "tyranny of tyranny" than the "tyranny of structurelessness." She also argued for the importance of cultural and psychic change, its interconnection with change in formal political and economic structures, and the role of the small group in enabling people to expose and tackle that interconnection. In particular, Levine stressed the role of the consciousness-raising group in linking personal struggles with the wider movement, building solidarity between women and carving out an autonomous women's culture.

All this confirms an important role for participatory, movement-based democracy as both a means and an end of feminist politics. However, Levine failed to counter Freeman's criticisms about the informal elitism and lack of accountability that can emerge in participatory democratic forms. A difficulty here is that the debate became polarized between the advocacy or rejection of structure. I would suggest that the key distinction was really between *different types of structure*: hierarchical or nonhierarchical. Freeman was right to point to the costs of failing to make non-hierarchical structure explicit or rigorous, but this does not necessarily demand a return to hierarchy. Indeed, some of Freeman's suggested principles of democratic organization—rotating leadership, delegation of specific authority for limited tasks, rational allocation of tasks on the grounds of ability and interest, diffusion of information, equal access to resources—are all compatible with nonhierarchical structure (1984: 14–16). Thus Levine and Freeman may not have been as far apart as they originally appeared.

Those criticisms of expansive, participatory aspirations that do have some purchase do not necessarily invalidate the entire project. Rather, they point to inconsistencies in its formulation and inadequacies in its implementation. Indeed, I propose that the major weakness in second-wave feminist movement democracy was not too much participation but too little; not that democracy was too expansive but that it was not expanded far enough. Both the form and scope of democracy were compromised by an aspiration to consensus and idealization of movement unity that made it very difficult for women to express their genuine differences when participating in dialogue. Phillips characterizes this as a problem of face-to-face meetings, in which people can be intimidated and prevented from expressing their opinions (1991: 130–132). Patricia Hill Collins asserts that the early second-wave "emphasis on women's coming to voice via the process of consciousness-raising" generated unresolved tensions between individual and collective voices that still dog contemporary feminist debates (1997: 380–381). I see both problems as symptomatic of the more general tendency, criticized by Alberto Melucci (1989, 1996a), to assume that social movements are unified political actors that express a coherent will. I suggest that this tendency was reinforced within second-wave feminism by an emerging assumption that women were structurally positioned in similar ways and that they had common interests and identities waiting to be uncovered. This would have encouraged the expectation that women's voices should converge within the movement, producing a collective actor that spoke with one voice.

In addition, the expectation of unity and consensus was heightened in feminism because it is "a movement that exhibits an important departure from other social movements, that is, it is led by women. . . . [F]eminism is meant to value, support and unite women" (Ryan 1992: 62). The belief that women within the movement could or should "do" politics in a more solidaristic and less conflictual way than men was exemplified by the notion of "sisterhood" (e.g., Morgan 1970, 1985). This exhorted a familial "concern and a personal care for women as a group" (Papandreou 1988: 335) and implied "a common heritage, some shared experience that sets us apart" (Phillips 1993: 33). Such an assertion of solidarity and commonality was intended to challenge the structures that kept women divided and in competition with one another (Cassell 1977: 56–71). Yet critics have argued that it set impossible standards for political collaboration based on familial affection (Phillips 1993: 32–33). It has also been argued that the claim to sisterhood rested on the denial of any meaningful differences between women, thus obscuring the relatively narrow identifications and agendas of many self-identified feminists and removing power relations within the feminist movement from democratic scrutiny (e.g., Mohanty 1998: 258–264)

It is thus not surprising that a series of schismatic convulsions arose in second-wave feminism. Vitriolic divisions have long been discerned between reformist and revolutionary sectors of feminism, constantly undermining the rhetoric of unity (Ryan 1992: 40–41; Taylor 1983: 436–438). Further subdivisions within the reformist sector include careerist, liberal, and social democratic feminism; the revolutionary sector can be broken down into marxist, socialist, anarchist, radical, "politico," and cultural strands (e.g., Ferree and Hess 1994: 49–51; Ryan 1992: 55). Each grouping is understood to have a distinct analysis of women's oppression and competing strategies for change, with ideological differences compounded by the tendency for wounding, personalized criticism, or "trashing" (Ryan 1992: 62). These ideological and organizational divisions now appear to have been superseded by divisions stemming from *identity*, with the proliferation of autonomous groups established by working-class, black, Asian, third world, lesbian, and disabled women. The claims of these women about the distinctiveness of their experiences feed into the long-standing marxist-influenced argument that women as a group are so stratified by class, status, and ethnicity that it makes little political sense for them to act collectively (e.g., Bujra 1978). They are also reinforced by the influence of postmodern theory on feminism and its emphasis on the fracturing of experience and fluidity of identity. All this has led many commentators to assert that "there is no overwhelming reason to assume an underlying feminist unity" (Delmar 1986: 10), and it seems difficult to talk about "the feminist movement" in the singular with any degree of empirical accuracy or theoretical sensitivity. We have instead a multiplicity of collective actors and identities. Movement democracy is thus reconfigured as the recognition of the irreducible plurality of "feminisms."

However, this is a somewhat misleading reading of the development of feminism. Melucci's constructivist approach to movements, introduced in previous chapters, is again useful here. Movements are revealed as typically fragmented, heterogeneous, and dynamic forms of collective action, their representation of themselves as collective actors always painfully and continually reconstructed and contested through complex, diffuse, socially embedded channels. Thus it is likely that there *never* was a homogeneous entity called feminism, able to act with a single will, although some feminists may have attempted to present it in that way. It is not correct to attribute that homogeneity and unity of will to individual, apparently distinct feminist mobilizations today, nor should it be presumed that these mobilizations are entirely disparate. They remain connected to each other insofar as they are engaged in the ongoing struggle to reconstruct feminism. A central part of that struggle, as asserted in my Introduction, "is the (re)definition of woman's identity." Although the identities that emerge may be increasingly plural and strategically shifting over time and space, their emergence from "the historical effort, individual as well as collective, formal and informal, to redefine womanhood in direct opposition to patriarchalism" implies a "fundamental commonality" to feminism (Castells 1997: 175–176; see also Riley 1988). This imparts a form of collective agency and identity to feminism and some coherence to it as a collective actor, but it needs to be recognized that this collective agency and identity is not unitary, stable, or prepolitical but heterogeneous and continually reconstructed through political struggle.

Democracy must play a crucial role in such struggle if collective agency and identity is to be negotiated, accountable, and open to change. I would argue that the fragmentary tendencies of the later second wave are thus a healthy development insofar as they involve a reaction against the democratic inadequacies of earlier movement politics, just as second-wave feminism itself was spurred on in part by the democratic inadequacies of the New Left movement. Although the democracy those feminist pioneers created turns out also to have had its limitations, it remains to be seen whether more recent attempts to renegotiate the relationships between feminists can offer a more participatory and inclusive formulation. The next section focuses on one trajectory of debate on these issues, found in the work of black and third world feminists.

Black and Third World Feminist Interventions

The phrase *black and third world feminists* is intended to encompass feminist-identified "black" women, "women of color" and "third world" women. None of these labels is unproblematic. Establishing criteria for what counts as feminist is always potentially exclusionary. Moreover, several prominent black and third world women thinkers have explicitly resisted the label and/or put forward alternatives (such as *womanist*). This is because of the racist history of feminist movements; because self-identification as a feminist appears to privilege struggle with women against men; because the content and style of black women's struggles are perceived to be different from those of white women; and because anti-racist struggle is seen as equally, or more, important (Walker, A. 1990; (charles) 1997: 278–285, 292–294; Mohanty 1991a: 4). The difficulty with terminology is compounded by the fact that racially based labels are necessarily essentializing, simplifying, and potentially reificatory (Collins 1990: 19–21). Further, the term "third world" is somewhat anachronistic since the collapse of the "second world" of the Soviet bloc. Increasing recognition of the geographical ambiguity of the term, and the way it "flattens heterogeneities, masks contradictions, and elides differences," has led many commentators to abandon it in favor of the more malleable but perhaps less political concept of the "postcolonial" (Shohat 1996: 322–323). Finally, grouping together diverse work according to the authors' skin color and geographic location may reinforce the racist practice of homogenizing a nonwhite, non-western Other and contrasting it to an uninterrogated white western norm—a danger that is particularly acute in the context of this book given my location as both white and western.

However, my use of the label *black and third world feminism* can, I think, be justified on two main grounds. First, it is intended to indicate a "common structural location" (Mirza 1997: 3), giving rise to "structural commonalities of struggles" (Shohat 1996: 332) and rooted in global patterns of power, notably slavery and imperialism and the ways in which these still shape contemporary capitalism and the state system. Second, it remains important in the subjective formation of an "imagined community" (Mohanty 1991a: 4–5), "a self-consciously constructed space where identity is not inscribed by a natural identification but a political kinship" (Mirza 1997: 3). In sum, black and third world feminists write from standpoints that have been defined or positioned as nonwhite and/or non-western and female in a world of racialized and gendered hierarchies, and they have had to struggle to redefine and reposition themselves. They are engaged in the innovative deconstruction and reformulation of feminism, among other things, in the light of those experiences.[1]

I am exploring the implications for feminism of this body of work, rather than others, for several reasons. Black and third world feminists are widely acknowledged to have pioneered debates about the marginalizations of the feminist movement. Further, although similar themes have emerged from postmarxist- and postmodernist-influenced perspectives, black and third world feminists have developed them primarily through engagement with movement practices rather than through participation in relatively abstract philosophical debates. Finally, unlike other activism-oriented, identity-based approaches in feminism, black and third world feminist work is distinctive in drawing attention to issues of geographic and territorial location. This is because it constructs identifications with non-western, non-European parts of the world: with indigenous peoples forced to the margins and diasporic populations whose dispersal demands the critical scrutiny of insider/outsider categorizations and notions of belonging. These aspects of black and third world feminist thinking are particularly important in Chapter 6. Here I want to begin with critiques of racism in the white-dominated, western-centric second-wave feminist movement.

Many examples of explicit racism in first-wave feminist organization have been documented, such as the eugenicism of the British birth control movement (Amos and Parmar 1984: 13), the support of Canadian white women's groups for anti-immigration policies that prevented wives from joining their husbands (Agnew, V. 1993: 219), and the efforts of white women's suffrage organizations in the United States to defeat the Fifteenth Amendment granting the vote to black men (Caraway 1991: 139–157). In contrast to this "overt racism that conjures active dominance and enforced segregation," contemporary white feminism stands accused of "a more subtle 'white solipsism' that passively colludes with a racist culture" (Donaldson, L. 1992: 1). This is despite the involvement of many white second-wave feminists in anti-racist struggles, such as the U.S. Civil Rights movement.

White solipsism dogs the four areas of feminist analysis highlighted in Chapter 3. On the issue of *power*, Gemma Tang Nain argues that "the concept of patriarchy . . . has provoked the greatest antagonism from black feminists" (1991: 5). It is seen as positing intrinsically conflictual male-female relations and as prioritizing their operations in the realm of family life and sexuality. This does not mesh with black and third world women's experience of multiple oppressions that cut across male privilege and female subordination, and it is particularly criticized for marginalizing the operations of racism. The ways in which white women may be complicit with, and benefit from, racist power are obscured. In addition, the concept of patriarchy is understood to jeopardize the necessary allegiance of black women to black men in the anti-racist struggle (e.g., Amos and Parmar 1984: 8–9; Carby 1997: 46, 48).

On the issue of the *location and scope of politics*, black and third world feminists have criticized analyses of the public/private divide that emphasize the association of women with the domestic sphere and child-rearing as the key source of their vulnerability and invisibility. The accompanying tendency to caricature families that differ from this model as deviant or "backward" has also been criticized. Black and third world feminists insist rather that the construction of the public and private, and of home and family, differs according to historical and cultural context and has been intimately shaped by the operations of many forms of power, not just by patriarchy. For example, the institution of slavery and the racist political economy that developed out of it have systematically structured black women into similar forms of work as black men outside the home, as well as into care and domestic roles in white women's homes. Furthermore, it has left a legacy of state intervention in the reproductive and family lives of black and third world women, including forcible sterilizations and abortions and the removal of children. Thus the family home is reaffirmed as a site of political struggle, but this is because it needs to be actively protected from external sources of power, because its capacity to offer sanctuary needs to be strengthened, and because it is a source of black and third world women's resistance (Collins 1990: 46–55; Amos and Parmar 1984: 9–15; Bhattacharjee 1997: 312–314, 322–329; Carby 1997: 46–47).

These arguments link to criticisms of white western feminist arguments about the *political actor* on the grounds that they marginalize and even eradicate the agency of black and third world women. This eradication has occurred partly because undifferentiated theories of patriarchy, when applied on a global scale, feed into racist stereotypes by constructing a monolithic picture of black and third world women as passive victims of their culture (Lorde 1983). There is also a deeper problem here in the form of an unreflexive anthropological approach to difference in academia, encouraging white, western feminists to constitute black and third world women as the objects of study with little attention paid to the power relations involved in such objectification (Amos and Parmar 1984: 6–7; Mani 1990: 36–39; Mohanty 1991b).[2] A related point is the tendency to assume that the feminist movement is a *white* movement, which black and third world women can be "invited" to join. This reflects a failure to "acknowledge the struggles of Black sisters both within the women's liberation movement and outside of it" (Amos and Parmar 1984: 7; Parmar 1989: 56).

Finally, such struggles often point toward different kinds of *strategies for change* than those put forward by a white-dominated feminist movement. The liberal feminist strategy of gaining access for women to the existing system has been accused of a bourgeois individualism that benefits only a white elite (hooks 1984: 1–3, 8, 19–22). Radical feminist struggles to reclaim an autonomous sexuality for women have little purchase for black women who are already hypersexualized as the exotic Other and who also, paradoxically, have been rendered sexually invisible. For example, campaigns for abortion on demand do not protect black women from enforced abortions, and reclaim the night marches can reinforce racist stereotyping about black sexuality by marching through predominantly black inner city areas (Hammonds 1997; Amos and Parmar 1984: 11–15). Black and third world feminists have instead prioritized anti-racist struggle, or they have striven to integrate anti-racism into feminism so that the latter is reconstituted as "struggles to free *all* women: women of color, working-class women, poor women, disabled women, lesbians, old women—as well as white, economically privileged, heterosexual women" (Smith, B. 1990: 25).

These arguments can be read as confirming my claim that the major problem with early second-wave feminist democracy was not too much democracy but rather too little. Democracy was not expanded to confront racialized relations of power in society and the movement. Structurelessness in organization masked underlying structural inequalities and militated against efforts to organize in ways that compensated for them. Participation was limited to a white middle-class elite who universalized from their own experiences to speak for others. One response from this elite has been the essentially defensive attempt to reestablish the distinctiveness of women's oppression and the coherence of feminist struggle "under the single 'mistress narrative' of gender domination" (Frankenberg and Mani 1996: 360). Another response has been the development of "additive" or reformist strategies, which add the experiences of black and third world women into existing analyses and networks without challenging core categories or practices (criticized in Spelman 1988: especially 114–159; Uttal 1990; Zinn et al. 1990). Others have retreated into silence. Such responses have provoked anger and frustration on the part of black women and led to many confrontational episodes in feminist conferences and campaigns (e.g., Sandoval 1990). Combined with their experiences of marginalization in other movements, many black and third world women have consequently felt compelled to organize autonomously. As the trailblazing Combahee River Collective insisted:

> no other ostensibly progressive movement has ever considered our specific oppression as a priority or worked seriously enough for the ending of that oppression. . . . We realize that the only people who care enough about us to work consistently for our liberation are us. (Combahee River Collective 1983: 275)

The Collective labeled their strategy "identity politics." However, separate organization on the basis of identity has proved to be problematic for black and third world feminists, as for feminists in general. Linda Briskin argues that "the problem of identity politics is not its appeal to identities, for in the first instance such a recognition of diversity is a healthy and critical response to the ideology of an unmediated sisterhood among women" (1990: 104). Or as bell hooks puts it, "We all recognize the primacy of identity politics as an important stage in the liberation process" (1991: 19). The problem occurs when experience and identity are naturalized and reified as the source of political unity and strategy, rather than recognized as contested and political in themselves.

A group constituted on this basis is likely to face fragmentary pressures as the women within it find their experiences do not mesh with those of others and as they assert a still more specific identity. For example, the Organisation of Women of African and Asian Descent was formed in Great Britain in 1978 by women who named themselves "black." As Heidi Safia Mirza comments, this "was an empowering act in an empowering time." Ultimately, however, "the legacy of that reductionist naming of 'blackness' was to shift the racial discourse . . . towards the struggle to be heard among ourselves. . . . OWAAD folded under the pressure from within to assert heterogeneous identities" (Mirza 1997: 8). As with feminism more generally, this tendency toward organizational fragmentation should, to some extent, be recognized as a healthy and necessary dynamic. Rather more problematically, identity politics gave rise to a rhetoric of a "hierarchy of oppression" whereby the more oppressed a group was seen to be, the more legitimacy it could claim for its vision of reality and strategies for change (Parmar 1989: 58). This meant that "black women, being the victims of 'triple oppression,' were the keepers of the holy grail" (Mirza 1997: 9). It functioned to silence women from groups perceived to be less oppressed and, most worryingly, to delegitimize the experiences of those not readily identifiable with one particular group, such as women seen as "not *really* Black, not authentic" (Zook 1990: 91).

In the light of these developments, many black and third world feminists have begun to develop more inclusive and democratic modes of organization. Their ideas can be mapped onto the four themes highlighted above: the operations of power, the scope of politics, the nature of the political actor, and strategies for change.

Democratic Innovations (1)

Toward an Interactive Theory of Power

Although black and third world feminist writings are critical of theories of patriarchy, they share a commitment to the view that power is pervasive throughout society. However, they reject monist or parallelist understandings of how power operates, insisting that power has more than one source and takes multiple forms. This insistence on pervasiveness and plurality encourages the conclusion that power necessarily operates *within* oppositional movements like feminism. These movements can never be entirely "innocent," power-free forces of resistance.

At least two approaches to power can be discerned within black and third world feminist literature. One is "cumulative" or "additive." It identifies several autonomous but overlapping structures and relationships of power deriving from gender, race, sexuality, and class, the combined weight of which is understood to press down more heavily on those situated at points of convergence. This can lead to efforts to identify one particular form as weighing heaviest on black and third world women (King 1988: 47). Such a view also lies behind the rhetoric of a hierarchy of oppression. An alternative approach sees power as "interactive" (King 1988: 47), "intersecting" (Frankenberg and Mani 1996: 359), or "interlocking" (Collins 1990: 222–230). Multiple sources of power are understood to manifest themselves simultaneously in context-specific ways to produce particular conjunctures, rather than hierarchies, of oppression. Although many black and third world feminists remain wary of the concept of patriarchy, I believe that the interactive approach enables its reconceptualization. Patriarchy was defined in Chapter 3 as a systematic form of gendered power that resides and results in the domination of men and masculinity over women and femininity. Now it is clear that the shape, effect, and degree of patriarchy are likely to change radically according to social context and the specific ways in which it overlaps with other forms of power.[3] Those other forms will be similarly varied and contradictory in their impact. This approach demands study of the context-specific manifestations of power. It necessitates a recognition that the "importance of any one factor in explaining black women's circumstances thus varies on the particular aspect of our lives under consideration" (King 1988: 48).

This emphasis on specificity and complexity has led some commentators to stress a convergence between black and third world feminists' theories of power and postmodernism (Frankenberg and Mani 1996: 360–361). Yet there are tensions here. Many black and third world feminists clearly remain convinced that there is structural fixity to power. They see it as sedimented and concentrated in predictable ways throughout society, with race, gender, and class routinely identified as major sites of oppression (e.g., King 1988: 47; Carby 1997: 45). This indicates that white dominance, patriarchy, and capitalism can be identified as macrolevel sources of power having an impact in patterned ways on black and third world women's lives.[4] Further, black and third world feminists stress the material effects of power on bodies: the ways it is constitutive of, experienced, and resisted through blood, sweat, and tears; the sheen of skin color; the bulk of bodies; the taste and smell of food; the intimacies of sex. This is what Nancie Caraway (1991: 9) identifies as the "fleshiness" of black and third world feminist theory. Seyla Benhabib's distinction between weak and strong forms of postmodernism, introduced in Chapter 2, is perhaps helpful here. Many black and third world feminists clearly hold to a strong postmodern view of power. However, it seems to me that the interactive approach is generally more compatible with the weak postmodern skepticism about essentialist and monocausal explanations of macrolevel phenomena, embodied experience, and social continuities than with the strong postmodern insistence on the discursive construction of the subject, the fluidity of relations of power, and an exclusive focus on microsocial practices and historical disjunctures. Further, many black and third world feminists share a postmodern skepticism about the idea that coercive power relations can ever be entirely abolished. I would suggest that this stems less from their adherence to a strong postmodern agonistic social ontology than from what could be seen as a weak postmodern belief in the multiplicity and complexity of operations of power—and from the experience of marginalization within liberatory movements. The need is reaffirmed for the continual contestation of power wherever it occurs.

A Politics of Location and Connection

The black and third world feminist commitment to the view that power is pervasive also confirms an "expansive" notion of politics. Writing about the U.S. context, Patricia Hill Collins argues that "Black women have had an enduring interest not just in resisting racist and sexist laws and customs, but in changing a broad segment of the rules shaping American society" (1990: 156). Thus the everyday rebellions of domestic workers against their employers; the caring practices that enhance children's self-esteem; the commitment by black women teachers to educate others in the community; and the collective organizing by black women in labor, feminist, and Civil Rights movement—all are interpreted by Collins as part of the spectrum of black women's resistance (1990: 139–156). Actions like these can be recognized as contributing to democratic politics if we recall the earlier expansive definition of democracy as the contestation of coercive power relations in even the most intimate areas of life and the construction of more participatory and inclusive relationships between the individual and the collectivity.

The insistence in black and third world feminist critiques that power is *interactive* as well as pervasive encourages the important modification that democratic practices must be *located* as well as expanded. According to Collins, black women are likely to:

> engage in . . . strategic affiliation and reject ideology as the overarching framework structuring our political activism. This does not mean that Black women lack ideology but, rather, that our experiences . . . foster a distinctive

form of political activism based on negotiation and a higher degree of attention to context. (Collins 1990: 160)

This suggests an alternative to both the undifferentiated expansionist view that an oppositional movement should subject all aspects of life to the same form of democratizing impulse and the conservative confinement of democratic politics to the familiar sphere of the polity or state. Collins's analysis implies that strategies to contest power and the inequalities it produces, including within a movement, need to be developed according to the socially and historically specific ways in which systems of power intersect in a particular context. Such strategies should be determined by activists in situ and not by some prior metatheoretical, universalizing theory. Of course, there is no guarantee that activists will have an accurate understanding of the context-specific operations of power, or that they will devise an appropriate strategy. As modified standpoint theory (of which Collins is a prominent exponent) insists, this knowledge has to be struggled for. Further, Collins insists that all standpoints generate only partial knowledge (1990: 234–237). In other words, it is simply not possible to have a bird's-eye view of the "totality," of the whole matrix of power relations. All claims about the way power operates are made from a position within the matrix and are likely to reflect the priorities and interests of that position. Therefore it is only through context-specific struggle that an accurate analysis and appropriate strategy for that context becomes a possibility at all. At this point, the interactive approach to power adds a further stipulation. Those strategies that are most attuned to the multiple and potentially complex interrelationships of power over time and space are most likely to be able to mount an effective challenge and to provide a democratic alternative.

This framework can aid the interpretation of quite diverse moments of feminist activism. Take, for example, the efforts of Sisters in Islam, a group of women lawyers in Malaysia, to reconstruct aspects of Islamic law along women-friendly lines. This strategy can be seen to be more radical and democratic in its thrust than a wholesale, secularist challenge to Islam, which would be likely to reinforce western ideological hegemony in third world contexts (Ong 1996: 130–134). On the other hand, the decision of the British group Women Against Fundamentalism (WAF) to agitate against a march endorsing the Iranian *fatwah* against Salman Rushdie can be seen as an appropriate democratic response to certain articulations of Islam within the British context. WAF's actions were informed by an analysis of the restrictive impact of all kinds of religious fundamentalism on women's lives in the United Kingdom, demonstrating awareness of the multiplicity of power, and they were combined with campaigning against the anti-Islamic attitude and racism evident in less critical anti-fundamentalist positions (Sahgal and Yuval-Davis 1992: 17–18; Yuval-Davis 1997b: 128).

None of the above should be taken to imply that individuals or groups from outside a particular location can have nothing of value to offer to activists within it. On the contrary: Collins's argument about the partiality of all standpoints is accompanied by the insistence that the knowledge each standpoint generates should be compared to others, in a dialogue aimed at the collective generation of fuller pictures of reality (1990: 234–237). This is primarily an epistemological argument, but it translates into a demand for a politics of *connection*—for the construction of strategic linkages across particularities of context. Collins's argument here needs to be put in the context of the growing literature on alliances and coalitions by black and third world feminists, which has arisen in response to the difficulties of identity politics. Bernice Johnson Reagon offered an early and influential articulation of this approach. She asserted that a politics based on the creation of a safe space, of a "barred room," is "nurturing but it's also nationalism. . . . Coalition work is not work done in your home. Coalition work has to be done in the streets. And it is some of the most dangerous work you can do" (Reagon 1983: 358–359). More recently, Chéla Sandoval has called for "weaving 'between and among' oppositional ideologies," undermining the appearance of mutual exclusivity between resistances and reconceptualizing them as "*tactical weaponry for confronting the shifting currents of power*" (1995: 217–218). Collins herself calls for the construction of "principled coalitions" (1990: 36). She specifies that such coalitions require participatory, open dialogue, rooted in an acknowledgment that all participants speak from partial perspectives and necessitating efforts to overcome existing power inequalities among participants that might distort access to dialogue and its outcome. I would add that principled coalitions also demand the development of mechanisms to ensure that participants acknowledge the partiality of their knowledge, such as measures to divide speaking time equally among participants and to facilitate intensive one-to-one dialogues.

Nira Yuval-Davis claims that Women Against Fundamentalism is a good example of a principled coalition. It was founded originally by diverse groups from black and third world diasporic communities, and has since expanded to encompass groups from other ethnic and religious backgrounds. Yuval-Davis argues that the organization maintains a non-assimilative respect for the differing concerns of participating women in the course of constructing a common opposition to religious fundamentalism and racism wherever it occurs (1997b: 128–129).

I propose that the movement form in general is a crucial site and source of a politics of location and connection. At this point, it might be objected that black and third world feminist arguments emphasize alliances and coalitions rather than movements per se. However, this seems to me to be a terminological rather than substantive distinction, reflecting the general tendency to misconceptualize movements as unitary and static. This tendency has perhaps been heightened by claims by proponents of identity politics of a prepolitical unity. As we have seen, the movement form is more accurately seen as fluid, heterogeneous, and continually (re)constructed. Melucci has argued that processes of movement construction take place primarily in face-to-face "submerged networks," as noted in Chapter 2, but others have criticized this view because it "localizes the process of the construction of meaning completely within the group of participants that constitute a social movement," thus ignoring the impact of exterior social processes, public discourses, moments of mass collective action, and interaction with formal political structures (Klandermans 1992: 80–81; also Mueller 1994; Bartholomew and Mayer 1992: 152–155). Further, other analyses of the development of movements in modernity have drawn attention to the dissemination of forms of communication that enable simultaneous participation in movement construction by people in disparate geographic locations. Although the connection of print media to the emergence of the hierarchically organized movements of modernity has been most emphasized, recent developments in telecommunications and computing are more compatible with the "decentralised, segmentary and reticulate" structure Melucci believes typical of more recent movements (Melucci 1996a: 113; Gerlach and Hine 1970: 33–55; see Chapters 1 and 2). These modifications enable us to see that movement construction can now extend far beyond face-to-face relationships, through processes that are large-scale but still indirect and extremely diffuse, and with essentially independent, disparate groups still connected to and identifying with one another.

Several feminist sociologists have argued that such a structure is typical of second-wave feminism, proving highly effective in sustaining feminist participation and in achieving movement goals (Taylor 1983: 438–440; Cassell 1977: 106–121; Roseneil 1995: 72–73). Black and third world feminist critiques indicate that feminist movement construction may thus far have been more limited, less inclusive, and less sustainable than many white feminists have realized. However, many black feminists remain committed to the possibility of forging more expansive, inclusive, and sustainable movement connections. The literature on principled coalitions could thus be read as offering a prescription for more demo-

cratic feminist movement construction. It also indicates the need for connections *between* movements, a point to which I shall return below.

Situating the Actor in Movement Politics

Although black and third world feminists strongly restate the view that
power is pervasive, they generally do not subscribe to a picture of total
oppression, insisting rather on the possibility and necessity of transformatory agency. As bell hooks argues: "sexism has never rendered women
powerless, it has either suppressed their strength or exploited it. Recognition of that strength, that power, is a step women together can take towards liberation" (1984: 93). This chimes with the view explored in
Chapter 3 that power has a creative as well as a coercive dimension and
that women, however constrained, can still exercise power. However,
hooks modifies this argument in two important ways. She insists that
women, when given the same opportunities and conditioning as men,
are just as liable to exercise masculinist, coercive modes of power. Further, women's potential capacity to exercise a creative and constructive
form of power does not stem from a putative association with (white,
bourgeois) feminine traits and roles, but from their participation in struggles against coercive power (hooks 1984: 83–94). A space for conceptualizing such struggles is opened up by an interactive approach to power
that recognizes that multiple forms, intersecting in complex ways, can
produce contradictory and unpredictable results, including empowerment and resistance as well as repression. For example, Deborah King
points out that black women's long history of unpaid and coerced slave
labor and poorly paid participation in the workforce has "promoted egalitarian relations with black men" and a degree of self-reliance, as well as
encouraging the pathologization of black and third world women as deviant and exacerbating their structural impoverishment (1988: 49–50).

The interactive view of power also demands context-specific study of
the ways in which agency is both facilitated and constrained. It implies
the deconstruction of universalizing, abstract assumptions about women
and close attention to the ways in which different women act in different
locations. Thus Chandra Talpade Mohanty criticizes white western feminist texts because they "discursively colonize the material and historical
heterogeneities of the lives of women in the third world, thereby produc-
ing/re-presenting a composite, singular 'third world woman'" (1991b:
53). She insists on the need for attention to the ways in which specific
conjunctures of power constitute diverse women as the "subjects of their
own politics" (1991b: 76, note 7). The picture is further complicated by
the recurring insistence in black and third world feminist thought that individual identity and subjectivity, formed at the intersection of several,

shifting forms of power, are complex, plural, contradictory, and never fully determined. Race, gender, and other aspects of our selves will never be uncontested, singular, and static foundations of the person. They are likely to coexist in complex ways, the relative importance of each shifting over time and according to context. As June Jordan puts it, "[E]very single one of us is more than whatever race we represent or embody and more than whatever gender category we fall into. We have other kinds of allegiances, other kinds of dreams" (interviewed in Parmar 1989: 61).

These arguments about the self bring black and third world feminist critiques to another critical conjuncture with postmodernist ideas. Some black and third world feminists have moved toward a thoroughgoing strong postmodernist acceptance of the fluidity and fragmentation of the subject, forged through the never-ceasing play of competing discourses. This shift has been fiercely attacked by others who fear the erasure of embodied experience and of their hard-won efforts to articulate it (Ram 1993). I would suggest that Benhabib's distinction between weak and strong postmodernism is again useful here. It allows for the recognition of a productive convergence between weak postmodern and black feminist arguments for the social construction, situatedness, and plurality of the agent, without demanding acceptance of the strong postmodern formulation that "the subject is merely another position in language." There is another point of convergence in that most black and third world feminists remain united in their *aspiration* to contest fixity in formulations of the political actor and enable imaginative, physical, and social mobility. Rather than reducing such mobility to a matter of the play of language and representation, the facilitating role of involvement in movement politics is stressed. Social movement struggle enables both "a form of consciousness in resistance" (Sandoval 1995: 222) and "creative, expansive self-actualization" (hooks 1991: 15).

This argument overlaps not only with weak postmodern frames but also with the developmental ontology of leftist political traditions. As we saw in previous chapters, the latter emphasizes the radicalizing and humanizing effect of participation in oppositional politics. However, as hooks insists: "Opposition is not enough" (1991: 15). Particular kinds of oppositional struggle are necessary. Thus hooks is critical of the ways in which black liberation struggles in the United States have tended to "imitate the behaviour, lifestyles, and most importantly the values and consciousness of white colonizers." She also argues that black liberation has been equated with the liberation of black *men* (1991: 15–16). Sandoval asserts that "hegemonic" feminist practices and efforts to classify them have reified movement struggle into opposing ideological ghettos and required the repression of more mobile identifications and strategies (1995: 211–214). Both theorists call for a more reflexive and democratic kind of organizing along the lines outlined above, based on a recognition that collective identity and agency is constructed and strategic and must be continually open to challenge and to connections with other struggles. The effort to connect, they argue, has been a historical pattern in black and third world women's mobilization, notwithstanding the turn to identity politics. To take an example from U.S. organizing, many white first-wave feminists insisted that their struggle for suffrage was in competition with the black struggle and should be prioritized over it. Black women attempted to combine support for both (Caraway 1991: 139–157). The construction of connections between movements may be especially crucial to facilitating black and third world women's agency, emerging as it does at the point at which many structures of power converge.

These arguments offer a way out of some of the problems of feminist democratic theory with its focus on representing women in institutions and the dilemmas of individualism, essentialism, and elitism to which this gives rise. The black and third world feminist image of the individual actor as situated, complex, and struggling for mobility through movement politics indicates that the meaning of categories such as "woman," "black woman," and "black women," and the extent of their/our shared experiences, cannot be determined through prior theoretical resolution or complex institutional mechanisms. Feminists should adopt a principled and pragmatic recognition of the central importance of social movement activism to any feminist agenda, because such activism provides a forum through which individual and collective identities can be renegotiated.

This points us back toward the early second-wave emphasis on the feminist movement as central to the reconstruction of democracy. However, early efforts to construct democracy *within* the feminist movement can now be recognized as flawed because they were intended to facilitate the participation of women perceived to have essentially the same interests and the same identity. In contrast, black and third world feminists insist that participatory processes within movements need to be developed that enable diverse participants to negotiate plural and shifting interests and identities. Black and third world feminists also confirm the second-wave argument that feminist activism is necessary for democratization *beyond* the movement itself, because it inserts women's voices into political processes in society. To some extent, the notion that the feminist movement can itself be regarded as a collective actor is rehabilitated. However, black and third world feminists also emphasize the pain and conflict involved in the construction of feminism. This reinforces Melucci's argument about the need to abandon the idea that collective actors are coherent unities able to act with a single will and speak with one voice. Rather, attention needs to be paid to the processes by which a collective actor is continually reconstructed and to the multiplicity of demands and perspectives to which it can give rise. Additionally, in an important departure from early second-wave orthodoxies, black and third world feminists refuse to privilege feminism as the most important agent of change for women. A plurality of movements, and the active construction of connections between them, is seen as crucial in enabling the political agency of black and third world women and in creating a more democratic society.

Democratizing and Radicalizing Political Change

Black and third world feminists emphasize the necessity of transformatory change with an urgency that stems from an acute awareness of their vulnerability to multiple structures and relations of power. This is a timely riposte to reformist complacency and to strong postmodern refusals of the possibility of radical change in favor of micro-resistances or the reduction of politics to a "language game" (Collins 1997: 381). Black and third world feminist arguments about transformatory change operate on weak postmodern terrain to the extent that they reject conventional revolutionary strategies. This abandonment stems from the recognition that it is impossible to grasp the totality of power relations, that coercive power is unlikely to be abolished in all its forms, and that it is likely to stratify liberatory movements ostensibly struggling against power. This encourages the view, first identified in anarchism and restated by some early second-wave feminists, that radical reconstruction cannot be deferred until after some putative future convulsion. Rather, the construction of alternatives has to begin in the here and now, within the movement for change. Thus the construction of a democratic politics of location and connection should be considered both the means and the end of black and third world feminist struggle. Furthermore, the abandonment of revolutionary strategy is accompanied by a refusal to privilege one site of struggle and force for change. As we have seen, the interactive analysis of power leads to a strongly pluralistic emphasis on the context-specific ways in which the operations of power are identified and oppositional movements developed.

Nonetheless, three sources of power receive particular attention as targets for change in the literature I have examined. This is because their interconnections with patriarchy and white dominance are particularly brutal in their effects on most black and third world women. First, the need to challenge the operations of the global economy is stressed. Strategies range from the organization of women working in factories or in privatized working environments to the establishment of programs for community relief, and from redefinitions of the meaning and place of work to the recovery of third world women's relationships with nature and their habits of frugality and resourcefulness (Mohanty 1997: 22–27; Shiva 1989: 38–95; Chai and de Cambra 1989: 60–61; hooks 1984: 95–105). Second, black and third world feminists emphasize the need to struggle against cultural dominance. This is not a merely aesthetic argument. The expression of difference is seen as necessary to preserve psychic health and to ensure community survival. Strategies to counter cultural dominance include retelling history and myth from black and third world women's perspectives, highlighting the contribution of black and third world women as knowers and teachers, developing black feminist cultural criticism, and reinstating Afrocentric and/or women-centered value systems (Collins 1990: 145–154, 206–219; Anzaldúa 1990a: xxiv; hooks 1991: 1–13; Chai and de Cambra 1989: 62).

These goals are compatible with early second-wave, movement-based arguments for change developed by white feminists, which also sometimes emphasized the substantive dimension of democracy and the need for the creation of alternative cultural resources and for long-term cultural change. But black and third world feminist writings point to a third site of struggle that many white radicals would prefer to bypass: the state.

Undeniably, many black and third world feminists reiterate a strong antipathy toward the state and its coercive potential, emphasizing "the crucial role of a hegemonic state in circumscribing their/our daily lives" (Mohanty 1991a: 10). The state is depicted as a coercive, militarized, bureaucratized source of power in itself, as well as a centralized nexus of racial, patriarchal, and economic power, which means that poor women of color are acutely vulnerable to its effects. This is evident in analyses of diverse policies, including child welfare systems, immigration restrictions, police brutality, the use of torture, the suppression of feminist movements, and frequent forcible attempts to control women's fertility (Tijerina 1990: 172; Alexander and Mohanty 1997: xxi–xxvii; Agarwal 1988: 12–14, 20–24; Panjabi 1997; Bhattacharjee 1997: 314–319). Consequently, we find in black and third world feminism, particularly in western contexts, a widespread rejection of reformist strategies that operate through state institutions and sometimes an explicitly oppositional, antistatist politics, as manifested in the "everyday battle" of black and third world women "with the state apparatus" (Aida Hurtado quoted in Sandoval 1995: 219).

Yet it should be noted that many black and third world women in western contexts have pursued change through institutional channels, on the rare occasions when this opportunity has been made available to them (Collins 1990: 155). Furthermore, in third world contexts from China to Nicaragua, Mozambique to Palestine, women have participated in large numbers in anti-imperialist, nationalist struggles to gain control of the institutions of the state, notwithstanding the frequently ambivalent gendered implications and results of such struggles. Feminist movements have also been closely associated with such struggles and have joined in the consequent maneuvering for state power (Heng 1997; Shohat 1997; Jayawaradena 1986). These divergences reinforce the need for a politics of location according to which it must be recognized that state-centered strategies will be more appropriate and even necessary in some contexts. On the whole, black and third world feminist arguments confirm a skeptical and strategic approach to the state, in an echo of the postmodern and postmarxist frameworks currently filtering into feminist thought. More distinctively, they indicate that access to the state and state-led change is always likely to be highly circumscribed for black and third world women by the interactions of the state with the structures and relations of capitalism, white dominance, and patriarchy. Thus the point is not simply that state-centered strategies are appropriate only in specific circumstances. They should retain their legitimacy only if they are one of a range of participatory movement struggles encompassing those who are most vulnerable to sources of power like the state and aiming ultimately to transform those sources of power to enable the vulnerable to gain control over their own lives.

This leads, finally, to the point that black and third world feminist strategies for transformatory change are neither relativistic nor parochial. The emphasis on enabling a plurality of struggle does not mean that "anything goes" or that everyone should "do their own thing." The emphasis on specificity of struggle is, after all, combined with an argument that power also has macrolevel continuities in origin and effect, and that these give rise to an inescapable simultaneity of struggle in some women's lives. Further, the partiality of all knowledge about the ways in which power operates has been stressed. All this means that the need to create connections between multiple movements is crucial. In effect, black and third world feminists reject both the modernist, monist prioritization of unity in a single struggle and the strong postmodernist reification of the differences between movements given the fragmentation of forms of power. They tread a path between particularism and the imposition of unity in the pursuit of social change by insisting on the possibility and necessity of the democratic construction of solidarities between diverse movements.

Conclusion

Black and third world feminist arguments about democracy and social movements are summarized in Table 4, where they are compared and contrasted to early second-wave, white-dominated orthodoxies.

TABLE 4 Feminist Movement Democracy

	Ideal-type Democracy	Operations of Power	Terrain of Politics	The Political Actor	Strategies for Change	Role of Movements
Second-wave Feminist Orthodoxy	participatory contestation of coercive power in the most intimate areas of life, and the construction of egalitarian and inclusive relationships	pervasive in social life; emphasis on patriarchy, its effects on private life, and interactions with capitalism	expanded into social life, including intimate relations; same mode of action required throughout	women constructing a common identity and voicing common demands; feminism also seen as key actor	immanent in feminist activism linking personal, cultural, and institutional; wariness of state-led change	feminism as site and source of democracy; aiding women's agency, bridging public and private, and politicizing the domestic
Black and Third World Feminist Alternative	participatory contestation of coercive power in all aspects of life, and the construction of egalitarian and inclusive relationships	pervasive in social life; taking multiple forms that interact in context-specific ways, including within movements	expanded into social life in differentiated ways; strategy devised in specific locations and in dialogue with others	the situated, complex, and plural self, striving for mobility in activism; movements also key actors but recognized as complex and contested	immanent in diversity of movements and links between them; priority to economic and cultural change; skeptical but strategic view of state	movements as sites and sources of democracy, aiding complex agency, bridging disparate struggles, and politicizing diverse issues

Notwithstanding their experiences at the sharp end of the failures of feminism, black and third world feminists have not given up on the promise of expansive and participatory movement-based democracy but are instead striving for innovative ways to make that promise real. Movements are reinstated as a *site* of democracy, with renewed stress on the cultivation of participatory mechanisms and modes of dialogue within them. There are two main reasons why movement democracy is seen as important by black and third world feminists. First, it can enable open-ended processes of identity and interest construction for the individual and for the collectivity. This is seen as particularly crucial in enabling the agency of black and third world women who are subjected to and produced by multiple forms of power. The notion that democracy within movements will uncover a shared, static collective identity, and will lead to the expression of a unitary will, has been rejected. Second, participatory and inclusive dialogue within movements can enable the construction of alliances between diverse, context-specific forms of activism. These distinct struggles could otherwise be dominated or suppressed by more powerful forces, or be doomed to parochial and ineffective isolation.

Movements are reinstated also as a key *source* of democratization in society. Early second-wave feminism reiterated the anarchist idea that movements could prefigure democratic relationships in the wider society, and they insisted that feminism, in particular, could enable the individual and collective agency of women by politicizing the boundary between the public and the private arenas. Feminism could thus also expand democracy into the most intimate realms of social life. Black and third world feminists insist that *all* movements could potentially enable the development of diverse and radical subjectivities, if they are constructed democratically and if they forge democratic links with other movements. Further, it is recognized that the movement form enables collective contestation of pervasive power relations in a variety of social sites, not just in intimate life. This is because of the capacity of movements to straddle all kinds of social locations and to link spatially separated struggles. The construction of connections within and between movements enables more adequate knowledge of the complex ways in which power operates and the development of broader solidarities, thus enabling power relations in society to be tackled more effectively on a variety of fronts.

Perhaps most important, black and third world feminists reject the second-wave idealization of feminism as *automatically* constituting a site and source of democracy. The uncovering of the workings of racism within feminism indicates that movements also contain anti-democratic and exclusionary tendencies. Democracy within and beyond the movement must thus be constantly and reflexively striven for if it is to be made a reality.

Such arguments offer useful correctives to those of feminist democratic theory explored in Chapter 3. Although feminist democratic theorists were right to point out the problems with a monolithic view of pervasive patriarchal power, they have responded by downplaying its operations outside of the state. Black and third world feminists put forward instead a view of power as pervasive, multidimensional, and interactive, producing complex, context-specific matrices of oppression in all areas of life. Whereas feminist democratic theorists' wariness of the undifferentiated expansive view of democratic politics led to a retreat to the public sphere, black and third world feminists retain a commitment to expanding democracy but through a complex politics of location and connection. This means that collective struggles must be formulated in specific social and geographical locations, but democratic connections must also be sought between them. In contrast to the forms of political agency in feminist democratic theory, which tended toward individualism, essentialism, and elitism, black and third world feminists are keen to enable the expression of differences within and between individuals while retaining the notion of collective and transformatory agency. They develop a situated and multidimensional notion of the individual and stress the need to seek ontological and imaginative mobility through democratically constructed movement activism. This process can enable a plurality of voices to be heard. Finally, feminist democratic theorists reacted to early second-wave state skepticism and the corresponding emphasis on the transformatory potential of the movement by becoming largely state-centric and reformist. In contrast, black and third world feminists insist on the possibility and necessity of social transformation through multiple movement struggles in diverse social sites. They have a strategic and skeptical view of the state, which allows for the possibility of engagement but only in the context of broader movement activism.

However, there are still some important questions left unanswered. In particular, I am interested in the applicability of black and third world feminist ideas *across territorial borders*. Most of the approaches I have discussed in the last four chapters assume that the nation-state is the foundation and backdrop of democracy and the home of social movement activity. Surprisingly perhaps, even some of those with more expansive visions accept the territorial boundaries of their particular state as defining the extent of their reach. For example, Sandoval's analysis of the development of subjectivity through different and apparently opposing struggles draws on "*U.S.* Third World feminism." Now there are strong historical and sociological reasons why the territorial boundaries of the state we find ourselves in should shape the scope of our inquiry and the extent of our political ambitions. However, these boundaries have also been naturalized and placed beyond the bounds of critical scrutiny, a testament to the ideological pervasiveness of methodological nationalism and statism in academic and political life.

Subjecting such assumptions to critical scrutiny seems particularly crucial given that a persistent anarchistic skepticism toward the state has snaked through second-wave feminist organizing and has reappeared, in a modified form, in black and third world feminist arguments. The latter insist that the state cannot and should not always be bypassed, but it must be approached with wariness. It certainly should not be allowed to define the boundaries and focus of political struggle. As I hinted above, national and statist categories are disrupted by the efforts of black and third world feminists to construct identifications with marginalized and non-western peoples within and beyond the states in which they are located. Furthermore, the black and third world feminist formulation of a politics of location and connection cuts across the usual static, spatial delineation of political life into appropriate spheres and would seem, ultimately, to challenge its confinement into those spaces called states. These are strong indications that states could and should be an analytical component, rather than the outer shell, of a framework to understand the relationship between social movements and democracy.

The next chapter examines the growing literature on the ways in which the state is being challenged or reshaped by processes of globalization. This is the backdrop to the emergence of significant, sustained attempts to reframe the possibilities for democracy and social movements in a global context.

Notes

1. My focus on the implications of black and third world feminist thought specifically with regard to the second-wave western feminist movement is not meant to imply that the former exists *only* as a critique of the latter, which is thus implicitly posited as prior and white. Black and third world feminist-identified praxis has been a presence within white-dominated feminist campaigns and in autonomous organizations in the West, particularly in the United States, since first-wave campaigns began. It has also developed out of and within other movements worldwide, shaping their development, from movements pursuing national self-determination and human rights, to those organizing against imperialism, racism, exclusionary immigration practices, and exploitation.

2. As Sara Suleri indicates, this argument can lead to an essentializing "claim to authenticity" in academic research, implying that "only a black can speak for a black." This is not particularly reflexive about the differences in lived experiences between the object of research and the researcher and, as Suleri stresses, ducks the fact that objectification is unavoidable in claims to capture the "ethnic voice of

womanhood," whoever makes this claim (1996: 338). The modified standpoint epistemology underpinning this thesis indicates that it is valid to expect the analyses of black and third world women about their own lives, and the lives of black and third world women more generally, to be particularly insightful. However, it rejects the idea that it is illegitimate to comment on anything outside one's own immediate experience, or that accounts of that experience should not be subject to critical comparison with accounts by and about others.

3. Many other strategies have been developed by feminists attempting to reconceptualize the relationship between gender and power. One is to adopt what Judith Allen calls the "adjectival mode" (quoted in Bulbeck 1988: 13), whereby the term *patriarchal* is deployed to describe an often unspecified quality shared by apparently unconnected moments. Alternatively, patriarchy is abandoned altogether in favor of what purports to be a more neutral descriptive term for relations between men and women, such as Sheila Rowbotham's *sex-gender relationships* (1981: 75–77), R. W. Connell's *gender regimes and the gender order* (1987: 119–142), or Hazel Carby's *sex/gender systems* (1997: 51). My concern is that this approach decenters the question of power and the fact that gender relations are hierarchical and unequal. Power remains a central analytical focus in the work of those feminists adopting a strong postmodern framework, but this framework has brought different problems in its wake.

4. I am using *white dominance* here as analogous to patriarchy, indicating a form of power. The more widely used term *racism* seems more analogous to sexism, indicating a form of prejudice. Some commentators would reject this fomulation, insisting that racism is not just a matter of prejudice but includes the systematic power of implementation. They conclude that "black racism does not exist" (Feagin and Vera 1995: ix). Floya Anthias and Nira Yuval-Davis modify this by arguing that "although Blacks may be racist in terms of believing that some groups are endemically inferior, they do not usually possess the power to effect change. On this basis it does not seem reasonable to consider their racism as the same type as that exercised by dominant groups over subordinate ones" (1992: 16). I suggest that distinct terms would therefore be helpful. The phrase "white dominance" is taken from Ruth Frankenberg (1997: 5).

5

Globalizing Democracy, Globalizing Movements

The reification of the state has proceeded so far in our imagination—and in the practices in which we are engaged day to day—that all of us have trouble thinking about a politics that defies its logic. But, fortunately, our practices are more advanced than our theories. The actual politics of social movements is a continual challenge to the enclosures established by the state system.

(Magnusson 1993: 124)

Surely we have had enough of a politics of little boxes.

(Walker 1995: 324)

Introduction

Modern understandings of both democracy and social movements have been fundamentally shaped by the experience of living within a world of states. State borders have been seen to demarcate the reach of movements and the boundaries of democratic institutions, and they have largely captured the political imagination. However, their hegemony over theory and practice has not gone unchallenged. There have long been movements and democratizing efforts that have reached across state boundaries, as well as efforts to theorize movements and democracy in a global context. This marginalized legacy of contestation has gained in significance in recent years, in the light of analyses of globalization that assert that states no longer control many processes affecting the populations within their borders, and that populations are increasingly questioning the legitimacy of those borders and the capacity of state institutions. It would seem that globalization is producing significant democratic deficits and innovative, and sometimes violent and exclusionary, movement mobilizations in response. These developments have led to

145

widespread pessimism. They have also encouraged a proliferation of proposals aimed at strengthening democratic institutions and at enabling the participation of ordinary people in globalizing processes.

Such proposals include a revived version of liberal cosmopolitanism, a global framework for "demarchy," and globalized versions of marxisms. These all draw on modernist traditions of thought. There are also post-marxist- and postmodernist-influenced schemes for global civil society and for a politics of connection. Each is discussed in this chapter with regard to its treatment of the now-familiar themes of the operations of power, the location and scope of politics, the role of the political actor, and the possibility of social change. It will become clear that proposals indebted to modernist traditions tend to replicate certain modernist limitations and that globalized postmarxist and postmodernist approaches offer more fruitful lines of inquiry. I argue that a weak postmodern approach to movements, which insists on the possibility of transnational connection between them as well as the importance of difference, is particularly insightful. This "postmodern politics of connection" extends the black and third world feminist claims developed in Chapter 4, but it could also be fleshed out by them in ways that will be pursued in the final chapter. I begin here by mapping claims about globalization onto the central features of modernity identified in previous chapters, examining the ways in which globalization is having an impact on democratic institutions, social movement activity, and social and political thought.

Epochal Change (3)

Globalization

"To some extent, no doubt, globalization is a buzzword, a term as ambiguous as it is popular" (Scholte 1996: 45). However, several shared themes do emerge from the "globo-babble." The first is that of social interrelatedness:

> Social, political and economic activities are becoming "stretched" across the globe, such that events, decisions and activities in one part of the world can come to have immediate significance for individuals and communities in quite distant parts of the global system. On the other hand, globalization also implies an intensification in the levels of interaction, interconnectedness and interdependence between the states and societies which constitute the modern world community. (McGrew 1992a: 68)

In other words, global social relations bring more people into relation with each other, more of the time. The second theme is the reconfiguration of space and time. This phenomenon is variously referred to as "distanciation" (Giddens 1990: 17–26), "time-space compression" (Harvey 1989: 284–307), or "a phenomenology of contraction" (Waters 1995: 62–63). The basic idea is that social interactions have accelerated, with huge distances drastically compressed by developments in transport and communications technology. Locations and social relations that were previously geographically separated have been brought into new proximity. Jan Aart Scholte adds that a new location has been created, a "supraterritorial" realm characterized by distanceless and instantaneous interactions (Scholte 1996: 45–49). A third theme is "the intensification of consciousness of the world as a whole" (Robertson 1992: 8). This is interpreted as both a product of globalization and a contributor to it. Exposure to geographically disparate influences and to issues framed in a global context can encourage the reflexive scrutiny of localized traditions and behavior patterns and lead to the construction of new social relationships (Luard 1990: 191; Rosenau 1990: 333–387; Giddens 1994: 5–7).

More concrete claims about the ways in which globalization is affecting modernity can be mapped onto the five headings identified in Chapters 1 and 2.

i. The Economy. Transnational corporations can geographically fragment production processes and market goods on a global scale. Levels of international trade rise. Post-industrial and post-Fordist developments are concentrated in the West. The financial sector mushrooms, with instantaneous transactions outstripping state control and revenues. Three broad global classes emerge: "the integrated, the precariously linked and the excluded" (Cox 1997: 58). These are internally heterogeneous and cross-cut by migration. Ideologies of technological progress, liberalization, and ecological risk are diffused worldwide (e.g., Mittelman 1994; Strange 1994; Waters 1995: 65–95).

ii. The State and State System. States are increasingly permeable to and constrained by economic, ecological, and military forces. They exhibit varying levels of incapacity to carry out welfare and security responsibilities. The post–Cold War globalization of neoliberal orthodoxy enforces the restructuring of state responsibilities and capacities. Pressures from below for fragmentation coexist with pressures from above to pool sovereignty in supra-state bodies and with the global convergence of policies and political culture (e.g., Luard 1990; Scholte 1995b; Held, D. 1995: 99–135; Waters 1995: 96–123).

iii. The Household and Family. Uneven processes of modernization lead to reduced family size. Contested western ideologies of domesticity, romantic love, and sexual intimacy are globalized, encouraging an increased role for trust and communication in relationships. Families headed by women constitute one-third of households worldwide by the early 1990s. Women generally remain responsible for domestic and family maintenance, including marginal agricultural production, while increasing numbers are incorporated into the globalized economy and assume sole "breadwinner" responsibilities in ways that both draw on and undermine traditional gender roles (e.g., Giddens 1990: 112–124; Seager 1997: 19–23, 59–71; Mies 1998: 112–144; Peterson and Runyan 1999: 130–147).

iv. Culture. Global cultural homogenization is evident in the formation of a transnational elite and the convergence of mass aspirations and identities around globally marketed consumer goods and through globalized media monopolies. Increased heterogeneity takes the form of revived or reconstructed particularist and defensive identities and the spread of hybrid cultural forms. All are "relativized," defined by participants in relation to the West (e.g., Smith, A. 1990; Hannerz 1990; Pieterse 1995; Waters 1995: 123–157).

v. Ontology and Epistemology. Processes of individuation undermine communal and holistic notions of the self and encourage their defensive reformulation. Conceptions of the self as fragmented and plural are encouraged and complicated by processes of hybridization that bring geographically disparate worlds into new proximity. Claims to authoritative knowledge are challenged by the proliferation of stories of reality and bolstered by a revival of aspirations to universal truths and global explanatory concepts (e.g., Mlinar 1992; Smart 1994; Scholte 1995a; Harvey 1989: 39–65).

Many of the above arguments are strongly contested. Realist international relations theorists assert that the state system remains the defining feature of global politics, capable of adapting to the very limited changes that have occurred (Gilpin 1981: 211–244; Smith, M. 1992: 260–261). Some social democrats acknowledge that more dramatic change has taken place, particularly in terms of economic relationships. However, they insist that the economy is being internationalized rather than globalized and that it remains amenable to the interventions of states and interstate organizations (Hirst and Thompson 1996: especially 1–17, 176–194). Marxist critics argue rather that capitalism has always been intrinsically globalizing, as recognized by Marx himself (1977: 222–225). The current intensification of this dimension of capitalism reveals the limits of reformist attempts to tame it. Variations on this view receive more attention below.

There are also significant disagreements among those who agree that globalization is occurring, that it amounts to more than the latest stage of capitalism, and that it is having profound social effects. One dispute revolves around timing. Did globalization precede modernity or emerge during it? Is it symptomatic of an uncertain transitional period, or is it ushering in a qualitatively new postmodern epoch (Robertson 1990: 20, 26–27; Larochelle 1992: 157–161; Waters 1995: 4)? Perhaps the most convincing view here is that globalization emerged in the course of modernity, accelerating in recent decades, and that the contours of a new epoch are visible along with countertrends (Giddens 1990; Scholte 1996: 46–47). Another debate revolves around the impact of globalization on the state. Although some claim that "the nation-state has become immobilized and at worst obsolete" (Freeman quoted in McGrew 1992a: 92), others agree with realists that this overstates the point. They insist that states have been interdependent since their inception, with many in permanent structural crisis. Further, some states are able to manipulate globalization processes quite effectively in their own interests, and certain coercive state capacities may be expanding (Ruggie 1993: 164–165; Saurin 1995: 246–250; Hurrell and Woods 1995: 458–460; Smith, M. 1992: 256–257). Scholte concludes that sovereignty, as classically understood in terms of the untrammeled authority of a state within a specific territory, may now be at an end and with it the sharp demarcation between inside and outside the state. Yet the state remains central to the organization of those aspects of contemporary life that remain territorially bounded (Scholte 1995b: 4–8). Thus instead of celebrating the demise of the state, or asserting that it is entirely unchanged, we should be retheorizing its changing power and place in a world no longer divided into inside and outside universes.

The Global Triumph of Democracy?

It is in this context that we need to understand the challenges faced by democratic practices and institutions. In some ways, democracy is thriving in conditions of globalization. One of the most commented-upon phenomena of recent years has been the spread of liberal democratic institutions throughout the world. Samuel Huntington (1991: 21–26) has identified a third "wave" of democratization, beginning in the mid-1970s in Southern Europe, spreading to Latin America, and then, with the collapse of the Cold War and the Soviet bloc, encompassing East Central Europe and parts of Africa and Asia. David Potter's survey of the 1975–1995 period reveals that the number of states that were either "partial" or liberal democracies jumped from 32 to 90 percent in Latin America and from 0 to 81 percent in the former Eastern European bloc. The number of liberal democratic regimes in Asia tripled from three to nine in the same period and in sub-Saharan Africa "nearly 67 per cent were either partial or liberal democracies" by 1995 (Potter 1997: 8–10).

Political scientists' explanations of this phenomenon fall into three main categories: modernization theory, political elites theory, and a structural approach (Potter 1997: 10–22; Luckham and White 1996: 5–6). Modernization theory posits the prior level of socioeconomic development in a country as the most crucial factor. Often regarded as precursors of globalization analysis (Waters 1995: 13–19), proponents of modernization theory stress the one-way diffusion of socioeconomic processes from the West to the rest and tend toward a reductive functionalist and liberal reading of capitalism as unproblematically providing the conditions in which democracy can flourish. Arguably, Francis Fukuyama's analysis of "the end of history" (1989) represents an idiosyncratic, neo-Hegelian variation of this view, positing liberal democracy as the endpoint of human ideological and institutional development, its success bolstered by the "spectacular abundance of advanced liberal economies" and the end of socioeconomic contradictions. In contrast, the political elites approach deals more directly with why democratization occurs when it does, by examining the calculations and actions of the major actors involved. This can be extended to encompass the interplay of elites within and *across* states: the role of the United Nations in setting up international interim governments and overseeing transitions to democracy (Potter 1997: 17), the involvement of the International Monetary Fund and the World Bank in negotiations over economic policy (e.g., Luckham 1996: 88–84), and the shift in U.S. policy from a somewhat sporadic and instrumental advocacy of democracy to more systematic and consistent support since the end of the Cold War (Whitehead 1996: 245–248). The structural approach to democratization deals with many of the same phenomena but puts them into the long-term historical context of changes in structures of power. Recent formulations of this approach have emphasized class relationships and realignments; the changing shape and scope of state power; and the interconnections of both with reconfigurations in transnational power such as the crisis in the communist world, the end of the Cold War, and the emergence of a U.S.-dominated international system (Potter 1997: 18–22).

One problem with all these approaches is that the role of social movements and popular unrest in democratic transitions has almost entirely dropped out of the picture.[1] Yet there was extensive activism during the transitions in East and Central Europe, particularly in the early stages, as Paul Lewis points out:

> Regardless of the stance of party leaders and policies of the communist authorities, social forces in Eastern Europe showed a growing capacity for self-

> organization and an increasing ability to challenge state power. Starting in
> the late 1970s, they took a different form in each country (predominantly in-
> dependent political party formation in Hungary, trade unions in Poland,
> protestant churches in East Germany, artists and intellectuals in Czechoslo-
> vakia) but nonetheless jointly reflected the emergence of a comparable civil
> society in several countries in Eastern Europe. (Lewis 1997a: 403)

The impact of social pressures such as these is difficult to quantify.
Lewis concludes that the transitions in East and Central Europe remained primarily elite-driven, although he also emphasizes the influence
of the Solidarity movement in Poland (1997a: 403–409; 1997b: 449). However, his analysis serves to prompt inquiry about movement activity in
transitions in other regions. It draws attention to the fall in levels of popular participation across East Central Europe since the transitions, raising
questions about the depth and security of the democracy achieved
(Lewis 1997b: 450–455). Furthermore, Lewis highlights the "significant
transnational component" of the mobilizations that occurred (1997a:
103). Several dimensions to this can be identified. Direct linkages were
forged between movement actors in different states in East and Central
Europe and those in the West. Movements also exerted an indirect influence on each other, as part of a phenomenon characterized as "snow-
balling" (Huntington 1991: 100–105) or "contagion" (Whitehead 1996:
250–252), whereby changes in one country were publicized in another, in-
spiring local social forces to press for change. Anthony Giddens points
out that the impact of transnational forces on social pressure for democratization can be even less direct, in the form of "the expansion of social
reflexivity and detraditionalization" across the globe. Expanding reflexivity means that populations are less likely to accept old stories of political legitimacy. They tend to be "better informed about the political domain than they were before" and "that domain becomes for them one
among multiple points of reference, local and more global" (Giddens
1994: 111). Giddens concludes that "it is globalization, with its attendant
transformations of everyday life, which surely underlies pressures towards democratization in the present day" (1994: 110).

In spite of the aspirations of many participants in movements for
change, it is perhaps a particularly weak version of democracy that has
been institutionalized on a global scale—liberal democracy in its most
elitist, least developmental form. Significant here is the close association
of democratizing processes with economic aspects of globalization, particularly the expansion of neoliberal orthodoxies (Brecher et al. 1993:
xii–xiii; Dagnino 1993: 239). Although Fukuyama is right to point out that
the diffusion of democracy has been bolstered by the material and symbolic attractions of global capitalism, he fails to recognize the alienating

effect of the gap between formal and substantive democracy so bitingly identified by Marx and entrenched by the neoliberal insistence on state withdrawal from economic planning, social provision, and redistribution. As Robert Cox points out, the shift toward neoliberalism was instituted by "a loose elite network of influentials and agencies," operating on the transnational level and enforcing compliance through sanctions and rewards, "largely unobstructed by democratic control or accountability" (Cox 1997: 60–61). This elite has, furthermore, linked liberalization to a limited kind of democracy, sufficient to guarantee compliance with market reforms but not to open up the possibility of contestation. Cox concludes that "much of the democratizing movement saluted in recent years is fragile, lacking a secure base in a participant, articulated civil society" (1997: 63). Further, national government autonomy is so constrained that the effect has been to "transform politics at the national level into *management*" and to circumscribe drastically the political choices of newly enfranchised citizens (Cox 1997: 63).

Although Cox emphasizes the paucity and fragility of a globalized *liberal* democracy, David Held's (1991, 1995) concern is with its *territorial and national* form, which other aspects of globalization are rendering anachronistic. The central argument here is that a coincidence between decision makers, their elective constituencies, and the impacts of their decisions can no longer be presumed now that "sites of power can be a continent away from the communities or constituencies which are the subjects of its exercise" (McGrew 1997a: 12). Thus Held asks:

> Whose consent is necessary, whose agreement is required, whose participation is justified, in decisions concerning, for instance, the location of an airport or nuclear plant? What is the relevant constituency? Local? National? Regional? International? To whom do decision-makers have to justify their decision, and to whom should they? (Held, D. 1991: 143)

As Held acknowledges, the globalization of forms of power is already being accompanied by a process of state adaptation whereby functions are shed upward and outward to supra-state and nonstate bodies. In other words, *state government* is already being displaced or overlaid by a structure of *global governance* (see Chapter 2). However, this process has not been accompanied by significant attention to democratization and, further, involves transferal of authority to bodies that may be particularly difficult domains to democratize according to principles developed within the state. Such bodies are, for example, frequently of significant geographical and emotional distance from those whose lives they shape. Interstate institutions tend to adopt an exclusionary technocratic approach to admittedly complex global issues. It is, at best, states that are currently represented within interstate institutions and this may be in tension with the representation of people, rather than complementary to it (Scholte 1995b: 51–55). Neither can territorially based principles of democracy be straightforwardly applied to increasingly globalized sources of economic power and authority. For businesses, the profit motive is paramount, accountability is "allegedly provided by the boardroom's responsibility to its shareholders," and "participation . . . takes the form of customer choice" (Scholte 1995b: 49). Given the paucity and incapacities of globalized democracy, then, the disaffection and innovative mobilizations found by new times theorists among the citizenry of established liberal democratic states seem likely to spread to the citizenry of the new.

The Globalization of Social Movements?

Globalization is also having an impact on social movements. As argued above, it has been a factor in the development and proliferation of pro-democracy movements. It has also played a role in the fragmentation and particularization of struggles, most notably in the case of those forms of collective action deemed central to modernity, workers', and nationalist movements. The constituency for class-based organization has been undermined by the relocation and dispersal of production processes and the partial privatization of work patterns. The practical difficulty of mass organization in this context, alongside increased workplace insecurity and the growth of consumption expectations, has encouraged co-optation and compliance (Cox 1987: 368–395). Mobilization around economic issues has reemerged in more dispersed, less coordinated forms, such as consumer organizations and diverse resistances. The latter range from "strategies for opting out of the global economy," like local currencies and bartering schemes, to a few "prominent instances of conscious popular revolt against economic globalization," like the Zapatista guerrilla uprising (Cox 1997: 64–65).

Nationalist movements, on the other hand, have transmogrified from a unifying struggle against external colonial control to fragmentary, cross-cutting tendencies based on narrower ethnic identities in already independent states. Many such states are suffering a crisis of legitimacy. They have been long held together by imperial conquest and subsequently by Cold War superpower interventions and authoritarian control. The cessation of both has left dangerous legacies of ethnic stratification. The submission of subsequent regimes to processes of economic globalization, regional integration, and cultural homogenization can undermine their legitimacy and state cohesion still further, making even long-established liberal democratic systems appear unresponsive to internal demands.

These dynamics have encouraged groups from the Scots to the Kurds to mobilize for control of the existing state apparatus, devolution of the state structure, or creation of a new state (Bretherton 1996: 104–114). In several contemporary nationalist struggles, particularly in East Central Europe and the Balkans and parts of Asia and Africa, the always ambiguous ideological combination of empowerment and exclusion involved in national and ethnic politics has been stitched into increasingly narrow and particularist notions of identity, often expressed in reactionary and violent ways.

Conversely, globalization has been a factor in the consolidation of movements on a global scale. To adapt Leslie Paul Thiele, a movement may be considered *global* "first, if it has an multinational membership and organizational structure; and, second, if its concerns and allegiances are explicitly global rather than solely national or local" (1993: 280). One example of a mobilization with multinational membership would be the indigenous peoples movement, the coordinating body of which draws participants from northern Europe, the Americas, Australasia, Japan, and the Arctic (Maiguashca 1994: 363–365). Thiele's framework needs to be adapted to encompass the fact that, even when membership is confined to a particular territory, a movement may be involved in strategic coalitions with other groups in diverse geographic locations. Thus the Movement for the Survival of the Ogoni People works with "supraterritorial environmental and human rights organisations" as well as "global retailers," the Body Shop (Scholte 1995b: 43). Transnational and transcontinental coordinating bodies have developed to make contact between disparate groups, from Development Alternatives for a New Era (DAWN) to People's Global Action (PGA—see Ford 1998: 10; Sen and Grown 1987: 9–13). Even more diffuse forms of coordination have been enabled by new communications technology: anti-smoking activists connect through a worldwide computer network, GLOBALink, and the establishment of free communications centers at the 1992 Earth Summit allowed activists to keep in contact with their constituencies (Stefanik 1993: 266–269).

Arguably, the issues on which such movements struggle are increasingly understood to be global in origins or effects, from ecological crisis to religious messianism. This can lead to the development of more expansive and inclusive identities, manifested, for example, in a revival of cosmopolitan identifications around the essential unity of humanity or planet Earth. Again, the picture is complicated by the fact that many locally rooted and community-oriented movements—from the aforementioned Zapatistas to Asian democracy and environment movements (Ichiyo 1993)—insist on the impact of global forces on their specific situation and consequently strive to forge connections with activists elsewhere (see also Alger 1992).

These organizational and ideological developments have been accompanied by the emergence of multilevel strategies oriented upward, downward, and outward from the state. On economic issues, the statist focus of modernist workers' struggles has been displaced in many contexts by the direct targeting of companies through litigation, boycotts, and direct action, or by attempts to withdraw from the system as documented above. Mechanisms of international governance have increasingly been the source and target of movement activity, as demonstrated by the dramatic rise in nongovernmental organization (NGO) affiliation to and lobbying of UN bodies and conferences (Alger 1994: 311–324), and by the efforts of indigenous peoples to press their claims through international law (Maiguashca 1994: 375–379). There have been autonomous forums established at the global level, such as the Permanent People's Tribunal in Rome, set up in 1976 to hold state elites to account (Falk 1987a: 182). Finally, Thiele reminds us not to neglect the less visible cultural aspects of movement practices, oriented toward deep-rooted "social osmosis" on a global scale (1993: 282). Examples range from exchanges between peace groups in Western and Eastern Europe during the Cold War, intended to humanize the enemy, to the everyday attempts of Greens to tread lightly on the Earth and of Islamists to develop distinctive autonomous cultural forms in the heart of the West.

Global Frameworks in Social and Political Thought

So how are frameworks in social and political thought adapting to reflect upon and analyze these developments? I want to return here to approaches to globalization. Although these can be classified in many ways, a broad distinction can be made between modernist and new times versions. The former draw on marxist or liberal traditions, operating within a monist or parallelist framework that privileges the state and/or economy as key sources of power. Consequently, modernist approaches focus on globalizing reconfigurations in the economy, their impact on the state, and their relationship to interstate institutions. I would suggest that this is characteristic of the bulk of the work on the topic in IR, politics, and economics. Depending on whether they draw on a liberal or marxist normative tradition, proponents tend to be either generally optimistic about the direction in which globalization is moving or wholly critical of it. Neoliberals claim that the expansion and deregulation of markets are likely to convey increased prosperity to all, whereas interventionist liberals and social democrats argue that the undoubted social costs are likely to be mitigated by increased interstate cooperation. Their marxist-influenced opponents rightly draw attention to the more oppressive and coercive aspects of globalization, but do so by depicting globalization as a totalizing system of economic power. Other aspects of globalization, and resistances to it, are reduced to superstructural effects, counter-tendencies, or contradictions.

New times approaches, on the other hand, clustered in sociology and cultural studies, depict globalization as a multidimensional, multicausal phenomenon, constituted by intertwined social, economic, political, and cultural forces. Disciplinary proclivities often encourage a focus on culture and identity, but some proponents also look at economic and political effects. A broader approach is certainly encouraged by the new times framework. An insistence on the multiplicity of forms of power encourages sensitivity to both the problems and possibilities of globalization, highlighting its coercive aspects and the fact that it is not monolithic. Resistance thus becomes both possible and necessary. Instead of being positioned as a counter-tendency, critical collective organizing can be recognized as partly a product of globalizing processes. Elements of both kinds of approaches to globalization are evident in the frameworks discussed below.

Another innovation in social and political thought to which I want to draw attention is the revival of cosmopolitanism. According to Alejandro Colás, cosmopolitanism is characterized by the view that:

1. Individuals are members of a single moral community by virtue of their humanity;
2. They therefore have moral obligations toward other human beings which transcend particular boundaries of ethnicity, creed or nationality;
3. These obligations require political activity to be carried out across these boundaries and imply the upholding of certain universal categories. (Colás 1994: 513–514)

This definition is notable for avoiding the caricature of cosmopolitanism as a belief in a world state. The crucial point is rather "the refusal to regard existing political structures as the source of ultimate value" (Brown 1992: 24), judging them instead by the standards of a universal moral code (Hutchings 1998: 12). Colás's definition also avoids the equation of cosmopolitanism with liberalism, although this remains its most developed form. Rooted in a theory of natural law as the basis of a universal morality (Hutchings 1998: 5–6), liberal cosmopolitanism developed into two main strands: "pacific internationalism," characterized by opposition to war and a belief that it could be eradicated by interstate cooperation and convergence; and "benevolent interventionism," which refused to prioritize peace and had less faith in gradualism, insisting instead on the need for occasional armed intervention in the affairs of other states to encourage liberal democratic values and self-determination. Proponents of both largely accepted a world divided into states, albeit one constrained by the universal standards of natural law and the development of international institutions (Smith, M.J. 1992; Donaldson, T. 1992; Ellis 1992; Doyle 1983, 1986).

There have also been leftist versions of cosmopolitanism, although the interpretation of marxism as cosmopolitan is heavily contested and anarchism is usually ignored.[2] The cosmopolitanism of both begins from assumptions about the social construction of the state system and the socially embedded and sociable nature of individuals, the latter providing moral standards for judging existing institutions. As R. N. Berki recognizes, the key point here "is not the over-debated, trite problematic of 'individualism versus collectivism'" but "the *extent* of the collective unit" envisaged as desirable—whether it encompasses humanity as a whole (1971: 94). Berki interprets Marx's argument about the limits of "political emancipation" within a bourgeois state, divided by class and the public and private distinction, to imply a critique of *all* political divisions, including those *between* states. He concludes that Marx's goal of universal human emancipation necessitates the transcendence of the state system (1971: 95–97; see also Femia 1993: 65). This is echoed in contemporaneous anarchist analyses that "deride national frontiers as artificial and dangerously inconsistent with the wholeness of its humanist affirmations" (Falk 1978: 67) and call for the "dissolution of all States and the creation of a universal federation of free associations" (Marshall 1993: 280). Alternatively, drawing on Marx's advocacy of workers' control over "their" state institutions and his support for nationalist struggles in Ireland and Poland, Alan Gilbert delineates a "democratic internationalist" marxist position. This envisages global unity as mediated through radicalized state institutions and national identities, rather than being transcendent of them (1992: 11). Finally, Peter Waterman identifies the subsequent development of a USSR-led "party internationalism." This "increasingly reproduced the model of diplomatic inter-state relations" by intervening in other states for largely strategic reasons and subordinating internationalist organizing to the interests of the Soviet state. As this approach became dominant, marxist cosmopolitanism of the transcendent or democratic internationalist kind was increasingly treated as a historical failure (Waterman 1998: 25, 40–42).

In the context of arguments about globalization, contemporary analysts are returning to cosmopolitan ideas and practices. Justification in terms of universal moral standards has largely been jettisoned in favor of the empirical argument that the distinction between inside and outside the state is being undermined, requiring a moral and political response (Miller 1998: 70–73). This means that, to a large extent, contemporary cosmopolitanism stands or falls on the perceived veracity of claims about globalization. Yet whether or not concrete realities are being drastically altered, the fact that theorists are turning to long-established traditions for normative guidance serves as a reminder that the project of questioning the status and role of the state is hardly new and that an absolute division between life inside and outside the state has always been open to question. But this reliance on older traditions, at least in the schemes I discuss below, also brings problematic modernist assumptions in its wake. As R. B. J. Walker has argued (1994, 1998), statist, spatial, and homogenizing conceptions of the political are reinstated, either by reaffirming a distinction between politics inside and outside the state or by transferring the notion of a political realm to the global level and presuming a universal identification within that realm. Further, the new cosmopolitans discussed here operate within a hierarchy of levels between global and local, universal and particular, systematically privileging the former. Finally, they tend to rely on a modernist view of globalization that emphasizes its homogenizing, unifying effects and downplays claims about increased complexity and fragmentation. Notwithstanding their claims that globalization is ushering in epochal change, then, proponents of a cosmopolitan revival tend to reproduce the theoretical options of modernism instead of subjecting them to critical questioning.

Modernizing Liberal Cosmopolitanism

The most high-profile efforts to retheorize democracy in the context of globalization are located within the liberal cosmopolitan tradition and include David Held's "cosmopolitan democracy" and the report of the Commission on Global Governance (CGG), entitled *Our Global Neighbourhood*. The latter stresses the economic dimensions of globalization, giving them a broadly welfare liberal or social democratic spin by asserting that problems are likely to arise that will necessitate and encourage closer interstate cooperation (Hurrell and Woods 1995: 448–452; CGG 1995: 7–39). Held gives a more complex, multidimensional interpretation of globalization, emphasizing growing "disjunctures" between the sovereignty claims of the state and international law, decision-making, and security structures; the world economy; and culture. These disjunctures are producing a "neo-medieval" world order of multilevel authorities and loyalties and leading to "democratic deficits" between those making decisions and the constituencies affected (Held, D. 1995: 99–140; 1991: 141–161). In response to these developments, Held and the CGG draw on liberal cosmopolitan ideas of both the pacific and interventionist variety. They advocate the diffusion of democratic regimes and development of interstate institutions, and exhibit "a Kantian commitment to the organisation of a co-operative league of constitutional democracies" (Falk 1995b: 563; Held, D. 1995: 226–231).

The strategies developed to implement these cosmopolitan aspirations have both ethical and institutional dimensions. The Commission insists on the need to develop a new civic ethic encompassing values that "all humanity could uphold" (CGG 1995: 49). This should be systematized into a regime of rights and duties and is likely to encourage the development of a more cooperative mode of politics (see generally CGG 1995: 41–75). Held begins by reconstructing the principle of autonomy, codifying it into a system of rights that should be claimed against seven sites of power—from the body to culture to legal institutions—and guaranteed by a "democratic public law" made global in scope (Held, D. 1995: 145–156, 167–201).

Strategies for institutionalizing these guiding principles focus on reforms of the UN system. Suggestions include widening representation on the Security Council and General Assembly and establishing new international courts. In addition, the Commission suggests the creation of a "Forum of Civil Society," a "People's Assembly," and a voluntary UN military force (CGG 1995: 225–334). Held envisages more radical long-term changes, including the establishment of regional parliaments, transnational referenda, and, ultimately, a global legislative assembly made up of representatives of democratic states and backed up by force (1995: 269–283). Another tranche of institutional proposals revolves around the democratization of the economy, with both the CGG and Held recommending the establishment of a global coordinating body alongside fairer systems of representation in Bretton Woods institutions and programs of debt alleviation. Held also wants to encode democratic rights into business procedures and the market. He calls for a range of measures to be imposed or facilitated by national, regional, and international governing bodies, from the minimum wage to consultation with workers and affected communities, from health and safety regulatory regimes to the global coordination of investment and aid (Held, D. 1995: 251–266; CGG 1995: 135–224).

These are innovative, detailed schemes, and they have been highly influential. The democratic aspirations of both are, however, significantly limited by their liberal roots and, in Held's case, by postmarxist modification. In the first place, globalizing capitalist relations are opened to modification but not to transformation. The Commission, indeed, sees recent economic developments as fundamentally benign and reins back its social democratic sympathies to conclude in neoliberal fashion that governments should limit themselves to providing a stable framework for the global market economy, with remaining disparities in resources being redressed through aid. The market and operations of corporations are thus largely exempted from democratic scrutiny (CGG 1995: 162–197; Falk 1995b: 570). Held, on the other hand, combines a liberal acceptance of market forces as the most efficient form of allocating resources with a much keener, postmarxist, awareness of the anti-democratic effects of market failures, inequalities in resources, and business influence on government. His proposals are intended to extend democratic principles outward into the market and businesses and thus to enable democratic autonomy in other realms of life (Held, D. 1995: 244–266). This echoes and builds upon the proposals of the postmarxist associative democracy scheme discussed in Chapter 2. In the same fashion, the point remains to introduce "new clauses into the ground rules of basic laws of the free-market and trade system" (Held, D. 1995: 255). However radical these clauses, the system itself is still not fundamentally challenged.

In the second place, and in contrast to the associative democracy scheme, states remain the primary containers and mediators of cosmopolitan democracy and the most important democratic actors in global politics. This is despite the fact that both Held and the CGG are explicitly committed to enhancing the participation of individuals. One factor here is the reliance on liberal cosmopolitanism, which carries an emphasis on the adaptation rather than transcendence of the state system and which, like much of liberalism, exhibits an ongoing "tension between state sovereignty and popular sovereignty" (McGrew 1997b: 245). Further, *Our Global Neighbourhood* remains locked into a methodologically nationalist worldview that gives politics radically different meanings in inside and outside realms. It positions individuals as active citizens within the state but as moral actors or "good neighbors" to those in other states. Recommendations for enhanced participation in interstate politics remain focused on the state itself, as in the reallocation of voting rights within the Security Council and other institutions. The stirringly named "People's Assembly," with its overtones of direct democracy, is to be constituted by representatives delegated from state assemblies (CGG 1995: 257–258).

Held's arguments are less circumscribed by methodological nationalism and statism. For example, his claim that there are seven sites of power carries with it an expansive notion of politics, in terms of struggles to maintain or challenge power in all those sites. As we have seen, particular attention is paid to the democratization of the economy (see also Held, D. 1995: 191, note 1). Further, Held is committed to a notion of citizenship that is exercised at "many different territorial levels depending on the issues that are at stake" (Miller 1998: 73). Yet his concrete proposals also remain focused on the role of states in constituting interstate institutions and, through these, in entrenching democratic public law in the seven sites of power identified. Like the Commission, Held exhibits "a liberal fascination with constitutional and legal solutions to problems which are essentially political in nature" (McGrew 1997b: 245). Or as Walker puts it (1994: 698), Held is committed to an analytical "hierarchy of levels" that privileges the global and legal/institutional over the local and participatory.

At this point, it might be objected that both the Commission and Held argue for a role for global civil society and the actors within it. This, it has been argued, "indirectly challenges the exclusivist, statist makeup of almost every international institution, and also recognizes the need to validate new modes of political participation" (Falk 1995b: 569). Yet the potential radicalism of this emphasis on global civil society is undermined by its specifically liberal formulation. Civil society is defined as "a multitude of institutions, voluntary associations, and networks," including economic interest groups but outside of the direct control of states (CGG 1995: 32–35, 62–63, 253–256; Held, D. 1995: 181).[3] For the Commission, this is becoming a globalized arena of political action. The naive pluralist assumption is then made that actors within global civil society interact with each other and with other actors on principally equal terms, encouraging an almost cavalier insensibility to disparities of capacity and influence between, for example, the World Bank and local voluntary associations (CGG 1995: 3). Also in line with liberal pluralism, formally constituted NGOs are emphasized, including those that are international in character (INGOs). Notwithstanding an impressive rhetoric of inclusion, urging the international community to "enable and encourage nonstate actors to offer their contributions to effective global governance" (CGG 1995: 55), proposals for concretizing this contribution remain thin on the ground. Civil society actors appear limited to a functional, supplementary role, supplying information to states and interstate institutions and implementing the resulting policy. The recommended "Forum for Civil Society" turns out to be a discussion body with no legislative powers and no formal input into the rest of the UN (CGG 1995: 32–35, 258–260).

Held, in contrast, makes an important postmarxist distinction between civil society "more broadly conceived" and noneconomic "civic associations," including "voluntary groups, charities and churches . . . political organizations and social movements" (1995: 181). Civic associations are recognized as a site of power in themselves. NGOs are distinguished from social movements, and both are granted a role in global politics. Nonetheless, that role remains limited. The historical participation of movements in struggles for economic rights is recognized (1995: 197) and a possible future role is envisaged in an international constitutional convention that would set the terms for a global legislative assembly, although this role is not extended to the assembly itself (1995: 274). Held's proposals are circumscribed by a legitimate wariness about the grander claims made on behalf of global civil society, and by his awareness of power relations and particularizing tendencies within civic relations (1995: 124–126, 181). More problematically, they are also limited by the aforementioned commitment to a hierarchy of levels. This militates against a study of the impact of social movements in global political processes. Thus Held insists that "the problems of global governance from above cannot be solved through the extension of grass-roots democracy alone. . . . An appeal to the nature or inherent goodness of grassroots associations and movements bypasses the necessary work of theoretical analysis" (1995: 285–286). Although he is correct that idealization of the local and of movements is not helpful, there is no "necessary work" here on the interrelationship of the local to the global, of grassroots movements to transnational activism, or of activism to global institutions.

The hierarchy of levels also circumscribes Held's proposals for change toward and within a liberal cosmopolitan system. William Outhwaite notes that Held stresses the need for local transformation but that his listed objectives focus predominantly on the domains "upward" of the nation state. The establishment of a global legal and institutional framework is clearly a political priority (Outhwaite 1997: 180–181). Although one "impetus to change" in these domains is identified in "the development of transnational, grass-roots movements with clear regional or global objectives" (Held, D. 1995: 237), the activities of such movements do not receive significant attention. Ultimately, Held lapses into a classic liberal reformism, emphasizing the influence of rational argument on elites. He distinguishes between short and long-term measures "in the conviction that, through a process of incremental change, geo-political forces will come to be socialized into democratic practices" (McGrew 1997b: 251; Held, D. 1995: 278–283). He also resorts to a "thought experiment" to prove the logical attractiveness of democratic principles (1995: 160–167). This distracts attention from the coercive and complex realities that need to be taken into account if change is to be made into a concrete possibility.

Our Global Neighbourhood also relies on the self-interest of elites in the context of globalization to facilitate change (Falk 1995b: 575). This neglects the possibility that elites may have an interest in upholding the current system or that inequalities of power and conflictual relations between them may be exacerbated by globalization (McGrew 1997b: 245). The Commission does, however, recognize the need for popular pressure and calls on civil society to *demand* change from elites (CGG 1995: 352). Yet such demands must not challenge the economic, political, and moral framework that the Commission has already endorsed. It should be noted here that the civic ethic is not seen as something that has emerged from civil society but as a disciplining standard to which civil society must adhere—lest unruly INGOs should "make effective global governance difficult" (CGG 1995: 55). Thus we are left with a thin view of the possibilities of global democracy in which civil society is greatly constrained and existing elites left largely in control.

Demarchy on a Global Scale

According to Anthony McGrew (1997b: 242–253), John Burnheim's proposals for global democracy offer a radical alternative to liberal cosmopolitanism. Burnheim shares the liberal concern with democratizing processes of global governance; although he doesn't use the term "governance," he insists that dispersed, plural modes of regulation should replace the centralized monopoly of state government (1985: 1). Indeed, Burnheim adopts an anarchistic stance in identifying the state itself as the source of the problems of democracy, rather than the weakening of the state in conditions of globalization. States, Burnheim argues, decrease the security of their citizens, produce inflexible bureaucracies, enforce social homogeneity, constrict the political agenda, and impose territorial stasis (1985: 19–50).[4] He also points out, in much less detail, the socially damaging effects of the capitalist economy (1985: 126–127). Further, liberal forms of democracy that have developed within the state and capitalist framework are inadequate because they limit popular participation to voting for parties, which is a crass barometer of complex interests. They also encourage the professionalization of politics, the mystification of issues, and elite power-brokering (1985: 82–106). Although Burnheim has clearly been influenced by anarchist and marxist critiques, these are also castigated for assuming that a revolutionary movement will spontaneously generate democratic procedures (1985: 12). Burnheim's global alternative to both liberal and leftist democracy is called *demarchy*.

Demarchy begins from the assumption that interests need to be disaggregated if they are to be effectively represented. Thus *"each citizen or group would have a say in each specific area of decision in proportion to its material interest in that area"* (Burnheim 1986: 227, emphasis in original). Rather than voting, interested individuals would be selected by lot from a statistically representative sample to sit on specialized functional agencies (Burnheim 1985: 9). A participatory emphasis is apparent in Burnheim's insistence that such agencies should remain small to encourage meaningful deliberation among participants (1985: 106–107). An anarchistic abjuration of coercion emerges in his argument that there should be no overarching body able to enforce and coordinate agency decisions. Agencies should rely instead on self-regulation and should respond to recalcitrance by withdrawing cooperation and funding. As Burnheim points out, this is not unlike the means by which contemporary international organizations gain authority (1985: 190, note 2; 1986: 230–231). In the most radical dimension of Burnheim's framework, such agencies would ultimately be granted control of the allocation and pricing of land and other natural resources, the profits of which could then be distributed to other functional bodies enabling the abolition of taxation, with overall coordination still ensured by the market. The agencies would also regulate financial and labor markets (1985: 132–155). Ultimately, global-level bodies made up of delegates referred from lower levels would be granted a remit to hear appeals and to restructure agencies according to changing circumstances (1985: 117–119). Although Burnheim appears to envisage a kind of halfway house in which states could be persuaded to farm more of their functions out to existing intergovernmental organizations, his ultimate goal is a world of overlapping authorities and loyalties not dissimilar to the "neo-medieval" globalized world Held describes. However, Burnheim's solution to the problem of order in such a world is to abandon entirely the territorial community and to abolish the state.

Given Burnheim's opposition to methodological nationalism and statism and his anarchistic sensibilities, it would be reasonable to expect movements to have a significant role in a demarchic world order. Yet this is not the case. The main actors in the demarchic system are individuals within agencies and agencies themselves. Burnheim does suggest that movements might consider reconstituting themselves according to demarchic principles, particularly the trade union movement; worker self-organization is seen as an important part of the transition to a more demarchic society. Further, movements reconstituted along demarchic lines could demonstrate to elites the effectiveness of this way of organizing (Burnheim 1985: 163–164; 1986: 235). Burnheim also emphasizes that the increase in "the opportunity to acquire and make significant use of a range of intellectual skills and capacities for co-operating with other people" in demarchy will encourage "a great increase in voluntary organizations and co-operatives of all sorts" (1985: 182). In other words, he expects demarchy to encourage a flourishing of civil society.

One problem with all of this is that it presumes a reformist, top-down model of change, reminiscent of liberal cosmopolitanism. Although he refers briefly to the self-organization of the workers' movement, Burnheim relies more centrally on the force of rational principles on elites. Movements are granted a role only insofar as they participate in the process of rational persuasion. This connects to an additional problem. In another echo of liberal cosmopolitanism, movements are assessed primarily in terms of their functional capacity. Thus Burnheim denigrates the "flamboyant interventions" of Greenpeace and recommends that the organization confine itself to setting up demarchically structured expert committees (1986: 235). This is hardly an adequate assessment of Greenpeace's direct action strategy, which combines intervention in ecologically damaging processes with efforts to capture the media agenda and thus influence public opinion. Burnheim is replicating here the disciplining insistence on good behavior that characterized *Our Global Neighbourhood*. What is more, his depiction of civil society under demarchy seems to offer little more than a liberal vision of a private realm of the pursuit of individual interest. There is no apparent role for civil society in terms of pressurizing or opposing governing bodies. Thus, as with liberal approaches, the cultural dimensions of movements and their more oppositional strategies are marginalized and even stigmatized as anti-democratic.

Burnheim's limited conceptualization of social movement involvement in demarchy indicates problems with his theory of democracy. To start with, demarchy is a technocratic, explicitly apolitical ideal that reduces democracy to the negotiation of regulations in committees. This derives in part from a legitimate disgust with the "pork-barreling" of party and interest group politics, but it also bears the trace of marxist and anarchist assumptions that power will disappear and that politics can be reduced to administration once a desired transformation has occurred. The inaccuracies and totalizing implications of such a view have been criticized in previous chapters. The more radical heritage of anarchism survives in the fact that Burnheim's framework is both participatory and expansive, involving people in the direct scrutiny of power relations within society and outward beyond the state. However, this is an undifferentiated expansionism, whereby the same democratic mechanism is deemed suitable for most locations and for the regulation of most social relations, including movements (Hirst 1986: 671, 673). Selection from statistically representative samples is clearly not an appropriate way to structure all movement activity, the strength of which often lies in its spontaneity and creativity.

Furthermore, Burnheim's scheme limits participation in important ways. First, although the individual is recognized to be a multidimensional political actor with diverse interests, it is still *interests* that are emphasized, albeit with a republican-style insistence that these can be reconciled through deliberation. Republicans, however, emphasize that reconciliation is possible because individuals have an investment in the community that shapes them. Their formulation was criticized in Chapter 1 for conflating community with nation, interpreted in a potentially homogenizing and exclusionary way. Burnheim's equally problematic response is to presume that the abolition of national identification is possible. He argues that the expected flowering of voluntary organizations under demarchy would compensate for this loss by enabling membership of a "rich variety of communities" (1985: 182). This is reliant on an entirely voluntaristic and de-territorialized notion of community. A more holistic notion of the political actor would surely have to take multiple identifications and deep-rooted belongings into account.

Second, participation is restricted to those individuals selected for committees. Paul Hirst complains that such a system is "ideal for busybodies" (1986: 671), but my concern is that those not on committees need to find ways of contesting the operations of power in their daily lives. One way of so doing is through participation in movement politics. Yet Burnheim is arguing that most of us should become passive recipients of agency decisions, while movements reorient themselves toward information gathering for institutions. Under closer scrutiny, then, Burnheim's vision of democracy is not as radical as McGrew believes.[5]

Marxism and the Globalization of Class Struggle

Another attempt at a radical global framework can be found in reformulations of marxism in IR and sociology, namely world systems theory and neo-gramscianism. These are both rooted in an interpretation of Marx's analysis of capitalism as intrinsically global in scope, and both share the fundamental marxist tenet that it is only through transformation of the current world system or global hegemony that meaningful, substantive democracy is likely to be achieved. From this point, though, their analyses diverge. World systems theorists rely on a base-superstructure framework, insisting that the "world economy existed prior to and always was largely beyond the control of (national) states, which were formed in important respects better to compete in the world economy" (Frank and Fuentes 1990: 154). States are thus reduced to a political subsystem of the capitalist world economy, their boundaries understood to coordinate with and reinforce core-periphery divisions of labor (Wallerstein 1986: 11–12). Neo-gramscians like Robert Cox allow more space for agency, and for political and cultural forces, by stressing the causal capacity of self-conscious classes and the complex ways in which capitalist hegemony has been globalized through the interactions of material capabilities, institutional forms, and ideas in the spheres of production, forms of state, and world order (Cox 1987: 355–358; 1986: 218–225).

There is a corresponding difference in approach to how world order is being or could be challenged. The dominance of statist strategy and goals within marxist-influenced workers' movements is interpreted by world system theorists, along with the rise of nationalist movements, as a product of "system-wide structural processes" originating in capitalism (Arrighi et al. 1989: 1–2, 30–33; cf. Frank and Fuentes 1990: 142–158). Judged relatively successful in gaining state power, these movements are also seen as compromised, the loss of their "anti-systemic" quality a prime reason for the rise of new movements since the late 1960s. NSMs are characterized as pursuing long-standing socialist goals through novel anti-bureaucratic or anti-statist strategies and, in the wake of structural changes in capitalism and the state system, as becoming increasingly transnational in scope and orientation (Arrighi et al. 1989: 34–51; Wallerstein 1990: 40–48; Frank and Fuentes 1990: 139–142, 162–164, 174). Although some world systems theorists urge caution about these developments, others remain optimistic about the capacity of NSMs to have an impact on the system and about the propensity of the system to ultimately collapse. Neo-gramscians are more skeptical. They agree that class struggle has been reconfigured by globalizing capitalism but insist that these reconfigurations have been primarily negative, functioning to fracture the working class and anti-systemic organizing. The seeds of counter-hegemonic forces can be found in marginalized and alienated workers, community resistance movements, and NSMs. However, these currently remain largely isolated and relatively ineffectual (Cox 1987: 368–395; 1997: 64–67; Gill 1995: 404–410; 1997: 59, 73).

On both accounts, class-based struggle remains paradigmatic. Marxist approaches, however sophisticated, are ultimately monist and, more precisely, economistic. They "consider the power relations in societies and in world politics from the angle of the power relations in production" (Cox 1987: ix). Classes arising from those relations remain *the* primary source of resistance and movement-led change. I argue in Chapter 1 that this has served to burden proletarian struggles of the nineteenth and twentieth centuries with overwhelming responsibilities, which they have rarely shouldered. It has also led to the marginalization or misinterpretation of other movements. The latter problem is reflected in the contortionist efforts of world systems theorists to depict NSMs as the inheritors of the class struggle mantle by squeezing their diverse goals into essentially socialist aspirations. The reductionism of such efforts is exacerbated by the structuralism of world systems theory whereby movements are seen as an effect of the structural logic of capitalism.

Neo-gramscians rightly jettison structural determinism but remain, nonetheless, economistic. It is precisely because they perceive a *lack* of continuity between class-based struggles of modernity and current movements that these theorists are not optimistic about the possibility of radical change. In particular, the fragmentation of class struggle and diversification of other movements is read as a sign of weakness in the face of the overwhelmingly powerful Goliath of economic globalization. But this relies on two problematic assumptions: that nineteenth- and early twentieth-century workers' organizations were indeed a universal emancipatory force despite evidence that this was always an idealized inter-

pretation and, further, that they remain an appropriate model for emancipatory struggle in what is admitted to be a very different world. Further,
this view relies on an interpretation of global capitalism as totalizing and
monolithic. Neo-gramscians might deny this, given their repeated insistence that the contradictions and social costs of economic globalization
have provoked a crisis in hegemonic control and provided the opportunity for the development of counter-hegemonic forces (e.g., Gill 1995:
418–423). Yet they downplay noneconomic dimensions of globalization
and neglect evidence that globalization can consolidate movements as
well as fragment them. Instead of exploring alternative movement possibilities, neo-gramscians stand by in despair as the possibility of counter-
hegemony appears to recede into the distance.[6]

Neo-gramscian pessimism is reinforced by the methodologically nationalist model of change implied by the concept of counter-hegemony.
As Cox makes clear, this concept implies the weaving of class influence
throughout society so effectively that state and society are stitched together into a "historic bloc" (1993: 55–58). Cox concludes that "the task of
changing world order begins with the long laborious effort to build new
historic blocs within national boundaries." This demands a radical,
broadly based class party oriented toward the state (Cox 1993: 65; 1987:
355). These arguments point to a two-stage model of change in which the
development of a national movement is a prior requirement to the development of internationalism. The possibility of a more dialectical relationship between the two is ignored. Also, Cox's argument does not consider
the possibility or desirability of constructing oppositional movements
outside of state institutions or of struggling against the hegemony of the
state on political life. A substantial chunk of contemporary movement activism is thus written out of the picture.

In contrast, it is precisely the transnational and nonstatist aspects of
NSMs that world systems theorists emphasize, comparing these favor-
ably to the statism and national form of earlier struggles. Immanuel
Wallerstein indicates that NSMs are predicated on a recognition that
power is not confined to the state and hint at the possibility of a genuine
world politics beyond narrow national identifications (1990: 46–48). Andre Gunder Frank and Martha Fuentes argue approvingly that NSMs
participate in a nonstatist politics (1990: 141–142, 177–179). However, the
strategic implications of these claims are underdeveloped. I suggest that
structuralist assumptions are again at work here. Given that states are effects of the capitalist system and help to maintain it, activism aimed at
gaining state power must be oriented toward the maintenance of the system, and nonstate activism must be anti-systemic. This is a simplistic for-
mula, neglecting the occasional progressive potential of the state, the role
of other forms of power, and the possibility of unforeseen and ambigu-

ous outcomes. Further, the assumption that movements too are a product of the capitalist system, albeit a contradictory one, encourages the marginalization of questions of movement strategy. The trajectory of movement development is already determined, and capitalism is likely to collapse in the end anyway through the contradictions that it generates.

This leads, finally, to the fact that neither world systems theory nor neo-gramscianism pays much attention to the construction of alternative forms of democracy. Underlying structuralist complacency discourages world systems theorists from concrete strategizing, and underlying pessimism discourages neo-gramscians from planning for an elusive future. Nonetheless, Cox perceives glimmerings of what he calls a "participative democracy" in the activities of some contemporary movements. These point to "the organisation of civic life upon the basis of a variety of self-governing groups that deal with the whole range of people's substantive concerns" (1996: 534). Cox's earlier elaboration of gramscian strategy points more specifically toward a combination of a "parliamentary" version of marxist democracy and democratic internationalism. This amounts to a call for a range of movements inside a state to join together with a class-based unifying party to construct a more substantive, participatory democracy within existing national civic and state institutions and then afterward within international institutions. This is a limited view of democracy, in part because the notion of counter-hegemony rests on the unification of movements. Although the tolerant, dialogue-based, and *democratic* nature of counter-hegemonic alliance is emphasized by neo-gramscians (Cox 1993: 57; Gill 1993: 15), it still involves the privileging of economic struggle and the leadership of a class-based party. However broadly constituted, this necessitates the subordination of other movements and the disciplining of their diverse goals. Further, marxist parliamentary democracy remains limited to national society and state, only reaching interstate institutions at a later point. This is an institutional and two-stage model of democracy that may be particularly anachronistic in conditions of globalization. It is also in contradistinction to more expansive visions, which insist that people need to be able to contest the operations of all kinds of power, not just economic power, in their everyday lives.[7]

Unsurprisingly, given its structuralist predilections, world systems theory reveals much less about democratic possibilities. Its anti-statism seems to hint at the need to combine a "participatory" version of marxist democracy with a transcendent version of marxist cosmopolitanism. The functions of the state system would be absorbed by communes organized on a participatory basis, which would then send delegates to multilevel coordinating bodies. However, Frank and Fuentes point in a somewhat different direction. They argue that contemporary movement practices offer a vision of "more participatory civil democracy and power in civil society and culture" (1990: 177). Their apparent approval of this development indicates a shift away from a marxist emancipatory framework toward a postmarxist radical civil society approach.

Globalizing Radical Civil Society

In recent years, the concept of *global civil society* has become fashionable among IR theorists. Huge confusion surrounds the use of the term, with theorists exhibiting a pick and mix approach to more established traditions. A radical version is the focus here, particularly as it has been articulated in the work of Richard Falk and Ronnie Lipschutz.[8] The former draws on liberal and anarchist influences and the latter on Gramsci, but the schemes of both also reflect the postmarxist formulation discussed in Chapter 2. Global civil society is depicted as a realm of social interaction between the global economy and state system and a potential site of challenge to both, constituted mainly by social movement activity (Lipschutz 1992: 392–399).

It should be noted that the term *social movement* is not used consistently. Lipschutz argues that civil society is "delineated by networks of economic, social and cultural relations ... occupied by the conscious association of actors, in physically separated locations, who link themselves together in networks for political and social purposes" (1992: 393). Falk, on the other hand, shifts to an emphasis on "transnational social forces" (1995a: 170). The key point remains, however, that their descriptions of networks or social forces are very close to characterizations of NSMs, depicting nonhierarchical, nonviolent, culturally oriented collective actors aiming to defend and expand global civil society (Falk 1987a; 1993: 19–21). Movements are, furthermore, seen as newly transnational in scope and cosmopolitan in orientation, dimensions that have arisen both because of globalization and in opposition to it. Theorized in terms of economic and cultural homogenization, political integration and innovations in transport and communications technology, globalization is understood to have encouraged the universalization of norms and identities, undermined state competence and the principle of territoriality, precipitated global-level crises, and encouraged citizens to develop autonomous capacities (Falk 1987b: 15–17; 1993: 24–33; Lipschutz 1992: 393–397, 404–418). Finally, in a divergence from NSM and radical civil society theory, movements are seen as nonstatist in orientation and also as actually or potentially *anti-capitalist*, a point to which I return below.

Falk and Lipschutz are concerned primarily with social change and resistance rather than democracy. Yet civil society is a motif of democratic theory and inevitably drags assumptions in its wake. I would suggest that what we have here is a globalized version of the democracy advocated by postmarxist theories of radical civil society and explored in Chapter 2, albeit without the elaborate Habermasian underpinnings. Democracy is expanded into global civil society, with movements seeking to democratize relations within civil society and to challenge the influence of the state system and global economy over it. A more participatory form of democracy is envisaged, involving increased opportunities for individuals to participate as global citizens in processes of decision making and in contesting global power relations through their involvement in social movement politics. What is more, movements are identified as key forces for democratization, in terms of both the engagement of their formal, institutional dimensions with state, interstate, and economic structures and their less visible impact on processes of cultural change. At this point, a key divergence from the nonglobal postmarxist version of civil society emerges, to do with the extent of change permissible. Whereas nonglobal versions posited that the liberal state and capitalist economy form the necessary framework of civil society, Lipschutz and Falk insist that both global capitalism and the state system must be open to challenge by the self-organization of society in movements if a truly democratic world is to be achieved. Thus Lipschutz characterizes global civil society as "a form of large scale resistance to the Gramscian hegemony of the international system" (1992: 399). He insists that "the code of global civil society denies the primacy of states or their sovereign rights" and that "resistance to the consumer culture of global capitalism . . . give[s] life and power to global civil society" (1992: 398, 418). Falk emphasizes that "[t]he essence of a political agenda at this historical time is the transformation of the state by non-violent means in the direction of peace and justice" (Falk 1987b: 23).

This goes some way to answering my earlier criticism about the boundaries imposed on movement activity by a postmarxist civil society approach. In its nonglobal form, this involved a reformulated doctrine of self-limitation that specified that movements must not challenge the boundaries established between civil society, the liberal state, and capitalist economy. Theorists of globalized radical civil society do not appear to accept this injunction and have a more radical view of the possibilities for long-term, movement-led change. However, my other objections to a civil society approach to social movements remain relevant. The tripartite distinction between civil society, the economy, and the state is still in place but at a global level. Further, the state system and global economy are privileged as the most important sources of power in the world, and global civil society is, more explicitly than in nonglobal versions, formulated as a sphere of *resistance*. As I argued in Chapter 2, this serves to obscure the reach of economic and state power within civil society, including the ways in which they penetrate and co-opt movement activity, while other forms of power and their structuring effect on movements are neglected. This militates against accurate analysis of movements, particularly those stretching across geopolitical divides. Such movements are likely to be profoundly shaped by the differential access and vulnerability of groups in different regions to centers of state and economic power, and by the hierarchical divisions imposed by imperial histories and racist attitudes. The civil society framework also imposes analytical boundaries onto complex political activities, which may be located simultaneously in disparate geographical spaces as well as in different social spheres.

A further problem is the imposition of a shared progressive and oppositional orientation onto movements. There are three reasons for this. First, the globalized radical civil society approach universalizes NSM characteristics to all movements or ignores movements that do not share these characteristics. This is despite the fact that NSM theory has already been criticized within sociology for obscuring movement diversity, particularly on a global scale. Clearly, not all movements worldwide are anti-capitalist or anti-statist. Second, the analysis of the impact of globalization on movements is simplistic. Although multiple economic, political, and cultural dimensions to globalization are recognized, there is also a modernist tendency to emphasize homogenizing and universalizing trends, encouraging an emphasis on the transnational consolidation of movements and a neglect of particularizing and fragmentary countertendencies. Third, the civil society framework rests on values implict in assumptions about appropriate political behavior, and about what constitutes a progressive agenda, which emerged in the western world. Notwithstanding the pressures of cultural and political convergence, these values are frequently not shared by non-western actors. R. B. J. Walker demonstrates this in his discussion of the Indian development movement, Swadhyaya. He draws attention to:

> the cultural specificity of the notion of self that informs the entire movement. This self is not separable from notions of the divine. . . . [A]lthough many of the achievements of this movement could be read as an attempt at a revitalisation of civil society, the civil society in question is not strictly comparable with the phenomenon invoked by Habermas or Cohen and Arato. Given the centrality of the spiritual impulse here, public life cannot be reduced to civic life . . . public life in this particular context must be infused with spiritual idealism in order to generate any kind of civic order, an assumption that would certainly generate considerable controversy elsewhere. (Walker 1994: 688)

The point here is not whether Swadhyaya is reactionary or progressive. It represents one response to a particular conjuncture of globalizing forces that is misrepresented under the rubric of global civil society or excluded from it altogether.

This points to limitations in the globalized radical civil society reconceptualization of democracy. Despite ostensibly expansive aspirations, democracy is de facto reduced to movement participation in and around economic and state structures and to movement dissemination of a global civic ethic. Although there is room here for more subterranean, oppositional, and unruly movement behavior, this disseminating role is not that far removed from the entreaties of *Our Global Neighbourhood*. The need for movements to democratize relations within and between themselves, and the question of how this could be achieved, is entirely neglected. We are back to the old leftist assumption that solidaristic relationships will spontaneously arise between progressive forces in the absence of the distorting forces of the state and capitalism. The foundations and boundaries of civil society are rendered prepolitical and not open to democratic contestation, functioning to confine democracy to a guiding ethic for the like-minded in their struggles against a predefined enemy. The difficulties faced by women in leftist movements and by black and third world women within feminism in getting their concerns taken seriously should serve as a warning of the anti-democratic implications of presuming that all structures of power and oppositional strategies have been identified in advance. Although there may well be many movements and viewpoints that need to be excluded from schemes for the globalization of democracy, the point is that such a question is political and needs to be democratically mediated.

Finally, Walker argues that the idea of global civil society as a sphere of democracy relies on the notion "that the world itself can be constituted as a bounded political community" that is "modeled on the state writ large" (1994: 696). In other words, it presupposes political cohesiveness, a collective identity, and a common public space. As Walker insists, this evades "most of the hard and interesting questions" about the creation of democratic politics in a globalizing world, such as exactly how community, authority, identity, and political connections can be reconfigured. I would add that it transfers a model of national citizenship to global-level civil society without taking account of people's continued attachment to national community or of the more complex possibility of multilevel identifications and loci of action. For Walker, movement politics point toward the possibility of treading a more ambiguous political path between globalism and nationalism, universalism and particularism. It is to his arguments that I now turn.

A Postmodern Politics of Connection

Walker's arguments about democracy and social movements could be characterized in terms of a "postmodern politics of connection." As evident above, Walker is centrally concerned with the limits to the political imposed by modernist reifications. Much of his work adopts the strong postmodern strategy of deconstructing these reifications within the discipline of IR, focusing particularly on the ways in which the concept of state sovereignty has been used to divide the world into inside and outside realms of life, domestic politics, and "anarchy," the universal and the particular (see especially Walker, R. B. J. 1990; 1993). Consequently, he seeks to explore:

> what it means to be caught up in practices of both universality and diversity; to negotiate alternative conceptions of self and other; to explore spatio-temporal possibilities not envisaged by the cartographers of containment or the children of Hegel's ghost. . . . It is in this context . . . that one might begin to read *some* social movements as practices in search of the political. (Walker 1995: 322–323)

This interest in social movements necessitates a shift from a strong postmodern deconstructionism and a focus purely on the discipline of IR toward a constructive analytical and political agenda that engages with diverse domains of political practice. Lene Hansen recognizes this duality in Walker's work, characterizing it in terms of "a pendulum shifting between theory and politics" (1997: 318). I see it rather as an ongoing tension between strong and weak postmodernist epistemological commitments.

Walker's major book on social movements has a recognizably weak postmodern framework of power. It identifies multiple structures—the state system, the economy, technologies, and culture—and characterizes them as global in scope, mutually constitutive, variable in effect, and giving rise to context-specific struggles (Walker 1988: 33–58). This framework is somewhat underdeveloped: It avoids the term *globalization* almost entirely, underplays the material effects of gendered and racialized power by lumping them into the realm of cultural power, and neglects the relationship of power to agency. Nonetheless, it avoids the more monolithic interpretations of globalization and the reductiveness of a strong postmodern approach to power as manifested only through discourse.

"Critical social movements" (CSMs) are identified as the key source of change within this framework (1988: 26–32). Walker, like other postmodernists, is acutely aware of the differences between movements and the dangers of definitional closure. This leads him to insist that the "meaning of 'critical' and 'emancipatory' has to be discovered rather than stipulated in advance" (1988: 31). Nonetheless, his characterization of CSM activity echoes NSM theory in its emphasis on nonviolence, skepticism toward the state and institutionalized politics, the creation of alternative identities and solidarities, and struggles over information and knowledge (Walker 1988: 81–107). Further, two central criteria for CSMs are specified. In contrast to "conventional forms of political life," CSMs "are less concerned with taking state power than with challenging more basic principles of everyday life," and with revealing the interconnections of state power with changing global structures and local relationships (1988: 78). Further, in contrast to reactionary movements, CSMs engage "in a politics of openness—to the complex connectedness of modern life, to the uncertainties of a world of imminent dangers, to the need for renewed vision" (1988: 78–79). This carries with it an insistence that CSMs should combine "both specificity and connection" (1988: 135), balancing their assertions of particularity, as emphasized by strong postmodern theorists, with an effort to construct solidarities with other movements. CSMs are also urged to extend connections *across* state borders and to connect *with* the state and interstate institutions when strategically necessary, avoiding both dogmatic anti-statism and unquestioning state centrism (1988: 107–114, 137–139, 157–163).

These arguments have complex ramifications for democracy. Walker is concerned less with the democratic deficits that have emerged under globalization than with the immanent contradictions in democracy itself: the contradictions between the universalizing ambition of democracy and its articulation within particularizing states (1993: 143), and between "the celebration of grassroots participation . . . and the effective erosion of the locale as a place where serious politics can occur" (1993: 152). CSM practices are interpreted as exposing these contradictions and as offering alternatives. Walker draws attention to their efforts to humanize and decentralize state and institutional modes of democratization and to democratize social relations usually seen as nonpolitical (1988: 137–142). More originally, he insists that CSMs effectively reconstitute political space. They repoliticize the local, uncovering the ways it is constituted by global forces and enhancing community participation, as in indigenous people's struggles to defend their local environment against the state and other forces. CSMs also extend politics beyond the state, as in the declaration by environmentalists of ecological regions, or peace movement efforts to create nuclear-free zones, thus bringing into being new territorial constituencies that do not map neatly onto state boundaries. Such movements also emphasize individual responsibility for the everyday reproduction of the world (1988: 84–87). Whereas global civil society theorists claim that transnational movements displace politics upward, to a space beyond the state, Walker is insisting rather that CSMs of whatever scale, location, and orientation expand politics *outward*, into the global and its manifestations in everyday life, by politicizing boundaries within societies, between states, and between the local and the global.

Finally, Walker implies that CSMs are not only sources of democratization but also constitute sites of democracy in themselves. This emerges through his argument that no general and final resolution between the universal and particular in political life is possible. Rather, the relationship between the two must be continually struggled with in ongoing political practices. Learning to live with such open-ended, uncertain political strategies is for Walker one of the most important challenges of the late modern condition. Although movements are a key site for working out the relationship between the universal and the particular, the hallmark of a *critical* movement is that it does not attempt a final resolution (Walker 1988: 163–170). In continually renegotiating the relationship between the two, critical movements could be seen as providing a democratic mechanism through which the exclusions imposed by universalizing tendencies or by attempts at closure are continually subject to collective scrutiny—and through which both counter-hegemony and parochialism are refused. Democracy is thus reaffirmed as an ongoing process as opposed to an end-state through which all ambiguities can be resolved.

Walker's claim about this characteristic of critical movements demands a close study of the concrete conditions and mechanisms necessary to achieve the successful mediation of the universal and particular. His failure to provide this is indicative of a measure of idealization and abstraction in his account of movements. This may be a result, yet again, of a reliance on assumptions about NSMs. There is also a problem here with the anti-foundationalist approach to the evaluation of movements. As Hansen argues, "there is in the end no way to decide whether a movement is critical or not, except by Walker's declaration of its status" (1997: 329). Although Walker is right that normative judgments about movements have no metaphysical foundation and emerge only from a study of movement practices, he does not approach movements without criteria about what is "critical" already in place, and it is surely necessary to be explicit about where these have come from and about the possibility of their modification in an encounter with movement activity. It is surely also necessary to undertake a more systematic study of movement activity. Walker's ambivalence on this point may be due to a continued strong postmodern skepticism toward the status of the empirical and an accompanying tendency to believe that alternative political possibilities will be revealed through ontological speculation rather than through more concrete social explorations (Hansen 1997: 323). This would mean that his arguments about the democratic implications of movement practices are likely to rely primarily on underlying philosophical predilections.[9]

A further problem is that Walker, like many others, does not pay sufficient attention to the differences *within* movements. He notes that movements "include a wide range of outlooks among their adherents and easily fracture," a feature he regards as positive given CSM suspicion of claims to unity (1988: 108–109). However, more detailed attention to the internal complexity of movements would reveal that some of the orientations within CSMs are much more "critical" than others (Stammers 1999: 83–87). It would also show that the fragile coherence of movements requires constant, reflexive effort if it is to be sustained. As Walker confirms, "A politics of connection is . . . absolutely crucial. Movements do connect, converse, learn from each other, and sometimes develop partial solidarities" (1994: 699). Chapter 4 confirmed that this kind of politics constructs relations *within* movements as well as between them—and it is where more elaborated models of alternative democratic practice can be found.

Conclusion

Walker's approach to social movements and democracy is compared and contrasted with other global approaches in Table 5.

All of these approaches start from the notion that globalization is de-centering the nation-state from its position in modernity as the foundation of society and the focus and container of political practice. This status was always socially constructed, historically specific, ideological, and contested. Now it is being increasingly challenged by processes that are also encouraging the reconfiguration of social movement practices and democratic institutions, in ways necessitating a reconsideration of the most fundamental political categories and aspirations. Efforts to do such rethinking, however, have not been as radical as might have been expected.

Yet again, this may be because the theorists under discussion are relatively disassociated from movement efforts to reconstruct politics on the ground, perhaps particularly so because of their disciplinary location in that eyrie of IR, with its pretensions to a bird's-eye view of the world as a whole. Most also fail to escape from limiting modernist assumptions about power, politics, agency, and change, replicating these through arguments about globalization and cosmopolitanism. Global liberal and marxist theories and postmarxist adaptations tend to privilege one or two sources and sites of power and to exclude others from democratic scrutiny. Factoring globalization into monist or parallelist approaches leads to simplistic analyses that emphasize one or two aspects and carica-

TABLE 5 Globalizing Theory

	Ideal-type Democracy	Operations of Power	Terrain of Politics	The Political Actor	Strategies for Change	Role of Movements
Liberal Cosmopolitanism	representative global governance in which states pursue shared goals in IGOs, aided by civil society	state/system as key source, needs to tame globalization. Held identifies seven sites of power in total	expanded upward to interstate institutions. Held also expands it outward to the economy	the individual as active, rights-bearing citizen within states; states primary actors in IR; some role for INGOs	imperatives of globalization and rational and moral argument influence elite-led change	reduced to formal INGOs located in global civil society, advising and aiding state elites
Global Demarchy	representative, participatory global governance by single-issue agencies constituted by people drawn by lot	state and capitalist economy as key sources	expanded outward to negotiation of functional issues in new institutions	the individual pursuing multiple interests in civic groups and agencies; the latter also key actors	gradual elite action, influenced by demonstration of demarchic principles in INGOs	formal INGOs have role demonstrating demarchy and advising elites; civic groups enable pursuit of interests
Globalized Marxism	worker control over global social life via delegation from self-governing workplaces or party control of state institutions	control of the mode of production; taking increasingly global forms in states, IGOs, and ideologies	expanded outward to global struggle for control of the means of production in society and state institutions	classes acting for themselves or parties / anti-systemic NSMs acting for them	contradictions in globalized capitalism increase crisis; exacerbated by class control or undermining of state power	unified workers' movement no longer likely; emancipatory potential of NSMs is disputed

Global Civil Society	participatory processes in global civil society enabling contestation of globalized power relations	state system and economy as major sources of power, both strengthened and under-mined by globalization	expanded upward to global civil society	the individual as active, rights-bearing citizen and movement participant; transnational NSMs also key actors	immanent in transnational NSMs, ultimately undermining state and capitalist framework	NSMs as key source of democracy, located in global civil society, with anti-capitalist and anti-statist goals
Politics of Connection	participatory contestation of globalizing power relations in all aspects of life	pervasive, global in scope, taking multiple forms that interact in context-specific ways	expanded outward in differentiated ways; strategy devised in specific locations and in dialogue with others	the individual, constituted by and resisting global power relations? CSMs also key actors	immanent in diverse critical movement practices and efforts to forge connections between them	CSMs as key sites and sources of democracy, expanding it outward and mediating the universal and particular

ture these as either wholly good or bad. (Held is an important exception here.) Further, global liberals and marxists may attempt to expand democracy beyond the state, but most also confirm the status of the state as the container and mediator of democracy as well as the major democratic actor in interstate politics. The demarchic framework requires the abolition of the state and application of the same organizational principle throughout global society to totalizing effect, in contrast to the global civil society framework, which reconfines democracy and movements to a fictive space between the state and economy. Most of these frameworks rely on understandings of individual agency that focus on political, civic, and economic dimensions and downplay complex communal identifications. Movements are conceptualized reductively, with analyses focusing on their formal organizational aspects or on class struggle, or stereotyping all movements as progressive, coherent, unitary actors. Finally, global liberal and demarchic frameworks put forward a notion of global change as top-down and elite-led. Global marxists cling to problematic notions of change as an all-or-nothing process of party-led, class-based counter-hegemony—or as structural collapse. Global civil society theorists advocate a more nuanced view of long-term transformatory change through social self-organization, but this relies on idealized and spuriously universalized notions of movement activity.

In contrast, a postmodern politics of connection recognizes the multiple forms taken by global structures and relations of power. It confirms the expansive character of movements and democracy as challenging all imposed boundaries on the political. It insists on a role for movements in enabling individual and collective agency and social change. It emphasizes the necessary plurality of movements and the necessary process of forging connections between them and, occasionally, the state, in processes of change. There are clear and striking overlaps on all these points with the black and third world feminist framework identified in Chapter 4. Indeed, Walker points to ways in which this framework could escape from its methodologically nationalist constraints. The pervasive and interactive theory of power could be expanded to encompass the global reach of many forms of power as well as their context-specific manifestations. A democratic politics of location and connection could operate across geopolitical as well as social locations. Indeed, transformatory change may necessitate the construction of movement connections beyond the state.

Conversely, black and third world feminist arguments illuminate some important ways in which Walker's work remains limited. Walker's analysis of power underplays racialized and gendered hierarchies and not enough attention is paid to their context-specific and often contradictory interactions and their implications for agency. He also fails to pay attention to the differences within movements and the often painful processes by which their apparent unity is constructed. Black and third world feminist arguments point toward the need to understand the ways in which connections between the global and the local are gendered and racialized. They also indicate that movements striving to make those connections are themselves inscribed with relations of power—which they need to struggle against. These arguments point to the need for detailed study of debates about and within transnational activism. Only then will it be possible to see how the world politics outlined by Walker might be made a democratic politics. It is in the light of these arguments that the next chapter returns to feminism.

Notes

1. According to Potter (1997: 14–15), the original formulation of the "political elite" or "transition" approach identified a prior stage where the role of social mobilization was crucial. This has dropped out of more recent formulations.

2. As Colás points out, cosmopolitanism "is usually associated with the language of Enlightenment ethics, with the rational, autonomous individual as its ideal agent," in contrast to socialist internationalism, "related to the economic determinism of 'scientific' socialism, where moral agency is shoved aside by the forward march of history" (1994: 516). Colás argues that this involves a caricature of marxism that denies its more moral dimensions. With regard to anarchism, Richard Falk draws attention to its global dimension and points out that this is often neglected by anarchists as well as by those interested in global change from a more conventional cosmopolitan perspective. Falk puts this neglect down to the domestic political priorities of anarchists and the association of anarchy with disorder, "precisely the opposite of the primary desideratum of global reform" (1978: 64).

3. None of the definitions of civil society in *Our Global Neighbourhood* explicitly includes economic actors. Business is granted "a role in global governance" rather than in civil society as such (CGG 1995: 255). Furthermore, the institutional proposals intended to enable the participation of global civil society do not appear to include economic actors. Nonetheless, the role of business is discussed within a section ostensibly on global civil society. This ambiguity may be a product of tensions within the CGG between the representatives of governments and businesses and those from NGOs. It may also reflect awareness of the distinction that has emerged in recent years between liberal and postmarxist versions of civil society. Held, in a postmarxist move, explicitly excludes corporations from his definition of global civil society.

4. It should be noted that Burnheim does not cite anarchist influences except in the form of one work that uses rational choice theory to justify anarchist assumptions about cooperation (1985: 120, 190, note 1). His assumptions about the state, though, are clearly more in line with anarchism than with either liberal or marxist forms of cosmopolitanism. His lack of sensitivity to other forms of power other

than the state, besides capitalism, also reflects orthodox anarchist thinking. Furthermore, it should be stressed that Burnheim's arguments about the state were formulated before globalization theory was much developed. However, he draws on an important precursor of globalization theory in the form of liberal functionalist literature, which posited that intergovernmental organizations were evolving to meet the needs of the international community. This is taken by Burnheim to open up possibilities for a demarchic world order (1986: 221–222).

5. McGrew reads Burnheim's model as social movement–led "radical communitarianism" (1997b: 245–249). It seems to me that he is conflating Burnheim's functionalist position with the more radical social movement-oriented approaches discussed below, perhaps because of their shared debt to modified versions of marxism and anarchism.

6. This problem may be exacerbated in Stephen Gill's version of neo-gramscianism because of the addition of foucaultian assumptions about the operations of power (Gill 1995: 402–404; see commentary in Stammers 1999: 74–75).

7. Cox's position seems to have changed in recent years. In a 1996 article, he urges a "dual approach" rather than a two-stage strategy, in which the struggle for counter-hegemony within states *coexists* with the struggle to create a new multilateralism (1996: 533). This is a significant moderation of methodological nationalism, but it does not answer the criticisms raised here. No significant role is accorded to transnational movements, and democracy at the global level seems still to be confined to institutions. In a 1997 article, Cox apparently reaffirms a methodologically nationalist, two-stage strategy, insisting that "a democratic movement . . . would have to be based upon a socially cohesive revivified civil society, and this will have to be generated *from within*. It would not be democratic if it were to be dependent upon infusion by well-meaning but *intrusive foreigners*" (1997: 69, emphasis added). In a more recent article (1999), Cox's argument shifts again. He insists on the fluidity of notions of civil society and regional differences in the impact of economic globalization. He also details diverse resistances to which, in several cases, he grants counter-hegemonic potential. This is a more nuanced account, pointing to a "regional" civil society model that I have not seen articulated elsewhere. However, control of the state is still seen as the appropriate goal for civil society counter-hegemonic strategies (see his comments on African movements, 1999: 25). And Cox's analysis remains locked within an economistic framework that privileges globalizing capitalism as the major source of power and primary target of struggle throughout the world.

8. For variations on global civil society theory, see Frost (1996), Wapner (1995), Sakamoto (1997), Macdonald (1994), and Shaw (1994; 1996). The last two authors are notable here because they develop gramscian approaches to global civil society that differ from those put forward by both Cox and Lipschutz. In contrast to Cox, Macdonald and Shaw both point to the emergence of a civil society that is transnational in scope, although they insist that this development is thus far limited and riven with conflicts and contradictions. In contrast to Lipschutz, anti-statist political conclusions are rejected.

9. Lene Hansen claims that Walker's underdeveloped notion of critical movements should increase our skepticism about the possibility of deriving judgments about political possibilities from movements. She sees the pendulum of Walker's

thought moving in this direction, as evident in his 1994 warning against "a romantic strategy of 'listening to the movements'" (quoted in Hansen 1997: 329). Actually, at the same time, Walker does provide a study of movement activity in the 1994 article in which he discusses Swadhyaya, although he uses his findings to subvert the universalizing pretensions of IR theory rather than to examine the vital question of constructive alternative political possibilities. In other words, he invokes Swadhyaya as a manifestation of difference, thus shifting back onto strong postmodern ground. However, Walker subsequently appears to reaffirm the need for attention to the political possibilities, and dangers, of movement activity (1995: 322–324). The pendulum evident in Walker's work has clearly not yet ceased to swing.

6

Reconstructing Global Feminism, Engendering Global Democracy

While the notion of transborder participatory democracy (one in which it is not the state but people themselves who emerge as the chief agents in defining the course of the global economic and political processes that structure their lives) has been low on the agenda of women's movements for democracy, perhaps this is an idea whose time has come.

(Alexander and Mohanty 1997: xli)

Introduction

From a feminist perspective, it is a glaring inadequacy that the proliferating literature on the globalization of democracy and movements rarely engages with its gender-specific dimensions. Academic gender-blindness may be exacerbated in the study of global issues because it is conventionally constituted as the "high" politics of war and diplomacy or macrolevel economic processes in which women do not appear to have a role (see, e.g., Tickner 1992: 1–5; Sylvester 1994: 4–9; Halliday 1994: 147–149; Peterson and Runyan 1999: 5–13, 48–61). Although the theorists discussed in the last chapter have expanded notions of democratic politics and movement activism into the global arena, the division between the political and the domestic, and the ways in which this may structure access to global processes and their impact, remains unquestioned.

What is more, women's and feminist mobilization is rarely granted more than a mention. In liberal cosmopolitan reconstructions, this is part of a broader neglect of movements. World systems theorists have paid some attention to women's class positioning and the economic mobilizations to which it gives rise (Ward 1988, 1993; Nash 1988). The neo-gramscian framework has been extended to encompass feminist activities but only through jettisoning its economistic foundations (Stienstra 1994:

22–42). Global civil society theorists do not look specifically at feminism, although aspects of it could fit with their arguments about the progressive potential of transnational NSMs. The postmodern politics of connection developed by R. B. J. Walker is potentially sympathetic to feminist concerns, but Walker refrains from "attempting to apply insights from contemporary feminist theory directly to the theory of international relations," partly on the grounds that feminism is "not a collection of insights that may be applied. As a fractured and heavily contested discourse, it remains a site of active political struggle" (Walker 1992: 196). Yet this welcome recognition of the political status and disunity of feminism hardly justifies the exclusion of the democratic insights it has generated.

This book is predicated on the assumption that a feminist perspective is essential for a radical and inclusive reconstruction of democracy on a global scale. The final chapter puts feminist arguments into a global framework. I begin by mapping out global and gendered patterns of power, examining the marginalization of women in newly globalized democratic institutions, the impact of globalization on feminist activism, and the ways in which feminist theoretical frameworks are responding, or not, to such developments. The second part of the chapter turns to feminist efforts to reconstruct democratic theory and the polity in the light of analyses of globalization. Finding only limited insights, I then shift to debates about the democratization of the feminist movement, this time on a global scale. I put forward a constructivist defense of the conceptualization of feminism as a global movement before exploring the insights that have emerged from efforts to democratize it. These are discussed under the headings of the operations of power, the scope of politics, the nature of the political actor, and the possibility of transformatory change. The arguments that emerge here draw on black and third world feminist interventions and expand on the idea of a postmodern politics of connection. They indicate that a more democratic feminist movement is already under construction and point toward a more general reformulation of global democratic politics.

Gendering Epochal Change

Patriarchy and Globalization

Feminists are relatively late entrants into globalization debates. Their efforts are indebted to longer-standing feminist critiques of development and neoliberal restructuring, and they frequently retain a focus on economic processes and the interstate system. This ties in with what was identified in Chapter 5 as a modernist approach to globalization, albeit with an added concern to illuminate its "narrow analytic terrain" and "narrative of eviction," which have ensured that the gender-specific consequences of economic and political processes on women's lives disappear from view (Sassen 1996: 10). Other relevant arguments can be gleaned from proliferating feminist debates about religion, culture, migration, ethnicity, and postmodernity. Taken together, these point toward a new times, multidimensional reading of globalization that is critical both of the more naive, sweeping claims made about globalization and of its more homogenizing and polarizing effects.

With other critical approaches, feminist interventions urge against the tendency to interpret intensified social interrelatedness in terms of a "mythic 'oneness'" (Eisenstein 1997: 143). They emphasize the ways in which contemporary globalization processes are reconstituting and reinvigorating older hierarchies of race, gender, and class (Alexander and Mohanty 1997: xxi-xxiv). We are reminded that globalizing reconfigurations of space, time, and territoriality have coercive effects and occur unevenly, with much of the world continuing to live according to slow rhythms, embedded within territories, and with others forcibly displaced. Further, feminist accounts attempt to re-embed ostensibly supraterritorial and "hypermobile" interactions within material social relations, revealing interconnections with recognizable, territorially located, and socially stratified places and processes, as well as opportunities and dangers for people depending on their location and embodiment (Sassen 1996: 15–20). In what otherwise remains a rather dark portrait of global reconfigurations as at worst violently detrimental and at best ambiguous for many women, feminists agree with other theorists of globalization that it is accompanied by increased awareness of the world as a whole. Globalization thus "allows for the subversive possibility of women seeing beyond the local to the global. This move puts male privilege clearly in view like never before" (Eisenstein 1997: 147). It also enables the construction of transborder identifications and organizations in response.

More concretely, feminist readings of globalization and its implications for women and feminist politics can be mapped onto the five key features of modernity identified in previous chapters.

i. The Economy.   Fordist textile and communications industries, post-Fordist homeworking systems, and service economies all rely on young, third world, and/or immigrant female labor. Women are stratified into marginalized class groupings and constitute the majority of the world's poor. Poorer women make up a large proportion of migrants, particularly as domestic and sex workers moving from second and third world economies to the Middle East and the North and West. Globalized ideologies of growth and ecological risk shore up women's role as consumers and mothers in the first world, while encouraging the regulation of third world women's fertility (e.g., Sassen 1996; Runyan 1996: 239–243; Pettman 1996: 157–207; Mohanty 1997: 3–29; Mies 1998: 112–144).

ii. The State and State System.   State restructuring, including cutbacks in welfare provision, the strengthening of coercive capacities, and the delegation of responsibilities to international institutions, functions to exacerbate women's poverty and labor burdens and intensifies intervention into the lives of many. The UN and international law help render women's lives visible and facilitate their activism while renewed nationalisms urge their domestication. State and transnational elites remain western and male-dominated (e.g., Alexander and Mohanty 1997: xxi–xxvi; Brodie 1994; Moghadam 1993: 336–346; Bhavnani 1993; Tinker and Jaquette 1987).

iii. The Family and Household.   Uneven processes of modernization lead to reduced family size. Contested western ideologies of domesticity, romantic love, and sexual intimacy are globalized, encouraging an increased role for trust and communication in relationships. Families headed by women constitute one-third of households worldwide by the early 1990s. Women generally remain responsible for domestic and family maintenance, including marginal agricultural production, while increasing numbers are incorporated into the globalized economy and assume sole "breadwinner" responsibilities in ways that both draw on and undermine traditional gender roles (e.g., Giddens 1990: 112–124; Seager 1997: 19–23, 59–71; Mies 1998: 112–144; Peterson and Runyan 1999: 130–147).[1]

iv. Culture.   The convergence of identities and aspirations around mass-marketed goods and images is stratified by gender and ethnicity. Processes of cultural homogenization and hybridity are mediated by women in their role as cultural reproducers and signifiers of cultural authenticity. Global media monopolies normalize idealized images of western women and commodify female sexuality. Reconstituted patriarchal traditions restrict and subordinate women's activities (e.g., Peterson 1996: 6–7; Pettman 1996: 185–188; Obiora 1997: 377–388; Sahgal and Yuval-Davis 1992: 1–11).

v. Ontology and Epistemology.   Conceptions of the self are revealed as gendered and raced. Attempts to reconstruct the female subject are complicated by the assertion of differences between women on a global scale and notions of fragmentation and plurality. Universalist claims are criticized by feminists as masculinist and within feminism as western, white, and class-biased in the context of the proliferation of many women's stories of reality (e.g., Alarcón 1990; Bordo 1990; Benhabib 1992: 211–230; Wekker 1997: 333–339).

In sum, feminists have provided compelling evidence that almost all aspects of globalization have a gendered dimension. Whereas women became visible mainly with regard to analysis of the family in nonfeminist approaches, a feminist reading factors them in throughout. Further, the argument here is not simply that globalization has gendered effects, distinctive for men and women, but rather that gendered structures and relations of power are tied into the very heart of globalization processes. They shape causes and trajectories as well as outcomes. What is more, they are not "superstructural" effects of other sources of power but have some autonomy in cause and effect and are systematic in form. The fact that this is still, overall, to the detriment of women relative to men points, as I argued in Chapter 4, toward the need to reinstate the analytical category of patriarchy and to recognize the potentially global reach of this form of power.

This need not imply a singular and monolithic gender hierarchy that is played out in the same way everywhere in the world. The interactive, multidimensional approach to power I have been advocating implies the need to pay attention to the context-specific manifestations of globalizing patriarchy, its interaction with other structures and relations of power, and its uneven and contradictory effects. Thus we find, for example, that neoliberal restructuring is being undertaken to a different extent and is having different gendered effects in East Central Europe compared to the newly industrialized countries (NICs) of Asia and Latin America. Increased levels of female employment in the latter, due to the relocation there of multinational textile and electronics factories, contrasts with mass female joblessness in the former, due largely to the collapse of the female-dominated public sector and state benefits (Moghadam 1993: 346–347). Further, conditions and wages in longer-established NICs may be improving, in part due to technological upgrading and the displacement of many female workers by males. This has encouraged a new wave of relocations to other parts of the third world where the workforce remains female-dominated and conditions atrocious (Agarwal 1988: 6–11; Runyan 1996: 240).

The Marginalization of Women in New Democracies

The dissemination of democratic discourses and institutions might have been considered one of the more positive aspects of globalization, but it has been limited in important ways. Some of these were discussed in Chapter 5. Here I want to draw attention to the marginalization of women in new democracies. This has been brought to light most starkly in the feminist literature on the recent wave of transitions in East Central Europe. The "asymmetrical gender consequences" (Posadskaya 1994: 4) of the changes in East Central Europe are graphically illustrated by the dramatic fall in the number of women in the new national representative bodies across the region, from an average of one-third of seats under "state socialism" to an average of less than 10 percent after the first supposedly democratic elections. Levels varied from 20.2 percent in the former GDR to 15.7 percent in Russia, 8.5 percent in Bulgaria, and 5.5 percent in Romania (Einhorn 1993: 150–151; Konstantinova 1994: 68; Watson 1993: 72). The Balkans yield an even grimmer picture, with the elections after the break-up of Yugoslavia producing only 2.9 percent female representatives in Bosnia and Herzegovina, and a mere 1.6 percent in Serbia (Papic 1992: 58). The point here is not that the liberal democratic assemblies are actually less democratic than their pretransition counterparts. No feminist commentator, to my knowledge, makes this claim. The point is rather that the democratic, representative credentials of the new institutions must also be open to question, given that women have almost entirely disappeared from view.

Feminist explanations of this phenomenon tend to stress the specific social and political situation in each country and the region as a whole. Attention is drawn particularly to the common heritage of state socialism and the legacy of its approach to "the women question." This approach was predicated on the view that "labour force participation was not only a necessary, but also *the sufficient* condition for women's emancipation" (Einhorn 1993: 20). Political equality was further enforced by the introduction of party quotas. As I argued in Chapter 3, quotas in this context meshed with one-party rule to impose a female presence that lacked legitimacy and autonomy, while political participation added to women's labor burdens. It has since been demonstrated that the integration of women into the labor force and legislature was driven primarily by strategic reasons rather than by a commitment to women's rights. Little effort was made to change cultural attitudes or to challenge the domestic division of labor. Ultimately, economic and political mechanisms to sustain the public role of women collapsed with the regimes that introduced them, and that role in itself was discredited (Eisenstein 1994: 19–20; Einhorn 1993: 151–153; Klimenkova 1994: 23; Voronina 1994: 41–47).

This emphasis on context specificity, however, cannot account for the fact that the marginalization of women has occurred in new democratic institutions in other regions. Further, this has resulted in levels of visibility that are now closer to the *norm* for levels of female representation in the so-called advanced or mature western democracies, except in Scandinavian countries (Einhorn 1993: 150–151). There are clearly more general dynamics at work here, albeit interacting with local particularities in context-specific ways. The few attempts to take broader contextual factors into consideration have adopted comparative frameworks (e.g., Waylen 1994) or examined transnational influences (e.g., Chowdhury, Nelson et al. 1994: 4–8). I suggest that a more holistic approach, drawing on a multidimensional and interactive approach to globalization, would be revealing. This would examine the ways in which globalizing forces for and against democratization intersect in a specific context such as East Central Europe.

Such an analysis would have to begin with the recognition that the philosophical underpinnings of liberal democracy—its underlying concepts of power, politics, agency, and change—contain gendered biases that militate against the participation of women. On top of this, an interactive analysis would need to consider the gendered inequalities built into the globalization processes that encouraged the emergence of liberal democratic regimes in East Central Europe. Thus, for example, attention would have to be paid to the overwhelmingly male composition of national and international elites involved in negotiating change. The gendered effects of global processes of detraditionalization and rising social reflexivity, which have encouraged pressure for change from below, would also have to be examined. Feminist studies of the East Central European context confirm that women's bodies have been a particular site of struggle over detraditionalization. Such studies emphasize the cultural impact of marketization, its association with western forms of liberty and, more specifically, with a form of sexual "freedom" involving the commodification of women's bodies and sexuality. The consequent proliferation of sexual imagery through globalized media and pornography networks, and the growth of the sex industry, seems to have spurred on the reactionary, defensive efforts of religious and nationalist forces to control women's sexuality and reproductive capacities and to limit their public role (Klimenkova 1994: 17–23, 31–32). This coincides with an apparent dramatic increase in the level of sexual and domestic violence against women in the region (Attwood 1997).

The close association of democratization with a specifically *neoliberal* form of capitalism, enforced by western and transnational elites, also deserves attention. Feminist studies of East Central Europe confirm that neoliberal conditionality has had especially detrimental effects for women. Their work burdens have been exacerbated and their economic security decreased by the importing of western labor practices, by cutbacks to the public sector, in which women were heavily employed, and by the end of forms of state support such as subsidized childcare and contraception. These developments have been reinforced by a context-specific backlash against women's work outside the home because of its association with state socialism. Women now constitute the majority of the unemployed and poor of the region, all of which enforces their economic dependence on men and constitutes a serious "situational constraint" on their political participation (Einhorn 1993: 127–142; Schaeffer-Hegel 1992: 106; Eisenstein 1994: 20–24; Watson 1993: 78–82). Further, the neoliberal effort to redraw a boundary between the political and economic has been accompanied by a redrawing of the boundary between the political and the *domestic*, due perhaps to the convergence of neoliberalism with a resurgent nationalism in the region. Democratic politics has been constituted as a "man's business" to which women are not suited. The new regimes have been given a remit to intervene in the domestic sphere in the form of legislation and constitutional clauses explicitly oriented toward "enabling" women to stay at home, limiting their capacity for reproductive self-determination and thus their access to the public sphere (Eisenstein 1994: 25–26; Voronina 1994: 53; Heinen 1992; Drakulic 1993: 124–126; Watson 1993: 74–77).

Finally, the emphasis on the effects of nationalism in the feminist literature on East Central Europe draws attention to the revived significance attributed to unitary national culture and autonomous territorial control in the process of constructing democracies in particular regions. This attempt to reassert a crude form of the territorial model of democracy may not only be of limited efficacy in conditions of globalization—it also appears to be particularly disadvantageous to women.

The Globalization of Feminism?

More positively, globalization processes are also shaping and being shaped by feminist mobilization for change. Perhaps the most dramatic development on this front has been the global proliferation of feminist mobilizations since the 1970s. Manuel Castells finds a pervasive feminist presence in institutions and in autonomous groups in every country in the West. He also detects signs of a revival in the former Soviet bloc; embryonic mobilizations in industrialized Asia; and an "extraordinary rise of grass roots organizations, overwhelmingly enacted and led by women, in the metropolitan areas of the developing world" (1997: 184–188). Although such organizations may not articulate an explicit feminist ideology, they are, according to Castells, engaged in "transforming women's consciousness and social roles" (1997: 184–188). This proliferation of feminist organization has, in some ways, brought diversification and fragmentation in its wake, evident in the apparent loss of unity and cohesion among national feminist movements in western states and in the efforts of women within and beyond the West to develop autonomous identities and strategies.

On the other hand, globalization has contributed to the consolidation of transnational feminist organizing. This is not an entirely new phenomenon. Vron Ware argues that "from the start, nineteenth-century feminism was an international movement in which women throughout Europe and America had received impetus and inspiration from one another" (1992: 160). Examples of international and internationalist first-wave organization include the International Congress of Women, which was established in Washington in 1888 and, by 1913, claimed 6 million members from twenty-three countries. Another International Congress of Women, held in The Hague in 1915 to work for peace, attracted 1,500 women from twelve different countries (Stienstra 1994: 48–51). There is also a long history of transnational feminist organizing in the Latin American context, with, for example, an international feminist congress being held in Buenos Aires in 1910 (Waterman 1998: 164). Nonetheless, recent decades have seen a diversification of the issues around which transnational feminist organizations develop. Thus groups campaigning around socialism, suffrage, peace, and education have been joined by others like the Feminist International Network of Resistance to Reproductive Technologies and Genetic Engineering (FINRRAGE) and the Women's Environmental and Development Association (WEDO) (Miles 1996: 121–123; Sturgeon 1997: 150–163). Such groups now draw participants from all over the world. WEDO has co-chairs from places as far apart as Barbados and New Zealand. Feminist organizing is also taking on more complex forms. Thus nationally or locally rooted groups can be linked with groups elsewhere through transnational coordinating frameworks, such as DAWN, which links activist-researchers across Asia, Africa, Latin America, and the Caribbean (Sen and Grown 1987: 9–13; Miles 1996: 113–114). Alternatively, local groups may forge transnational links with each other through direct contact and information exchange. For example, women's labor organizations from India and the Philippines have participated in a series of regional and international feminist conferences on women's labor world-wide (Mitter 1986: 144–156).

I would suggest that these organizational developments have been encouraged by the globalization of communications and transport technology and by growing awareness of the impact of economic globalization and liberalization on women. Another crucial factor has been the proactive role of the United Nations, and its organization of International Women's Year and the subsequent Decade for Women, 1975–1985. This gave rise to an enormous effort to gather information about women worldwide and provided public recognition of the gravity and global reach of women's issues. It was also the umbrella for three international conferences and accompanying NGO fora: at Mexico City in 1975, Copenhagen in 1980, and Nairobi in 1985.

These conferences were all highly politicized and conflictual, and some commentators feel that feminism came off the worst in its encounter with the "cold realist light of international, inter-state, relations": the Decade themes of equality, development, and peace were frequently eclipsed by debates about the New International Economic Order and Middle Eastern politics; women were used as mouthpieces for national establishments; and "the fissures in the women's movement were exploited and widened" (Newland 1988: 512–513; for a range of assessments see Tinker 1981; Pietilä and Vickers 1994: 75–83; Çağatay, Grown, and Santiago 1986; Tinker and Jaquette 1987). Nonetheless, there is also widespread agreement that International Women's Year and the Decade were "a milestone for the transnational women's movement" (Newland 1988: 426). They raised consciousness and expectations (Pietilä and Vickers 1994: 7) and encouraged an "exponential increase in the number and types of women's groups in every country of the world, and the complex of networks and organizations which unite them" (Tinker and Jaquette 1987: 426). Over 14,000 women and men participated in the NGO forum at Nairobi; the official conference was made up of 2,020 country delegates plus 600 delegates from both the UN and the 162 NGOs accredited to the Economic and Social Council (ECOSOC) (Tinker and Jaquette 1987: 419). The Fourth World Conference on Women, held ten years after Nairobi in Beijing in 1995, saw the trend for conflict and co-optation along national lines continue. Disputes over China's human rights record largely superseded substantive negotiations in the eyes of the world's media (Gilmartin and Brunn 1998; Howell 1997: 235–236). Less remarked was the continued, remarkable growth in the numbers attending: 17,000 delegates were registered at the interstate conference, including 4,000 representatives of NGOs, with more than 30,000 participating in the parallel NGO Forum at Hairou (Boutros-Ghali 1996: 1). The consolidation of feminist organizing on a global scale is clearly continuing apace.

As with other movements, globalization processes are also encouraging the diversification of feminist strategies upward, downward, and outward from the state. Many feminist groups are involved in mainstreaming feminist concerns within international organizations; for example, at least forty-five women's groups had been granted NGO consultative status within the UN by the mid-1990s (Stienstra 1995: 145–148). Others have participated in "symbiotic and simultaneous" events, such as Planeta Femea, the women's conference organized as part of the NGO Forum held parallel to the UN Conference on Environment and Development at Rio in 1992 (Ashworth 1995: 6; Braidotti et al. 1994: 91–92). Still others practice "a politics of disengagement," creating entirely autonomous, oppositional global fora, such as the International Tribunal on Crimes Against Women, held in Brussels in March 1976, or the independent women's news networks, ISIS (Stienstra 1995: 144; Miles 1996: 111–112, 118–119). More locally rooted mobilizations may struggle to oppose the global order through direct action and symbolic gestures designed to signify alternative cultural possibilities. The women at the Greenham Common peace camp, for example, protested against the deployment of U.S. nuclear missiles on British common land by encircling the U.S. airbase, weaving patterns into the fences surrounding it, and dancing on missile silos (e.g., Roseneil 1995). Other groups, perhaps particularly those in the third world, have developed pragmatic, problem-solving strategies to deal with the effects of globalization. In the context of worsening economic crisis, Women in Nigeria (WIN) has turned from campaigning activities to infrastructure projects, becoming involved in the construction of water supplies and a free legal aid clinic (Imam 1997: 294–295).

Rewriting Feminist Frameworks

Globalizing developments present important challenges to feminist theoretical frameworks. It often appears as if contemporary feminist debates are being pulled in two opposing directions, one particularizing and one universalizing. This is played out in several layers of argument. In the first place, as Anne Phillips points out, feminist analysis has emerged from a critique of the spurious universalisms of the Enlightenment and modernist thought that "offered us men in a gender-free guise." In other words, this is a particularizing moment. "The question then arises: how to correct for this bias towards men?" (Phillips 1992: 17). As Phillips indicates, a second layer of debate has then arisen between those who strive for the creation of a "genuinely gender-free world" and those who stress the need "to come to terms with bodily specificity" (1992: 18–19). This is the equality/difference debate touched upon in Chapter 3. The proponents of difference do not, however, entirely abandon universals; indeed, they rely on universal claims about women. So this is a universalizing moment in feminism. It has led, I would argue, to a third layer of argument, between those accepting such generalizations about women and those stressing the differences between them. Thus a universal/particular polarization is reinstated, this time within feminism. We saw this trajectory in feminist debates played out in Chapter 4 with the emergence of "identity politics" organizing. The third-level universal/particular polarization also seems characteristic of feminist approaches to analysis beyond the state. Some feminists stress that global dynamics are shaping the situation of women in the world as a whole, and they advocate a global response. Their opponents argue for a much narrower focus on particular groups of women and on their resistances in particular locations. This latter argument is frequently influenced by methodological nationalism and statism, which encourage the assumption that the nation-state is the container of women's lives and actions.

Both poles of the universal/particular debate carry analytical costs and generate political exclusions. Universalizing assumptions can operate to deny very real differences between women and to impose inappropriately uniform political agendas. Particularizing frameworks ignore globalizing tendencies and can lead to a politics of parochialism and exclusivist nationalism, involving the policing of group boundaries. Luckily, the polarity between these two tendencies may be more illusory than real, and feminists have other options. As Phillips demonstrates, surface rhetoric may mask the ways in which, say, theorists emphasizing female difference are aiming for more genuine equality (1992: 26–27). This argument can be applied to polarized discussions of the global and national/local. Many feminist claims about the global similarities between women and the need for global mobilizations do in fact strive for sensitivity to the differences between women and their mobilization, and many who stress national specificity do so as a political precursor to building a broader struggle.

Phillips concludes that the polarity between universality and particularity must be actively undermined and that feminists should strive, as many of them are already doing, to tread a more reflexive path through the middle (1992: 13, 26–28). I would suggest that black and third world feminists have been at the forefront of this move. As I argued in Chapter 4, much of their writing operates on weak postmodern terrain, between the unproblematic universalisms of modernism and the reified particularisms of strong postmodernity. I would also propose, following Walker's argument discussed in Chapter 5, that the relationship between the universal and the particular is not a metatheoretical issue open to abstract resolution. It needs to be constantly renegotiated through movement politics. All this suggests that feminists attempting to reconstruct understandings of democracy and social movements in the global context should seek to avoid both universalism and particularism by paying close attention to black and third world feminist debates and to the conduct of feminist activism.

Reconstructing the Polity in an Era of Globalization

It has to be acknowledged that feminist efforts to think through the reconstruction of the democratic polity in the light of arguments about globalization are thin on the ground. For example, feminist commentators on the East Central European transitions largely ignore the phenomenon of globalization when developing reconstructive strategies. Their suggestions are, however, worth a brief survey on other grounds. The Independent Women's Democratic Initiative in Russia puts forward several proposals, calling for "the organization of business and management schools for women and assertiveness-training courses," "the establishment of an insurance fund to support women living in poverty" and "the revision of pay scales and wage rates in 'women's' occupations" (Declaration . . . of Independent Women's Democratic Initiative 1991: 129–131). This comes close to what I identified in Chapter 2 as a social reformist or social democratic feminist approach, predicated on the assumption that parliamentary exclusion can be addressed only through reforms tackling women's general social disadvantage.

However, the social reformist feminist position is modified in the East Central European context by an evident wariness about state-initiated change and state-oriented politics. The Initiative outlined above aims to establish management schools and an insurance fund itself; it is not arguing that the state should do so on women's behalf (see also Bayer 1992: 113). This needs to be put into the context of the regional experience of authoritarian rule and state-enforced feminism. I would suggest that the influence of the dissident literature on civil society on the struggle against authoritarianism is also important. As we saw in Chapter 2, advocates of a civil society strategy argued for "a pushing back of the state-administrative forms of penetration from various dimensions of social life . . . [by] an independent or rather a self-organizing society aiming . . . at structural reform achieved as a result of organized pressure from below" (Cohen and Arato 1992: 32). Several East Central European feminists echo this sentiment by insisting that the mobilization and maintenance of autonomous feminist organization must be *the* political priority in the struggle to establish and maintain a more woman-friendly polity (e.g., Declaration . . . of Independent Women's Democratic Initiative 1991: 127; Drakulic 1993: 130; Posadskaya 1994: 6). This emphasis on movement-led change represents an important alternative to uncritically statist feminist democratizing strategies and is also a significant rebuttal to critics of a civil society strategy who have argued that post-transition problems in East Central European society indicate the need for a more state-oriented democratization strategy (e.g., Kumar 1993: 387–391; see also Stammers 1996: 27).[2]

The fact remains that, although the nationalist monopolization and statist orientation of the agenda for democracy is recognized as a problem by East Central European feminists, the territorial and bounded form of democracy is not. Their commitment to a focus on the particular conditions of East Central Europe appears to have meshed here with methodological nationalism and statism to reassert the grip of the state on the political imagination and to ensure that the challenges posed by global-

ization are ignored. Methodological nationalism and statism also circumscribe the more abstract, theoretical feminist literature that aims to reconstruct the democratic polity, as we saw in Chapter 3. There is one important exception here, in the form of recent reconstructions of citizenship
put forward by Ruth Lister (1997) and Nira Yuval-Davis (1997a, 1997b).

Both of these theorists put exclusions stemming from gender, ethnicity,
and national boundaries at the center of their critiques of existing formulations of citizenship, and they recognize that the state is under pressure
from globalizing processes of convergence and migration. In response,
they advocate a two-step reformulation of the concept of citizenship.
First, they argue that the universalizing pretensions of citizenship should
rest henceforth on the recognition of difference rather than sameness. For
Lister, this necessitates the adoption of a common grammar of politics,
the emergence of nonessentialist and pluralist conceptions of the self,
and the instigation of enhanced dialogue between groups. Yuval-Davis
also emphasizes the importance of acknowledging group difference.
Both theorists stress the need for the state to take action to combat marginalizing pressures on groups. This argument resonates with feminist
social reformism. It stops short of Iris Young's more radical idea that
groups should be granted rights of institutional representation, although
it seems to me that this is not incompatible with the overall framework
(Lister 1997: 66–90; Yuval-Davis 1997a: 8–11, 17–18). Second, citizenship
is reconfigured as a multilevel concept denoting the relationship of an individual to sources of governance above and below the state. Yuval-
Davis claims that this is less of a conceptual jump if we reinstate T. H.
Marshall's definition of citizenship as membership in a *community* rather
than a state (1997a: 5).

Perhaps surprisingly, this second dimension of the reformulation of
citizenship does not yield particularly radical conclusions. Although Yuval-Davis asserts the need to sever citizenship from its exclusive identification with the state, she also insists that the state "continues to be the
primary political target" and source of social power. The rights and duties she enumerates as part of the package of citizenship (voting, military
service, taxation) remain tied primarily to the state (1997a: 20–21). More
consistently, Lister extends citizenship rights to the international domain,
arguing for the development of international law to ensure that northern
states provide resources to the less fortunate in the world and that their
tendency to undermine the rights of migrants is curbed (1997: 56–62). Yet
apart from her brief reference to the significance of women's activism in
global civil society (1997: 62–63), this extension of the logic of citizenship
remains centered on membership of a state and on rights claims in law
that are implemented by states. I do not dispute the continuing importance of the state and of rights for much feminist activism as well as for

democratic politics more generally. However, my point here is that questions about membership in communities other than states, and particularly about participation or active citizenship in those communities, have largely dropped away. We remain, in the end, within a liberal, methodologically nationalist and statist framework. I suggest that there is also an issue here about the limits of the concept of citizenship itself. Although its close linkage with the nation-state may be historically specific, it remains a concept about membership in a *territorial community*. It cannot readily be stretched to tackle structures and relations of power or to encompass forms of identity that are not neatly segmented into territorial communities or that stratify such communities. In my view, it would be more useful and more radical to rethink notions about political agency entirely rather than starting from notions of citizenship with all the assumptions these already carry.

The beginnings of a more fundamental rethinking of democracy can be found in feminist international relations theory, although the reconstructive element of these analyses remains, as yet, underdeveloped. V. Spike Peterson (1995) provides a groundbreaking analysis of the intertwined impacts of both global dynamics and gender hierarchy on democracy and political identity. However, she does not consider how feminists might challenge the exclusions these produce. Betty Reardon (1993) factors a feminist perspective into proposals for a world constitutional order, but is concerned less with the details of how such an order is to be constituted than with the values underlying it. This echoes maternalist feminist democratic theory. Kristen Timothy (1995) focuses on the marginalization of women within the United Nations. She adopts what is in effect a political reformist defense of quota systems but without considering how this might affect the operation of the UN or broader global forces. Christine Sylvester (1998) examines the ways in which the "nostalgic idealism" of territorial democracy and the "nostalgic realism" of international relations reinforce one another and argues for the need to unsettle such nostalgia through social movement activities like that at Greenham Common. Her analysis focuses on the implications for IR understandings of world politics rather than on how such a politics is or could be specifically democratic. Finally, Donna Dickenson (1997) insists that conditions of globalization are encouraging women to organize above and below the nation-state in ways that challenge norms about political identity and community in liberal democracy and that undermine the public/private divide. Taken together, these last two approaches draw attention to the role of feminist movement politics in including women in global politics and in challenging the nature and limits of democracy. They echo the East Central European feminist emphasis on autonomous movement mobilization but point to the necessity and possibility of expanding such mobilization beyond state boundaries. In an effort to develop and critically interrogate this point, I now turn to the organization of the feminist movement on a global scale.

Reconstructing Global Feminism

Before discussing democratization within the global feminist movement, my assumption that such a global movement exists needs defending. This assumption has been increasingly attacked from within feminism as inaccurate and anti-democratic. There are legitimate and important concerns here given the evidently exclusionary implications of past efforts to conceptualize and construct a global movement. As Jan Jindy Pettman notes, first-wave western efforts were compromised by the fact that they "arose alongside an especially virulent phase of imperialism, and feminists laid claim to the vote and inclusion within an imperial state" (1996: 38). They frequently replicated imperialist and racist attitudes toward black and third world women inside Europe and America and beyond, undermining an expressed belief in the moral unity of women by positioning them as "little sisters to be saved." This is global feminism as "the white woman's burden" (Pettman 1996: 38; see also Ware 1992: 119–166).[3]

Second-wave efforts to reconstruct the basis of global feminism under the rubric of "global sisterhood" have also raised problems. In her influential radical feminist formulation of this position, Robin Morgan argued that a worldwide female solidarity was immanent in the common experience of a shared condition of the patriarchal control of female bodies (Morgan 1985: 4, 6–23). Conflicts of class, race, and nation were seen to be imposed upon women, and feminists were urged to link up their struggles to transcend male divisions and create their own autonomous, worldwide feminist revolution (1985: 18–19, 23–28). This formulation has since been criticized on the grounds of its radical feminist privileging of biology and sexuality as a site of power and for assuming that power operates in a monolithic way. The notion that women worldwide share a commonality of experience and that common experience generates a shared politics has also been attacked (Mohanty 1998: 258–264; Basu 1995: 3–4). What is more, as Chandra Talpade Mohanty puts it, "women as a unified group are seen as unimplicated in the process of history and contemporary imperialism. Thus the logical strategic response for Morgan appears to be political transcendence" (Mohanty 1998: 261–262). This obscures the differences in identity and power that still stratify relations between women and feminists. It is thus in danger of replicating the obfuscations of an earlier imperialist age.

In response to the problems with such formulations, many feminist activists and commentators have abandoned the attempt to construct and conceptualize a unity across borders altogether and retreated instead to small-scale, distinct mobilizations. Most often, this takes the form of an emphasis on the distinctiveness of national feminist organization. Countless country-specific studies of feminism simply assume the national model. Political opportunity structure theorists argue more explicitly for the centrality of state formation, and of state-level processes whereby elites jockey for power, in explaining feminist mobilization (Katzenstein 1987; Costain 1992). They receive support from the existence of country-wide organizations, such as the National Organization of Women in the United States and Women in Nigeria, and from the campaigns of third world feminists to establish indigenous and often explicitly national*ist* women's movements in the context of anti-imperialist struggles (West 1992: 566–576; Peterson and Runyan 1999: 187–193). Alternatively, some feminists have argued for the existence and importance of larger-scale *regional* feminist movements that spread to the boundaries of the West or third world, Eastern or Western Europe, and Latin or North America— but no farther (e.g., Keysers and Smyth 1992: 28–29). Others celebrate the fragmentation of feminism into mobilizations based on ethnic and social identity rather than geographical location.

Each of these different ways of framing the specificity of feminist mobilizations contains elements of truth and raises legitimate concerns about the power relations involved in talking about diverse activisms as part of a global movement. They also contain empirical inaccuracies and are based on reified ontological assumptions that can lead to conservatism. For example, although the nation and state are undeniably important in shaping distinctive paths for feminist mobilizations, the influence of methodological nationalism and statism can disguise the historically and geographically specific nature of state influence, the ways in which gender relations and feminism may shape and reshape the nation and state, and the possibility or necessity of challenging their hegemony over political life. It can also function to marginalize transnational facets of feminist mobilization, as highlighted above. What, for example, are we to make of the Latin American Encuentros? By 1990, they were attracting over 3,000 women from all over the region (Stienstra 1995: 150). The regional framework allows for such mobilizations but underplays the differences and contestations within regional activisms and the blurring of boundaries between them through processes of (re)colonization and migration. Along with the national framework, it can lapse into a static view of culture and solidaristic view of community, albeit on a larger scale. It may rely on a stark dichotomy between the West and the Other, one that constructs western feminism as unified and necessarily imperialist and one that "conceives of the West and non-West as autonomous spaces and thereby evades the thorny issue of their intersections and mutual implications" (Mani 1990: 31). Perhaps most danger-ously, both the national and regional models of feminism can stigmatize women pursuing a feminist agenda beyond the context in which they were born, or those who challenge received views of cultural authentic-ity, as "inauthentic" outsiders (Malti-Douglas 1996). Finally, as I argued in Chapter 4, the vision of feminism organized on the basis of distinct ethnic and cultural identities frequently relies on a prepolitical notion of identity that delegitimizes contestation and dialogue within and across identities. It also marginalizes women who do not fit neatly into a prede-fined category.

In sum, theorizations of the feminist movement have tended toward the poles of universalization or particularism—when this is continually un-dermined by movement practices. As argued previously, a path between these poles is preferable. This can be found in Alberto Melucci's construc-tivist approach to movements. As explained in previous chapters, Melucci characterizes movements as fragmented, heterogeneous, and dynamic forms of collective action, continually reconstructed through diffuse, de-centralized, subterranean networks. His approach indicates that feminism should never have been perceived as a homogeneous entity and that frag-mentation is a normal part of movement (re)construction. This does not mean, however, that feminism has no unity at all. Melucci's analysis also points toward the possibility that, however ideologically, socially, and ge-ographically distant fragments of feminist mobilization may appear, they remain woven unevenly into a broader web of feminist activism.[4] Further, critics have modified Melucci's emphasis on face-to-face processes of movement formation by pointing to the constitutive influence of interac-tion with exterior social processes and state-led institutions. This argu-ment can be extended to encompass the formative impact of feminist movement interaction with global institutions, such as the UN, as docu-mented above. Certainly, Melucci himself insists that feminism is a "plan-etary phenomenon" (1996a: 144), its "field of opportunities and con-straints of action . . . redefined within a multipolar and transnational system" through processes of globalization (1989: 74).

Although Melucci's interpretation of globalization overemphasizes its cultural and homogenizing aspects (e.g., 1996a: 7–9), a multidimensional and interactive approach to globalization makes clear two points. First, although experiences of globalization and the consequent articulation of identity and construction of movement activism are likely to be distinc-tive in each locality, "these are all located within global structures, and relations of power and penalty" (Pettman 1996: 83). Second, although ho-mogenizing aspects of globalization enable contemporary versions of western feminism to have an even greater reach and a more disruptive effect than old imperial formulations, there are also more complex, con-

tradictory, and multidirectional processes at work that are producing heterogeneous and hybrid feminist forms. Thus the vigils held by the Argentinean Mothers of the Plaza de Mayo are echoed in the vigils of the
Women in Black of Jerusalem, the latter held to protest the Israeli occupa-
tion of Palestinian territories. The Israeli group is then alluded to in the
formation of the anti-militarist Women in Black of Belgrade during the
Yugoslavian conflict in the early 1990s (Helman and Rapoport 1997;
Eizenstein 1997: 159–160). To give another example, the British group
Women Against Fundamentalism has given rise to a "feminist antifunda-
mentalist perspective . . . used increasingly as a frame for international
networking and solidarity. For instance, in 1989 a conference entitled
'Women against Fundamentalism' was held in India" and a similar conference was held a few years later in Canada (Miles 1996: 125). Rather
than presuming a relationship of imposition or a one-way diffusion, the
undoubtedly privileged position of white western feminism in the context of globalization is perhaps most usefully conceptualized in terms of
relativization, whereby feminists all over the world have to define themselves in relation to western cultural and political forms.

This combination of a constructivist movement framework and a multidimensional approach to globalization makes it possible to conceptualize a global feminist movement as a collective actor without implying a
homogenized and monolithic entity that can articulate unified demands.
This should not, however, be taken to imply that feminist efforts to construct such a movement have been free from exclusionary and universalizing tendencies. Although feminist conceptualizations of global activism
may have been analytically inadequate, they have had concrete effects on
political strategy. They indicate, in many instances, that the global feminist movement has not been constructed democratically. However, it
seems to me that a democratizing impulse is increasingly evident. There
is a now-familiar dynamic at work here. As we saw in Chapter 4, second-
wave western feminism developed partly as a reaction to the democratic
limitations of other movements and represented an effort to construct a
more genuinely democratic politics. Subsequent fragmentation within
the second wave pointed to the limitations of the democracy that had
been created. Ultimately, it encouraged the renewal of efforts to find a
way of building democratic bridges across differences.

I would suggest that this dialectical development is currently being
echoed in global feminism. The democratic limitations of efforts to construct a global movement under the rubric of the *white woman's burden* or
global sisterhood have unsurprisingly encouraged the proliferation of particularizing approaches on the basis of specific location and identity.
These are a welcome development insofar as they encourage reflection
on the democratic inadequacies that spawned them. Yet an emphasis on

specificity can also carry anti-democratic tendencies, reifying location and identity as prepolitical and precluding dialogue with others. In the light of these problems, efforts to reconstruct global feminist organization on a more democratic basis are now emerging, combining an emphasis on specificity of location with the aspiration to forge alliances across differences.[5] Relatively scattered and apparently unconnected moments of theory and practice can be recognized as part of a more general democratic impulse if we place them into the framework that was developed in Chapter 4 from black and third world feminist critiques. The rest of this chapter thus examines ways in which ideas about power, politics, agency, and change are being invoked and extended beyond borders.

Democratic Innovations (2)

Moving Against Global Power

I propose that there is a democratizing impulse in global feminist organizing that is rooted in an understanding of the operations of power of the kind this book has been attempting to sketch out. It involves an abandonment of monolithic, universalizing concepts of patriarchy in favor of a recognition that power may be global but that it also takes diverse forms that interact in context-specific ways. Such a shift was evident during the conferences held during the UN Decade on Women. The collection and dissemination of information on the lives of women during this period enhanced awareness of the global scope of power relations at the same time that negotiations during the conferences confirmed the complexity of the operations of power on the ground. Many white western feminists initially insisted that the conferences should be discussing "women's issues" such as sexual autonomy and equal pay rather than "political issues" such as the Israeli-Palestinian conflict and processes of economic development (e.g., Bernard 1987: 167–188). This stance gave way in many cases—though not all—under the weight of the insistence of black and third world feminists on the need to "create a feminist movement which struggles against those things which can clearly be shown to oppress women, whether based on race, sex, or class or resulting from imperialism" (Johnson-Odim 1991: 321; see also Bunch 1987: 283–305; Tinker and Jaquette 1987: 422). Cheryl Johnson-Odim claims that this move has resulted in a "broadening of the parameters of feminism" but that the problem remains of how and by whom the agenda is set within feminism in the first place. This "is primarily a question of power" (1991: 322–323).

 It seems to me that the UN Decade also encouraged recognition of the need to confront and dismantle relations and structures of power within the feminist movement—to "decolonize" feminism (Donaldson, L. 1992). This has involved a challenge to the dominance of white western women in transnational feminist organizing and in agenda setting. As Angela Miles points out, many white western feminists have resisted this challenge:

> Some US feminists with little international experience, for instance, were surprised and hurt to be challenged on U.S. government policies at the U.N. End of Decade Conference in Nairobi in 1985. . . . At the World's Women's Congress for a Healthy Planet in November 1991 in Miami, as well, some U.S. women who had spent most of their adult lives struggling against U.S. government policies were surprised that their experience did not entitle them to leadership roles in workshops. They were personally offended when women from other countries resisted their playing these roles. (Miles 1996: 161, note 9)

Miles suggests that a more appropriate response would involve privileged women working to be aware of, and to counter, inequalities of power from which we benefit. It would involve overturning the tendency to see Europe and the United States as the center of the world and to universalize context-specific concepts and theories via privileged access to transnational feminist networks. It requires willingness to learn from the perspectives of others. And it demands that the theory and activism of privileged women must be grounded within the territorial communities in which we live, with attention paid to the ways in which these communities are themselves shaped by global structures and relations of power, instead of presuming that the struggle against global power always takes place somewhere else (Miles 1996: 99–108; see also Bunch 1987: 328–345). As Charlotte Bunch puts it: "This is the challenge of bringing the global home" (1987: 329).

Bunch was personally involved in the establishment of the International Feminist Network Against Female Sexual Slavery, one attempt to put the above ideas into practice. This organization still reflects a western, radical feminist preoccupation with sexuality as a site of power, of the kind evident in Morgan's controversial formulation of global sisterhood. However, the radical feminist position is modified here in key ways. Although the network was initiated by three western feminists, it was founded and launched at a workshop in 1983 to which thirty women were brought from all over the world. Bunch's report of the workshop stresses that the "universal patriarchal oppression of women . . . takes different forms in different cultures and different regions" (Bunch 1987: 311). Although the primary focus of the group was intended to be "the violence and exploitation of women through the use of female sexuality," it was acknowledged that in some contexts these issues would need to be "approached in relation to other concerns, such as . . . the exploitation of women's work, female poverty, racism. . . . [W]e recognize that feminism needs to be expressed in different ways in different cultural contexts" (Bunch 1987: 318). The network explicitly rejected what it saw as the double standard of western feminism whereby prostitution in the third world was either excused because of economic necessity or focused on to the exclusion of oppressive practices in the West. It stressed the need for simultaneous analysis and action in third world contexts and in Europe and North America (1987: 319). Finally, the network was established as a nonhierarchical, transnational organization, intended to assist and coordinate local and regional groups from all over the world and not intended to direct them from on high or to enforce a shared outlook and set of priorities (1987: 319–320).

One problem here is that patriarchy and its effects on sexuality are still ultimately privileged. Although there is a recognition of the role of other forms of power, these seem to be regarded as secondary variables that operate in some areas rather than as integral to the way in which women's oppression is shaped worldwide. The radical feminist framework may be preventing the full implications of an interactive approach to power being accepted. Further, Bunch's report does not tell us the precise mechanisms by which such a transnational, nonhierarchical network can be sustained in the face of the continual stratification of feminist organizing by the operations of globalizing power. Other analyses of movement activism can provide more specific details on this point.

A Transversal Politics of Location and Connection

It is my view that increasing adoption of the global, interactive lens on power has encouraged the development of an expansive, participatory, but also *differentiated* approach to democratic politics, of the kind described in Chapter 4 as a politics of location and connection. Such an approach corresponds, for example, to the practice of "transversal politics." This has been highlighted by Yuval-Davis. As developed by the Italian Women in Black with feminist Serbs and Croats and with Palestinians and Israeli Jews, transversal politics is the name given to a process of coalition building in which participants seek to avoid both the enforced abandonment of differences in the construction of agreement and the unreflexive entrenchment of differences that allows no agreement at all, through processes of dialogue aimed at constructing a common perspective. Yuval-Davis identifies two key features of this dialogue in Italian Women in Black activities. First, "the boundaries of the groupings were determined not by an essentialist notion of difference but by a concrete and material political reality" (1997b: 129). In other words, there is a politicized, rather than reified, notion of identity at work here. Second, the dialogue entailed a process of "rooting" and "shifting," according to which "each participant ... brings with her a rooting in her own membership and identity, but at the same time tries to shift in order to put herself in a situation of exchange with women who have different membership and identity" (1997b: 130). The resonances here with the concept of a politics of location and connection hardly needs underlining.

The transversal model was developed in the specific context of feminist negotiations in situations of ethnic conflict, but it has wider ramifications for thinking about democratic politics. Yuval-Davis argues that it enables feminists to move beyond the "universalism/relativism dichotomy" plaguing contemporary debates (1997b: 125).[6] I would add that it avoids the constraining dichotomies of "international/national" and "global/local" and allows an imaginative leap beyond the concept of the "transnational," which still presumes that the state and state system provide the framework for all politics. Also, the prefix *trans*, which literally means across, through, or beyond, carries associations of movement and change. In sum, transversal politics is a useful shorthand to describe a process of political negotiation encompassing actors in disparate geographic and social locations. It involves the construction of a joint political project through dialogue that recognizes and respects the different subject positions of the participants and that is characterized by a critical stance toward territorial and social boundaries. It indicates, in effect, global movement democracy.

Transversal politics is intrinsically democratic because it is predicated on open, respectful, and participatory dialogue. Yuval-Davis (1997a: 19), following the ideas of black feminist theorist Patricia Hill Collins, emphasizes that such dialogue must be rooted in an acknowledgment that all speak from partial perspectives. As I argue in Chapter 4, this demands explicit attention to mechanisms for open dialogue, such as limiting speaking times and enabling intensive one-to-one conversations. On a transnational level, it also requires attention to linguistic diversity. Measures here could include efforts to communicate in more than one language or to supply translators, learning greetings in other languages, and devising nonverbal methods of communication.

As Collins recognized, open dialogue also requires efforts to tackle the power relations between participants that structure access to dialogue and shape its outcomes. Applied to transnational politics, this necessitates proactive efforts to redress the iniquitous geopolitical distribution of economic, social, and technological resources. Thus the locations of meetings and organizations should be made accessible to third world women and funds targeted to enable the poorest to participate. One acute problem is the relationship of "guilt and dependency" built into the supply of funds from and through northern feminist organizations to southern groups and communities. This is a much-debated issue among transnational feminist organizations. One suggestion is that recipients should be regarded as partners in establishing how money is spent (Waterman 1998: 180–183). Along similar lines, it has been proposed that "beneficiaries" should be redefined as "constituents," to whom donor groups must listen and to whom they must make themselves accountable (Butwega 1996: 256–257). Most fundamentally, as the quote above from Cheryl Johnson-Odim would suggest, marginalized groups need to be integrated into agenda setting rather than regarded as either recipients or beneficiaries of feminist attention. This would require resources to be made available for the institutionalization of systematic consultation mechanisms and for regular face-to face exchanges with groups from different geographical and social locations.

Practices along these lines have emerged from feminist mobilization against the North American Free Trade Agreement (NAFTA) and associated economic processes. A long and painful process of movement reconstruction has taken place in an effort to redress asymmetrical relations of economic privilege within the organization and to counter the geopolitical and racial privilege of Canadian and U.S. women relative to their Mexican counterparts, white women over Latino women, and Latino women relative to indigenous women. Trinational meetings have been held in Mexico. The group Mujer a Mujer has published several newsletters in Spanish and English (Waterman 1998: 160–171). Canadian groups have sponsored the participation of Mexican women activists in a joint tour to oppose free trade. The white-dominated Canadian National Action Committee on the Status of Women (NAC) has recruited more women of color to its membership and executive, electing Sunera Thobani as president. It also invited guests from as far afield as Nicaragua and South Africa to its 1992 general meeting. Analysts have concluded that these measures point in the direction of a more egalitarian and sustainable way of constructing transnational feminist alliances (Gabriel and Macdonald 1994: 549–554, 558–562).

Mobilizing Subjectivities Across Borders

A very specific notion of political agency is required for the successful implementation of the kind of politics described above. Here I turn from examples of feminist organizing to ontological and epistemological debates among feminist thinkers regarding their location within feminism and within territorial boundaries. Unsurprisingly, given the documented transnational organizational basis of feminism since its inception, the view that the political actor is first and foremost a national subject has long been contested by feminists. Indeed, many have rejected the idea that a national/state location is, or should be, in any way characteristic of women's and particularly feminist political agency. As Virginia Woolf put it, "as a woman I have no country. As a woman I want no country. As a woman my country is the whole world" (1938: 197). This has been described as a feminist version of the marxist cosmopolitan call for identification with a global community in the face of exclusion from state institutions (see Waterman 1998: 164). Although the exclusion of women is no longer so total, second-wave feminism has also exhibited a strong cosmopolitan streak, as evidenced in arguments for global sisterhood. Rosi Braidotti concludes that the "identification of female identity with a sort of planetary exile has . . . become a *topos* of feminist studies" (1994: 21).

Braidotti advocates instead a strong postmodern ontology rooted in the idea that the subject is fluid and multiple. She and others use "the term *mobile* rather than *multiple* to avoid the implication of movement from one to another stable resting place" (Ferguson 1993: 158). Rather than seeing all women as necessarily "unhomed" in a world of men, they insist on giving up the idea of "home" altogether (De Lauretis 1990: 138–139). Braidotti uses the political fiction of the "nomadic subject" to capture this idea. Although she may not be physically mobile, the nomad "has relinquished all idea, desire, or nostalgia for fixity" (1994: 22) and is particularly resistant to "the limits of one national, fixed identity. The nomad has no passport—or has too many of them" (Braidotti 1994: 33).

It is unclear here whether strong postmodernists are describing a mode of writing or a way of being associated with subordinated groups that feminist intellectuals can cultivate (Ferguson 1993: 172–175; Grewal 1994: 234; Braidotti 1994: 22–23). Both seem problematic. The first presumes "a common frame of reference in some unified (and implicitly equal?) transnational circulation of ideas and cultural products," which "is to refuse to address the inequities that shape global relations" (Mongia 1996: 7). The second privileges the "hybrid," migrant intellectual as the "only political-conceptual space for revisionist enunciation" (Loomba and Kaul quoted in Mongia 1996: 7). It seems to me that strong postmodernists are in danger of replicating the ethnocentrism of their cosmopolitan feminist predecessors. All downplay the fact that engagement in national/nationalist politics has been and remains significant in factoring many women into state-level and feminist politics and thus in enabling as well as constraining their agency. It is surely not insignificant that theories of cosmopolitan agency were formulated largely by white, western, middle-class women, reflecting their context-specific concerns about exclusion from the institutions of state and, in Woolf's case, the onset of war. The personal histories of theorists of the nomadic subject frequently span states, continents, and languages (e.g., Braidotti 1994: 8–15). I suggest that both approaches to female subjectivity are universalizing from relatively privileged social and geographical locations.

Transversal politics must begin with situating the self, as emphasized in black and third world feminist critiques. This means that the self should be recognized to be not only gendered and raced but also nationally and geopolitically located. As poet Adrienne Rich insists, "As a woman I have a country; as a woman I cannot divest myself of that country merely by condemning its government . . . a place on the map is also a place in history" (1986: 212). While reading Cuban poetry and visiting Nicaragua, Rich describes how she:

> began to experience the meaning of North America as a location which had also shaped my ways of seeing and my ideas of who and what was important, a location for which I was also responsible. . . . I could physically feel the weight of the United States of North America, its military forces, its vast appropriations of money, its mass media, at my back; I could feel what it means, dissident or not, to be part of that raised boot of power. (Rich 1986: 219–220)

This argument has been criticized by Caren Kaplan for blurring a "method of interrogating and deconstructing the position, identity and privilege of whiteness" with a "call to U.S. feminists to examine their investments in geopolitics." This implies that all U.S. women are equally privileged, erasing the specificity of the location of nonwhite women. Such a hegemonic effect occurs because Rich's argument was formulated *outside* of her home location (Kaplan 1994: 139–141). Nonetheless, her argument is still a useful starting point. What is necessary is a more nuanced formulation that recognizes that women's relationship to the states in which they find themselves is stratified by ethnicity, class, and sexuality. They may also be located over time and space in more than one social and national location, and they may have to struggle for "reterritorialization" in ways immensely complicated by globalization processes, including cross-cutting patterns of migration; the strengthening coercive capacity of states; and the emergence of violent, exclusionary versions of nationalism as well as hybrid, transnational cultural forms (e.g., Mohanty 1998: 267–269). As we have seen, the uneven impact of globalization ensures stasis and continuity for many people and violently enforces the mobility of others between and among national/state locations.

Black and third world feminists have extensively theorized the effects of *enforced* mobility on a global scale. Two images are recurrent. The first is the migrant, who is "homeless" in the sense that she cannot "call a country of adoption home, especially if the immigrant is a woman of

color in a white patriarchal society" (Grewal 1994: 250). Further, her location "disrupts the home/abroad and the margin/center constructs for
more complex positionings" (Grewal 1994: 235). The second image is the
mestiza, rooted in the "borderlands" between races and cultures, emotionally shaped by resistance to racist dualisms and to ethnocentric attempts to impose linguistic fixity (Anzaldúa 1990b: 377–379; 1987: 1–23;
Grewal 1994: 247–250). Both of these images resonate with strong postmodern strategies for reformulating subjectivity and have had great influence on them. However, black and third world feminists draw attention to the pain and trauma of processes of displacement and marginality
that have been evacuated from more abstracted postmodern accounts.
They also insist on the specific conjunctures of power shaping mobile
subjectivities in particular locations (Moya 1997: 128–135). Thus the image of the migrant should not be shorn of her association with physical
displacement, economic stratification, and subcultural defensiveness, nor
should the *mestiza* be uprooted from her historically and geographically
unique environment of "the Texas-U.S. Southwest/Mexican border"
(Anzaldúa 1987: preface). In other words, these notions of the political
actor are not locationless but have complex locations.[7] They cannot be
adopted as a matter of individual will by the writer eager to discard her
national and geopolitical identifications (Moya 1997: 132–133).

Nonetheless, social, physical, and imaginative mobility remains an aspiration for black and third world feminists, one requiring political struggle and not just textual exploration. The term *world-traveling*, coined by
Maria Lugones, captures this aspiration. "Only when we have travelled
to each other's 'worlds' are we fully subjects to each other" (Lugones
1990: 401). This metaphor combines a planetary allusion with an emphasis on the multiplicity of different communities and worldviews. "The simultaneous worlds of resistant, lively and diverse subjectivities that Lugones locates are not reducible to the common world of women that
Virginia Woolf called for" (Kaplan 1994: 150). Lugones suggests that
world-traveling has typically been the domain of the person outside
dominant society, the migrant and the *mestiza*, world-traveling out of necessity in the context of a hostile dominant culture. It is easy to avoid if
one is more integrated into that culture, able to judge others "arrogantly"
from a position of ontological complacency (1990: 390–394, 401–402; also
Lugones and Spelman 1983: 575–576). The white western feminist must
therefore make a willful, political effort to empathize across differences.
There are dangers here that must be avoided: the abandonment of one's
own location, the appropriation of other's experiences as one's own, or
the adoption of a vicarious "temporary tourism" whereby the other is
viewed as a spectacle before the tourist returns home (Ferguson 1993:
116; Sylvester 1995: 945–952). World-traveling requires critical awareness

of one's home location and the effort to construct sustained, strategic political struggles with those in other locations and in other movements. In
other words, it requires transversal movement politics.

Thus, for example, the white Canadian members of NAC could not
deny or transcend their Canadian location or their whiteness when constructing anti-NAFTA mobilization with Mexican groups. Through difficult processes of movement struggle, they have been forced to realize
that it is only through explicit recognition and negotiation of the complex ethnic realities of Canadian national identity, as well as the differences between Canadian and Mexican experiences of NAFTA, that a
cross-national alliance can be achieved—along with genuine world-
traveling for the participants.

All this confirms the point that feminists concerned to factor women's
agency into global politics need to highlight the potential of movement
form and to recognize the role of a diversity of movements in enabling
the ongoing construction and contestation of what it means to be women
in the world. Further, modes of collective identity and agency created
within movements should be recognized as hard won and transient and
they should be continually open to renegotiation. If it is continually reconstructed in a democratic, participatory manner, in the ways outlined
here, a global movement can enable the articulation of many voices in dialogue with one another. Feminist theory and practice is beginning to
point to ways in which this might be possible.

Democratic Change and the State System

Finally, I want to consider the implications of efforts to democratize
global feminism for thinking about transformatory change on a global
scale. It should be apparent that many feminist activists have not abandoned the struggle for such change nor forsaken an emphasis on the necessary role of the feminist movement in it. However, a conventional
model of revolutionary politics has been left far behind and with it the
notion of a definitive convulsive change. This seems particularly unlikely
once the complexity of the operations of power on a global scale is recognized. The transversal model of movement politics implies that the construction of alternative democratic relationships should not be left until
after coercive power relationships have been definitively challenged but
should be considered both the means and the end of struggle. Further,
transversal politics brings with it a strongly pluralistic emphasis on the
need for context-specific identification of the operations of power and the
development of localized movement struggles.

Having said that, black and third world feminist arguments for prioritizing change in the domains of the economy and culture, and for skepti-

cal but strategic engagement with the state, receive support from theorists and activists in the context of globalization. The damaging effects of the globalization and liberalization of the economy have been documented earlier in this chapter, along with the ways in which these effects are intertwined with and intensified by racial and gender hierarchies. For example, economic globalization has played a major role in the marginalization of East Central European women within emerging democracies and in the migration of significant numbers of vulnerable second and third world women. Thus third world feminist theorists M. Jacqui Alexander and Chandra Talpade Mohanty insist that the transnational feminist movement, and feminist democracy, must be anti-capitalist if feminists are to contest the reconfigurations of colonial relations of power within and beyond their movement (1997: xli). The framework for understanding power developed here, which emphasizes context-specific interactions, indicates that there can be no one struggle against capitalism, imposed as a priority in all contexts. Nonetheless, it points to the fact that more privileged first world women have a particular responsibility on this issue because of their position within the global capitalist hierarchy. As Miles recognizes, this position may have functioned as a historic block to the construction of commonalities of struggle with working-class and black and third world women, but it also locates us in the "'belly of the beast' . . . particularly well placed to resist Western exploitation. We are in a position to put direct pressure on the patriarchal-capitalist classes, governments, business and banks" (Miles 1996: 107). Examples highlighted by Miles of western activism in this area include North American feminist organizing against NAFTA, discussed above; the "Woman to Woman Global Strategies Group, founded in Vancouver in 1991 to research the impact of global economic restructuring on women's lives"; and the "Women for Alternative Economics Network, made up of women from diverse regions and organizations in the United States searching for economic alternatives to systemic poverty" in a global context (1996: 101).

Transversal principles also indicate that there is no one post-capitalist alternative. Rather, the point should be to enable many context-specific arrangements to develop. However, this is not to say that all strategies are equally effective and emancipatory. For example, a significant number of western feminist commentators have responded to the recent depredations of liberalized and globalized capitalism by arguing for the reestablishment of social democracy, involving the recovery of the much-reduced regulatory and redistributive powers of the liberal democratic state. Although some progress in this direction may well be an important goal in some contexts, this strategy has significant drawbacks as a response to economic globalization. For one thing, it is in danger of attempting to universalize a system that was always limited to only a few states and that may also have been dependent on relations of inequality between them and other states. Economic globalization means that, now more than ever, campaigns for economic protection and support within one country are likely to have significant ramifications for women and men elsewhere. Further, as indicated in Chapter 5, globalization is currently reconfiguring state capacities and nationalist ideologies in ways that strengthen certain coercive aspects of the state. A state-centric strategy for change may reinforce such developments rather than challenging them.

There is a more fundamental question emerging here, to do with how transnational feminism should relate to individual states and to the state system. Transnational feminist organizing remains divided on this issue, with no clear trend discernible. Many activists insist that states should be the focus of transnational feminist campaigns, however intransigent they may appear. This is the line followed by the editors of the proceedings of a 1996 conference that brought academics and activists together to consider the implications of the agreements reached at Beijing for women in Muslim societies:

> Experience suggests that state intervention on behalf of women can enhance women's rights and improve women's conditions significantly, particularly in the field of law, economics, and education. In the Beijing Platform for Action governments are made responsible for establishing the organizational structures . . . necessary for the platform's implementation. The prevailing sociopolitical conditions in Muslim societies, however, make it unlikely that governments seriously will promote women's rights and expand services for women without pressure. . . . It then falls on the international community to accelerate the human rights–women's rights momentum generated during and after the Beijing Conference, to give support to local activists, and to monitor the fulfillment of promises by individual governments. (Afkhami and Friedl 1997: xiv)

This statement implies that the primary role of the feminists within Muslim societies and beyond should be to pressure local states to fulfill their obligations to women. This is in contrast to the conclusion drawn earlier by several commentators on the Decade for Women. Critical of the co-optation and diffusion of feminist energies and agendas during the official conferences, and inspired by the creativity of NGO fora, these commentators insisted on the need to avoid subsequent entanglement with state and interstate institutions. They argued instead for the reestablishment of a women-centered orientation and a focus on building autonomous networks below and across the state (Newland 1988: 513;

Pietilä and Vickers 1994: 4). Jude Howell's analysis of the impact of Beijing on Chinese women's groups similarly emphasizes the impact of NGO activity, suggesting that this may strengthen demands for autonomy within the state-sponsored All-China Women's Federation and aid the growth of semi-legal women's networks in Chinese society (Howell 1997: 240–248).

I suggest that a way of building bridges between these diverse arguments about the state is provided by black and third world feminist arguments. As outlined in Chapter 4, these converge around a "skeptical and strategic" approach to the state. Such an approach stresses that differences in geographical and historical context are crucial in calculating how to deal with individual states and the state system; campaigns for greater access to the state, for the deepening of liberal democracy, and for state-led change may thus be more applicable in some contexts than in others. Given the hierarchical, coercive dimensions of the state and state system and their complex interactions with other sources of power, it should be recognized that engagement is always likely to yield limited results and to be fraught with danger. Thus engagement should always be combined with efforts to maintain links with broader, ultimately transformatory, movement struggles. It should be stressed that such a skeptical and strategic approach to the state and state system is being put forward here as an appropriate way of understanding the dilemmas of transnational feminist organizing; it has not emerged directly as an explicitly theorized position within such organizing. However, the need for such an approach to be adopted by activists gains support from commentary on feminist engagement with *interstate*, or intergovernmental, organizations (IGOs).

There is some evidence of an increasing effort in transnational feminist organizing to mainstream feminist priorities within IGOs. One analysis of the Beijing conference insists that this integrative strategy is giving rise to activist disquiet about co-optation and the attenuation of the relationship between feminist elites and their grassroots constituencies (Baden and Goetz 1998: 20–21). Similar tensions are revealed by Braidotti et al.'s conclusions about feminist participation in the Global Forum at the 1992 UN Conference on Environment and Development (UNCED). This led to an "unprecedented unitary statement of women across the board in the Women's Action Agenda 21." It was also based on claims about women's unity that reproduced "patterns of domination, relations of hierarchies and dualisms" that feminists are ostensibly committed to abolishing. One such dualism emerged between grassroots women's movements and professional, elite activists in male-dominated environment and development IGOs and INGOs. "Specific local women's struggles were used to illustrate the need to hear women's voices on environmental issues" and "many women in UNCED spoke 'on behalf of others' to push for consideration of women's perspectives," rather than striving to allow diverse women to speak for themselves (Braidotti et al. 1994: 175). This is not to deny that there is a recognition of the need to bring grassroots organizations into processes of global politics among feminists in transnational elites. However, this tends to slide down an agenda dominated by mainstreaming (e.g., Tahir 1997; Pak 1996). Clearly, the mainstreaming strategy runs counter to the wariness intrinsic to a skeptical and strategic approach to the state and to the accompanying insistence on the effort to maintain links to diverse, transformatory movement struggles. The limitations of mainstreaming indicate that such arguments need urgently to be translated to the interstate level.

Finally, black and third world feminist arguments emphasizing the need for cultural change are reinforced by anxieties about the cultural homogenization imposed by processes of globalization. Thus Ashoka Bandarage insists that "the global crisis requires a profound transformation in consciousness" and in ontological foundations, personal relationships, and community building. She suggests that the construction of innovative forms of creative arts and modes of communication would be an appropriate way forward (1991: 346–354). Feminists may disagree on whether to *prioritize* changes in intimate life and symbolic orders, but there is widespread agreement that such changes are essential to women's empowerment and to transformation in macrolevel social orders. Transversal principles indicate that there can be no one program for such changes on a global scale; rather, cultural diversity is to be expected and protected. Clearly, not all movements respect this principle or advocate progressive cultural change. It is specifically in a movement constituted according to transversal principles that expressions of difference are most likely to be respected and protected, and also critically interrogated. This is because the partiality of all perspectives is recognized and the relations of power within which they are embedded are explicitly tackled. This is the kind of approach adopted by the International Solidarity Network of Women Living Under Muslim Laws (WLUML), a transnational umbrella network that has had to confront both the diversity of women's experiences of living in Islamic cultures and western anti-Islamic feeling. According to Miles:

> [WLUML] enables diverse women to offer support to and accept it from each other in the knowledge that they are all contesting power in their own communities. It provides a space for women to adopt alternative interpretations of the world and to act on these. And it provides a way for women of Muslim heritage and/or faith to be strongly present in global dialogue *as Muslim women,* even while challenging their diverse Muslim cultures and

conditions. The explicitly Muslim context of their struggle enables them to gain strength from the support of women who are not living under Muslim laws without risking a diminution or loss of their specifically Muslim identification and voice. (Miles 1996: 124)

The WLUML example draws attention to the role of coalitions in global feminist theory and politics. From WLUML to DAWN, and from Women Against Fundamentalism to Women in Black, there is plentiful evidence of a widespread aspiration to forge concrete connections across specificities of struggle and territorial locations within and beyond feminism. Coalitions are stressed as central to the black and third world feminist approach to transformatory change outlined in Chapter 4, alongside the insistence that the character and goals of collaborative projects cannot be specified in advance but must be democratically constructed and open to contestation. Organizations like WLUML are putting this notion into practice through their efforts to ensure that different voices can speak and be heard within the group, within transnational feminist debates, and within global politics.

There is a framework for transformatory change through coalition politics emerging here that is agonizingly complex and long-term. But it also offers hope because it draws on the possibility of an alternative, more democratic future that is already immanent in feminist movement efforts to juggle universality and particularity on a global scale. In a world characterized by globalizing democratic deficits, patriarchal exclusions, and reconfigured colonizations, the feminist movement is already bringing new constituencies and issues into politics, politicizing boundaries between and within states, and enabling the participation of a wide variety of people in the contestation of the global power relationships structuring everyday realities. Such developments cannot be legislated for, guaranteed in international law, or achieved through vanguard politics. It should be stressed that progress toward the realization of movement potential is not inevitable or straightforward but, as the divisive debates and countertrends in feminism show, often painfully slow and subject to setbacks. Transversal democratic possibilities will thus only be deepened through an ongoing process of movement contestation for which there are no guarantees of success.

Conclusion

In this chapter, I have highlighted evidence of increasing efforts to reconstruct the global feminist movement on a more democratic basis. Such efforts remain, as yet, scattered, underdeveloped, and contested. However, put into the framework developed in Chapter 4 from black and third world feminist arguments, they point to ways in which that framework can be extended across borders and thus to a more democratic future for global feminism. They also indicate an alternative framework for democracy of more general applicability, as summarized in Table 6.

In sum, transversal feminist activism is predicated on an understanding of power as global in scope, multidimensional, interactive, and stratifying the feminist movement itself. This encourages the expansion of democratic practice outward, from intimate life to the global, but in a differentiated way. Strategy is formulated in specific contexts and combined with the pursuit of connection across differences through movement politics. Such a process is dependent on a notion of the political actor as embedded within gender, race, and class identities and as nationally and geopolitically located, but also as struggling for empathetic mobility through participation in movement struggles. Movements themselves are also emphasized as significant collective actors, albeit heterogeneous, multi-voiced, and continually reconstructed. Finally, this approach gives rise to a view of transformatory change that combines an emphasis on the necessary plurality of sites and sources of struggle with an insistence on the need to build more general alliances and maintains an oppositional stance toward state, economic, and cultural sources of power.

Such arguments differ sharply from most of the "malestream" schemes explored in Chapter 5. Those tend to rely on a monist or parallelist view of globalization that ignores gendered and racialized structures of power. They advocate an expansive approach to politics and democracy that is not expansive enough. They hold to one-dimensional notions of the individual and reduce social movements to their formal, class-based, or "new" dimensions. They also argue for state-centric reformist strategies for global change or lapse into despair at the receding prospect of totalizing revolutionary upheaval. When more nuanced transformatory strategies are put forward, they rely on an idealized account of movement activity. Only the postmodern politics of connection explored in Chapter 5 has close affinities with the arguments developed here, indicating that they operate on common weak postmodern terrain. Engagement with the nitty-gritty of feminist debates has enabled the fleshing out of the weak postmodern framework, particularly with regard to the operations of power, notions of individual and collective agency, priorities for change, and concrete strategies for the mediation of the universal and particular.

We have also moved a long way from the methodologically nationalist and statist feminist reconstructive proposals explored in Chapter 3. The ideas put forward here bear closer affinity to the early second-wave feminist argument for a participatory, movement-based democracy—albeit after the more totalizing aspects of those arguments have been jettisoned.

TABLE 6 Globalizing Feminist Movement Democracy

	Ideal-type Democracy	Operations of Power	Terrain of Politics	The Political Actor	Strategies for Change	Role of Movements
Transversal Feminist Activism	participatory contestation of globalizing, coercive power in all aspects of life, and the construction of egalitarian and inclusive relationships	pervasive, global in scope, taking multiple forms that interact in context-specific ways, including within movements	expanded outward in differentiated ways; strategy devised in specific locations and in dialogue with others	the territorially located, complex, and plural self, striving for mobility in activism; movements also key actors	immanent in diversity of movements and links between them; priority to economic and cultural change; skeptical but strategic view of states/IGOs	movements as sites and sources of democracy, aiding world-traveling, bridging disparate struggles, and politicizing boundaries

The way forward has been indicated by black and third world feminist arguments. The difficult process of constructing feminism on a global scale, in which black and third world feminists have played a pioneering role, has revealed ways in which these arguments are being, or could be, stretched beyond national and state boundaries to constitute a framework for democracy on a global scale. These arguments, although embedded in feminist movement practices, indicate a more general framework for global democratic politics in which feminism and other social movements must continue to play a central role.

Notes

1. This paragraph on the family and household is the same as an earlier one inserted into the discusion of globalization in Chapter 5 (pp. 147–148). As indicated in previous chapters, few nonfeminist commentators on modernity, new times, or globalization discuss the family and household; this has been a feminist-influenced addition to all of the contextual sections of the book. The contextual section in this final chapter brings feminist work center-stage. The point about the family and household thus remains the same, but gender relationships and the position of women also become visible in other domains.

2. The East Central European feminist skepticism about state-led change contrasts with feminist commentary on Latin America, where a civil society strategy was also widely invoked during anti-authoritarian mobilizations (Cohen and Arato 1992: 48–58). This strategy has since been called into question by feminists facing a transition "dilemma of 'autonomy versus integration'" (Waylen 1994: 339–340). Jane Jaquette argues that "autonomy alone is a weak strategy," and insists that women's groups must be integrated into parties and the political system (Jaquette 1994b: 232–235). It may be significant that the Latin American transitions saw a much broader mobilization of women outside the system than in East Central Europe: from the Mothers of the Plaza de Mayo to extensive "housewife" or "neighborhood" organization and regional feminist conferences (Feijoó and Gogna 1990: 86–107; Jaquette 1994a: 3–6; Jelin 1990: 191–193; Waterman 1998: 163–177). In the East Central European transitions, women were involved in movement activity but rarely at leadership level (Einhorn 1993: 158–161) and feminist organizations were relatively small and isolated, except in Eastern Germany (Schaeffer-Hegel 1992: 101–103). It may be more strategically viable for Latin American feminists to argue for post-transition integration precisely because a vibrant, autonomous movement has already been established. Nonetheless, the integrative turn carries significant risks, given that liberal democratic institutions are predicated on mechanisms and precepts that function to marginalize women as political actors and given that *"the turn to political society has potentially demobilizing consequences with respect to civil society,* as many participants and observers have noted" (Cohen and Arato 1992: 53, emphasis in original).

3. It should be noted that a minority of first-wave western feminists, such as the anarchist Emma Goldman, rejected inclusion within an imperial or racist

state. Others strove to build genuinely egalitarian transnational, interracial, and anti-imperialist alliances between women and men, as did the prominent African-American anti-lynching campaigner Ida B. Wells and her white British colleague Catherine Impey (Ware 1992: 167–224).

4. The metaphors of weaving and of a web are used deliberately here. They frequently recur in efforts to conceptualize a global feminist movement. As Chilla Bulbeck argues, "the world's women's movement need not be 'one' but can be many, modelled on the female symbol of the web or the patchwork quilt" (1988: 153). Or as Shima Das puts it, "We believe in the concept of spinning local threads, weaving global feminism. We may have different threads both in colors and texture from many local areas. . . . The diversity in design and color but woven into a single cloth will make us united and strong" (quoted in Miles 1996: 97).

5. Other attempts to acknowledge this democratizing tendency in feminism have invoked the idea of a "feminist internationality" (Vasuki Nesiah quoted in Gabriel and Macdonald 1994: 535) or of "inter-nationalized" feminist alliances (Runyan 1996: 250, note 4). I do not adopt either of these labels here because they still position the state and nation as the foundations of feminist interactions.

6. Yuval-Davis invokes the concept of transversal politics as a way of negotiating the universal and particular within feminist organizing. The links between this idea and her reformulation of citizenship are not made entirely explicit. She does indicate (1997b: 88, 92) that grassroots political activism should be constituted according to transversal politics and that groups thus constituted might then delegate representatives to state institutions. The implication is that such a process would help to concretize a model of citizenship that acknowledges ethnic and gender differences, by enhancing social processes of identity-formation and negotiation within groups and ultimately enabling their institutional recognition. One problem with this formulation is that it seems to rest on a division of citizenship into social and political dimensions, with feminist and other forms of grassroots activism characterized as part of the nonpolitical realm of the social until they have an impact on the public, political realm of the state. Transversal principles thus appear to be confined to the domain of the social. I have criticized this limited view of the political and the stage model of movement impact in previous chapters. Clearly, the overlap between transversalism and citizenship remains a fruitful area for further inquiry.

7. It is therefore puzzling that both Gloria Anzaldúa's formulation of the *mestiza* (1990b: 380) and Inderpal Grewal's discussion of migrant subjectivity (1994: 250) should echo Virginia Woolf's denial of national and state location at points. Although this may be particularly problematic for white European and North American women, it would seem to be a problem for most women given the capacities of nation-states to shape identity and political context. Even permanently stateless refugees living under UN passports are likely to retain national identifications and must unavoidably reside within a state. One can surely be born into and live within a nation/state without feeling at home in it, or one may have multiple or serial national/state locations. All of this shapes access to the world and engagement with others.

Conclusion

Throughout this book I have argued that the dominant traditions of social and political thought, including recent theoretical innovations, do not tell us much about the role of social movements in democracy. What they do tell us is largely reductive and inaccurate. Conversely, close attention to the activities and debates generated by social movements, particularly feminism, has illuminated the limitations of approaches to democracy in social and political thought. A focus on the feminist movement has pointed toward an alternative democratic framework, one that tackles the gendered and globalizing power relations that have so far rendered the promise of democracy hollow for many people. It also places social movements center stage as both sites and sources of democratic struggle.

The first question posed in the introduction was: What do social and political theorists tell us about the role and significance of movements in democracy? An examination of "modernist" traditions in social and political thought has revealed a variety of problems.

Within liberalism, including recent cosmopolitan reformulations, social movements are granted a role insofar as they can be reduced to their formal, organized, public dimensions such as parties, interest groups, NGOs, and international NGOs. These are seen as playing a necessary role in democracy because they enable individuals to group together and pursue collective interests and to participate in institutional politics. They also ensure that ruling elites have to compete for power and can draw on independent sources of advice and help with policy implementation. However, many liberals also fear these groups within the system, as well as extra-institutional social movement activity, as a threat to stability. Republicans, on the other hand, allow a role for civic groups that can operate as schools for democracy, inculcating the skills and outlook necessary for active citizenship. They too share the liberal fear of more unruly activism that may offer alternatives to the public identity of citizenship and disrupt the unity of the public sphere. An analytical polarization emerges here between those movements that are well-behaved and considered functional for democracy and those that refuse to be disciplined and are demonized as necessarily anti-democratic. This fails to explain the actual diversity of movement challenges to democratic institutions.

Marxists of various hues have recognized that movements are socially generated, socially embedded political forms that are not reducible to their institutionalized manifestations. However, marxists also overemphasize the role of class in movement formation and orientation. Further, a specific kind of social movement, namely the self-organized working class, is privileged as the agent of historical change and as the bearer of a more genuinely democratic future. Marxist frameworks thus reject the disciplining of movements by the status quo only to subordinate diverse movement goals to class struggle and to exclude many movement activities from serious consideration on the grounds that they are reformist froth. In the light of current global class reconfigurations, many marxists are gloomy about the possibility of radical change arising from movements. Anarchists are more optimistic—and more tolerant. They insist that anarchist struggle can take a variety of movement forms and that it must be constituted according to participatory democratic principles. The anarchistic reformulations of the New Left in the 1960s also drew attention to the subterranean cultural aspects of movements and pointed to their capacity to straddle the division in social life between the public and the private. Two key points about the role and significance of movements emerge at this point. Movements can themselves be constructed as sites of participatory democracy. Furthermore, efforts to construct democracy within movements can prefigure wider change by offering glimpses of a more democratic way of life that can be taken up by others in different contexts. The latter point is also made in the contemporary effort to globalize anarchist precepts through a "demarchic" framework. Unfortunately, demarchy slides into reformist timidity by emphasizing the prefigurative role only of those movements that are well-behaved and functionally useful for existing and future elites.

Moving onto "new times" approaches in social and political thought, those adopting a postmarxist perspective retain an anarchistic emphasis on the role and significance of diverse aspects of movement activity. However, postmarxists also replicate some of the difficulties of liberal, marxist and republican frameworks. Advocates of associative democracy, for example, grant a central role to well-behaved associations, particularly those representing economic interests in policy-making fora and the implementation of policy. Other aspects of movement organization and orientation are again excluded. The radical civil society approach, in contrast, also allows for the subterranean, cultural, and oppositional dimensions of movements. Movements are seen as enabling the collective contestation of power relations, operating to render state and economic power more transparent, halt their encroachment into social life, and expand democratic principles deeper into society. However, as with associative democracy, it seems that the liberal state and capitalist framework can be modified but not challenged. Rightly, the global version of radical civil society theory insists that many contemporary movements are actually mounting such a challenge and that this is an urgent necessity given the grossly iniquitous and damaging operations of the state system and global capitalism. I have argued, however, that the global civil society framework is incorrect in attributing this orientation to all movements, sharing with its nonglobal precursor the tendency to idealize movements and to see them as innocent of state and economic power.

Proponents of radical democracy take a different tack, combining a marxist prioritization of struggle against capitalism with a rejection of the privileged role of the working-class movement. Instead, in a shift toward a postmodernist framework, the increasing proliferation of movements is seen as a manifestation of contradictions in capitalism and of the accompanying expansion of democratic discourse. It remains unclear why diverse movements should combine against capitalism, and how they are to affect it, given that they are products rather than agents of discursive change.

Others reject marxism entirely for a more thoroughgoing postmodern approach. "Strong" postmodernist approaches characterize movements as operating on cultural terrain, their democratic impact residing in their manifestation of cultural difference and their tendency to challenge the boundaries of politics and to pluralize political identity. Although these are significant insights about movement possibilities, it is inaccurate to characterize all movements in this way. It is also problematic to reify the differences between movements and to give no grounds for evaluating those differences. International relations theorist R. B. J. Walker modifies these ideas when extrapolating their implications for global politics by shifting onto "weak" postmodern terrain. Walker insists it is specifically "critical" social movements that undermine the boundaries of the political and expand democracy into local life and beyond the state. He also claims that critical movements are engaged in the contestation of imposed universals and the search for solidarities across differences, involving the continual renegotiation of the relationship between the universal and particular.

One such critical movement is feminism. My focus on feminism in this book has stemmed partly from the recognition that feminism is both an intervention in social and political thought and a social movement, one that has exhibited a distinctive preoccupation with democracy. What has become clear is that most traditions of social and political thought outlined above have actually been generated by social movement activism and that such activism is frequently necessary to turn ideas about democracy into a concrete reality. This insight is often lost within the theoretical traditions themselves, particularly in the more conservative strands of liberalism and republicanism and in the postmarxist and postmodernist theories that have developed within academic institutions. The problem is exacerbated by an epistemology of abstraction, which fails to recognize the social generation of ideas. This disassociation from activism, I have argued, partly explains the failure of much social and political thought to generate radical democratic frameworks and to provide accurate analyses of the role of movements. This is more than an epistemological point about the need to ground theory in movement activism. It is also an argument that one important role of movements in democracy, unrecognized in most traditions of social and political thought, lies in their capacity to generate democratic ideals and to struggle to implement them.

Feminist democratic theory, I have argued, has also largely lost sight of its relationship to movement activism and consequently pays little attention to the role of movements. Rather, it was through a discussion of debates about the democratization of the feminist movement itself that a more complete picture of the potential significance of movements in democracy emerged.

Debates about the democratization of feminism begin with the confirmation of the anarchistic point that movements can themselves be sites of participatory democracy. In an important modification of this view, black and third world feminist arguments about racist exclusions in feminism, and their efforts to build a more inclusive feminist movement, reveal that movements are also sites of democratic struggle. In other words, the democratic character of movements cannot be presumed but has to be fought for. The ongoing effort to construct mechanisms of participatory, inclusive dialogue plays itself out on two axes. On the one hand, such mechanisms should enable the negotiation of the relationship between complex individual subjectivity and contested constructions of collective identity; on the other hand, they should inform the construction of alliances between spatially separated, context-specific activisms. These dimensions of movement democracy can both be seen as aspects of the negotiation of the relationship between the universal and the particular to which Walker drew attention—a particularly crucial issue in the construction of a democratic movement on a global scale.

Feminist movement debates also confirm the role of movements as sources of democratic change in society more generally. The anarchist claim that participatory movement forms prefigure wider democratic possibilities finds backing in feminist arguments. In addition, early second-wave feminists assert that movements enable women's political agency. Because movements are forms of political activism in everyday life, capable of bridging the public/private divide, women can participate in them without abandoning their gender roles and traits. The feminist movement is seen as particularly crucial because it politicizes the public/private divide, enabling women to act collectively to contest gendered power relations in the public arena and to legitimize their individual struggles in the home. Black and third world feminists add that movements in general can allow diverse, complex, and radical forms of subjectivity to develop, if they are constructed democratically and if they construct democratic connections with other movements. Attention is drawn to the fact that the movement form can straddle disparate social and geographical locations, linking diverse, context-specific struggles and enabling people to combine or move between these struggles in ways that reflect plural and shifting identities and interests. Finally, feminist debates confirm that movements expand democracy into new areas of society. Although early second-wave white feminists tended to emphasize the role of feminism in democratizing intimate life, black and third world feminist arguments stress the role of multiple movements in expanding democratic struggles to encompass the contestation of multiple forms of power. This maps onto Walker's weak postmodern argument about movements challenging the limits of the political and expanding democracy outward. Walker also indicates that this move could pose a challenge to global power relations and their manifestations in local contexts.

I am now in a position to consider the second question posed in the introduction: What can close attention to movement activism, particularly feminism, tell us about the limitations of democratic frameworks in social and political thought—and what alternatives do they point toward? Four main problems with existing approaches to democracy have been identified in the course of this book.

The first centers on the theorization of power. The diversity of movement goals worldwide and the contemporary shift in western movement activism pose a challenge to "monist" and "parallelist" arguments about power. Such arguments are characteristic of liberal, republican, and marxist approaches to democracy, and those new times and globalization approaches that remain heavily influenced by them. These limit coercive power to the state and/or capitalist economy. Monism reappears in a different form in the strong postmodern reduction of power to discourse. The feminist movement has challenged these approaches by drawing attention to how patriarchal power functions to marginalize women within democracies in ways that have been neglected and reified by other movements and theoretical traditions. Black and third world feminist critiques have then indicated that the monism of a focus on state or economic power or discourse is not adequately replaced by a monist focus on patriarchy. They demand recognition of the plural forms that power takes and analysis of how these interact to produce different effects on different women, including those within the feminist movement itself. Furthermore, simultaneous trends for the fragmentation and transnational consolidation of the movement form, charted by globalization theorists and visible in feminism, indicate that movement activists, including many feminists, are responding to the ways in which power is being increasingly globalized.

The second limitation of social and political thought, highlighted by a consideration of movement debates, has to do with the location and scope of democracy. Monism and parallelism in the theorization of power have resulted in partial constructions of democracy in social and political thought and the subjection of only state and/or economic power to collective scrutiny. Alternatively, discourse is privileged as a site of democratic struggle. This encourages the marginalization and even suppression of those movements that prioritize other forms of power. Many new times and globalization theorists have responded to movement refusal of this logic by arguing for the expansion of democracy into civil society and emphasizing the role of diverse movements. However, the civil society framework tends to reify the liberal state and capitalist economy as the necessary framework for such an expansive project, and it still makes assumptions about certain shared goals and values among movements. Many movements, particularly those outside Europe, do not accept this framework or operate with these values. Further, the arguments above about the movement form indicate that part of the democratic potential of movements lies precisely in their manifestation of a plurality of values and identifications. What is more, their socially embedded, diffuse, and heterogeneous organization transgresses and challenges boundaries set up to limit the political.

The feminist movement, I have argued, attempts to expand democratization into the intimate sphere and in other directions beyond the state. Within feminism, critiques have emerged of an undifferentiated expansionism that would pursue the same goals and insist on the same mechanisms in every social site. While feminist democratic theorists have drawn attention to the drawbacks of subjecting all aspects of our intimate lives to democratic scrutiny, black and third world feminists have emphasized the problem of imposing the same agenda in different social and geographical locations, particularly on a global scale. Their criticisms of the white, western dominance of the feminist movement lying behind such universalizing strategies also draw attention to the fact that movements are not innocent forces for democracy but are themselves structured by power and should therefore be sites of democratic struggle.

This brings me to a third problem with social and political thought: the conceptualization of the actor in democracy. Modernist traditions of social and political thought tend to hold to a reductive view of the actor, which privileges certain aspects of personhood in the form of the citizen or the worker. This reductive view is challenged by the pluralization of identity and agency represented by multiple movement struggles. Such struggles may, for example, draw on a person's role as a carer, his or her ethnic identity, or his or her religious affiliation. The feminist movement has generated critiques of the citizen and the worker as specifically masculine constructs that function to marginalize women's political agency. It has been pointed out that women have tended to participate in greater numbers in movement struggles than in democratic institutions. I have suggested that this is partly because the movement form can straddle the public/private divide. This is one reason why the turn in feminist democratic theory toward the citizen and institutional representation is problematic. Another is the argument from black and third world feminists that participation in movements enables the individual to articulate complex and plural identities and forms of agency. Additionally, black and third world feminist interventions confirm that feminism and other movements are significant collective actors in democracy, although this does not mean they should be thought of as coherent entities able to speak with one voice.

What is more, feminism and other movements challenge the notion that territorial community is the sole basis and the boundary of individual and collective identity, and thus of democracy. This is because movements can disrupt the illusion of communal unity by offering alternative identifications and because they often function across state boundaries, politicizing the reification of borders and giving rise to new forms of subjectivity. However, black and third world feminist arguments about the need to acknowledge the geopolitical location from which one acts have undermined more straightforward cosmopolitan claims about identification with a global community as the basis of political action.

The fourth and final limitation of social and political thought revealed by a focus on movement debates is an inadequate understanding of the processes and possibilities of change. The traditional revolutionary model, requiring a unified struggle by a universal class, has been challenged by the diversity of movement goals and the shift in western movement activism away from mass class organizations and a focus on the state. Although many marxists continue to search for the revolutionary subject, I have argued that this relies on a monist privileging of one source of power and change. This has anti-democratic implications because it justifies the forcible suppression of movement heterogeneity to achieve a supposedly genuinely democratic future. This future is expected to exhibit no fundamental social conflict, an expectation that is likely to ensure that social movement and other expressions of dissidence remain delegitimized. The expectation of social solidarity apparent here, often replicated in anarchist analyses, is continually challenged by actual movement struggles. Further, black and third world feminist arguments imply that it is not possible to grasp the complexity of all the operations of power from a location outside of them, nor to second-guess their manifestations, and thus it is not likely that power can be abolished in the modernist revolutionary sense. Continual struggle against coercive power in whatever form it may take is thus required.

Movements also challenge the limits of reformism by refusing to be well-behaved and to renounce extra-institutional activism and contestation of the system. Indeed, the argument above that movements function to politicize the boundaries imposed on the political and to expand democracy outwards suggests that reformist strategies miss precisely what is significant about movements and are fighting a losing battle in seeking to contain movements and limit democracy. This is not to say that the state, the focus of much reformist and revolutionary effort, has been entirely abandoned. Statist strategy is still pursued by some movements and some strands within otherwise anti-statist movements. Feminist arguments about the patriarchal, capitalist, and racist character of the state suggest that a wary and selective engagement with the state needs to be combined with the long-term struggle to transform it.

Black and third world feminist arguments stress the urgency of transformatory change more generally, given global patterns of capitalism, patriarchy, and white dominance that have devastating effects on many women's lives. I have suggested that this insistence presents a challenge to strong postmodern skepticism about radical change. Such skepticism is rooted in the notion that we are all subjects of discursive power, which we reproduce rather than challenge, and it elides democracy with the celebration of difference, thus undermining any possibility of solidarity in struggle. Black and third world feminist arguments, in contrast, indicate the possibility and necessity of a more substantive and solidaristic model of struggle for change.

This leads finally to consideration of the alternative democratic framework that a focus on movement activism points toward. My answer here is derived specifically from feminist debates about the democratization of feminist activism on a global scale, particularly black and third world feminist contributions. It was summarized in Table 6 under the heading of transversal feminist activism.

First, transversal feminist activism rests on an understanding of structures and relations of power as pervasive, plural, increasingly global in scope, and interacting to produce context-specific effects. Second, it demands the multidirectional expansion of democracy, understood as the participatory, collective contestation of coercive power relations, outward from the polity and into the home, the economy, international arenas, and movements themselves. It also involves the construction of alternative inclusive and participatory relationships in all of those domains. This is not, however, an undifferentiated expansionist model. Strategies for democratization need to be developed in situ by autonomous, diverse, context-specific struggles, which should also strive to construct common political goals, interests, and identities with struggles elsewhere. This process must start from the recognition of the partiality of the perspectives that all context-specific mobilizations generate, with agreement across differences sought through open, participatory, and inclusive dialogue. Commitment to such a dialogue requires the establishment of appropriate and imaginative procedures and attention to their substantive preconditions. It demands efforts to overcome differential access to information, resources, and agenda setting imposed by geopolitical, ethnic, and class locations.

Third, transversal politics draws on a notion of the political actor as a situated, complex self, striving for mobility within and across social locations and state borders through movement activism. This entails a recognition that movements are complex, continually renegotiated, multivoiced collective actors that can straddle geopolitical and other boundaries but need to be constructed in more democratic ways. The possibility of such democratic construction is immanent in some contemporary movement practices. This brings me to the fourth dimension of the transversal framework: the approach to change. Efforts to challenge and transform coercive patterns of global power should be maintained through a plurality of movement-led strategies in a variety of social sites and through the construction of democratically negotiated connections between them. It has been suggested that the operations of globalized capitalism and processes of cultural homogenization may need to be prioritized as targets for change, because of the impact of their interactions with patriarchy and white dominance. Further, context-specific formulation of strategy may determine the need for strategic engagement with the state and state system. Such engagement is most likely to retain its radicalism if efforts are made to retain links within broader transformatory struggle and extra-institutional movement activism. Finally, the transversal model represents both the means of struggle toward a more democratic world and the goal of such a struggle. It is democracy as process, democracy in movement.

It is perhaps necessary to underline why this framework is specifically feminist and what advantages it carries for women. The most obvious point is that it encompasses an analysis of patriarchy as one of several globalizing power structures that interact to militate against women's participation in existing institutional forms of democracy. It also privileges the movement form. Movements appear to be the most effective channel for incorporating women and their concerns into politics given that women tend to participate more extensively in grassroots community-based movement activism than in routinized, formalized institutions. I have suggested that this is because movements transgress the boundaries between the public and the private, enabling women to become "subjects of their own politics" through their traditional roles and traits rather than despite them. The movement form also enables, although it clearly does not guarantee, the collective contestation of those roles and traits. Further, the movement form enables the construction and continuing renegotiation of the collective identity and agency of women as a group. And, of course, the transversal democratic framework has been derived from ongoing processes and practices within the feminist movement. It draws on the role of feminism as a key site of struggle for women, as an ongoing effort to politicize and challenge the identification and positioning of women, and as a mechanism for incorporating women into global democratic politics.

Transversal democracy also seems to be immanent in the practices of other movements. Admittedly, I am on more speculative grounds here. Nonetheless, there are some striking echoes to be found. For example, editors of a collection on worldwide movement activism identify a shared interest in democratization among many movements. This rests on a view of democracy that insists it must be expanded into social, cultural, and economic practices. Democracy must also elevate the individual rather than the state as a political actor, this time incorporating diverse aspects of personhood. Further, it must contest increasingly global power relations and their reification in international institutions (Brecher et al. 1993: xvii–xviii). In the same volume, writing about the Latin American context, Eve Dagnino stresses the centrality of diverse religious and leftist social movements in the transitions there to liberal democratic regimes. She describes a process whereby movements struggle to build a common identity through processes of egalitarian direct democracy that avoid institutionalized representation and leadership and respect the autonomy of different groups. She then analyzes the role of movements in constituting rights and citizenship. Her argument here is the now-familiar one that citizenship must be broadened beyond the state to constitute a range of groups as "social subjects" and to expand democracy into society (Dagnino 1993). In an address to a gathering of people's organizations of the Asian-Pacific region, Muto Ichiyo extends this argument to the global, calling for "transborder participatory democracy" (1993: 155). This is rooted in "a community-based democracy through which the people build power over the things that matter in their lives" (1993: 150). It also involves the construction of bridges with movements in other locations in recognition of the need to confront globalizing power relations, particularly capitalism, and the power of the state (1993: 150–161).

The kind of diffuse democratization agenda I have outlined here, one that constantly struggles to balance the universal and particular and does not center on the state in the pursuit of change, has been seen as a defining characteristic of NSMs in western societies. I agree that this agenda indicates a shift in contemporary movement practice, although with antecedents in anarchism, in the context of new times restructuring of society, movements, and democracy. However, the examples above indicate that such an agenda can be found also in non-western contexts, in societies that have not been restructured along postindustrial lines and in movements that do not fit new social movement characteristics. Within feminism, which itself resides rather unhappily in the category of new social movement, the transversal agenda has developed specifically from the interventions of black and third world feminists, marginalized within the western context and reacting to their encounter with feminism outside the West. Black and third world feminists have emphasized the need to come to terms with diversity within the feminist movement globally rather than presuming a unified agenda and identity. The crucial point here is surely that the transversal framework has emerged in the context of the globalization of power relations. This has had different effects on different societies, requiring divergent movement responses but also producing some common reconfigurations in patternings of power and throwing people and movements together in new ways. I suggest that this has encouraged innovation in political strategy and the diffusion of ideas in a variety of directions. It has also led to an urgent need to create a politics that can make sense of the differences between movement activists who have been brought into new proximity.

Of course, not all movements, or strands within movements, have responded to these processes by developing transversal principles. It is important to emphasize the diversity in movement activism worldwide, including within feminism, and to be cognizant of the more problematic movement developments that have arisen in the context of globalization. These include religious and nationalist fundamentalisms of various kinds, which are hierarchically organized and exclusionary. They propound the supremacy of some ways of being over others, often striving violently to universalize these principles. The contemporary world order is bloodied and scarred by the activities of such movements. Two necessary clarifications flow from this point. The first is that there must be no presumption that transformatory change of the kind outlined here is obvious and inevitable. Such a presumption often filters into contemporary social and political thought about movements. It takes the form of a tendency to idealize movements as the bearers of an emancipatory future, which involves characterizing them as all sharing the same view and as all intrinsically progressive. Although I share a belief in the emancipatory potential of the movement form, as well as of feminist goals, it is clear that this potential is frequently unrealized. The framework for transversal participatory democracy, after all, has emerged from black and third world feminist critiques of their experiences of racist exclusion within the feminist movement.

The second clarification is that the transversal democratic framework is not compatible with an uncritical celebration of movement diversity when some movements are clearly so threatening to its survival. Although I have emphasized the need to enable the context-specific discussion and resolution of political strategies, this should not be taken as a recipe for relativism. As Yuval-Davis reminds us, transversal politics are "never boundless"; they are limited by the desire to construct a common political project (1997a: 19). Yet I have also emphasized that there are no metaphysical grounds for ascertaining boundaries or common goals. Rather, these must emerge through social movement struggle. Some pointers are provided by feminist debates, which indicate that the participants in transversal democracy should challenge the status and sanctity of reified hierarchies such as the state/system and gender relationships. They should strive to localize and concretize elusive global power relations rather than limiting their contestation to institutions that may be distant from lived realities. They should subject the power-stratified relationships within the movement to scrutiny via egalitarian participatory mechanisms for dialogue and accept that collective identity must always be open-ended and contestable. They should make efforts to forge democratic connections between autonomous struggles. Thus movements are not compatible with transversal principles if they seek to entrench existing structures and relations of power, to enforce a naturalized and exclusive political identity, and to remain parochial and separatist. Coalition with such movements or strands of movements may not, therefore, be possible or desirable. The question of how such forms of activism can be engaged with, challenged, or constrained so that they do not subvert democratization processes, including the increased participation of women, remains the great challenge. It is not one, however, for which a clear, universally applicable, a priori strategy can or should be devised. That would be against transversal principles of contextual specificity and the epistemological principle that such judgments should be grounded in ongoing movement practices.

The implications of these arguments for future academic research are straightforward. Clearly, the kind of attention to the political implications of activism I am urging here requires a commitment to interdisciplinarity. As we have seen, there is already a vast literature on social movements located within sociology and another on democracy within political theory, but these two have been kept largely distinct from one another. Further, disciplinary divisions reinforce selective academic blindness to gendered exclusions and to globalizing patterns of power by containing them within women's studies and international studies, respectively. Both globalization and questions of gendered marginalizations refuse containment in this way by leaking across disciplinary concerns. They have enormous implications for how we think about social movements and democracy. And they are already generating responses within movements themselves, including within feminism, which should not be ignored.

In addition, more specific studies of movement activism are required. My strategy in this book has been to think about the democratic implications of debates within feminism writ large, illustrating specific points by alluding to specific moments of feminist activism. The arguments that have emerged are necessarily partial and sketchy, given their sweep. They necessitate, I have come to realize, critical interrogation through more specific studies of particular mobilizations and the debates they generate. This implies the need to study "direct theory" more directly: talking to participants in movements to document their life histories and viewpoints and to reflect on what they tell us about the ways in which movements operate and about the gendered and territorial deficits of democracy. More generally, this kind of research program demands that academics recognize the ways in which political ideals are generated by and institutionalized through social struggle. Political argumentation that is constructed only with reference to the requirements of logic, or to mythical social contracts, original positions, and ideal speech situations, is likely to be limited. It tends to produce thin, bloodless political visions that often misrepresent or marginalize movement activity and have no realistic possibility of social impact. A more democratic future will not be attained simply through the rational force of ideals. Further, it is not adequate to rely on an understanding of movement activism formulated in the last century, to set this up as a standard for radicalism, and to renounce the possibility of change when contemporary activism fails to reach it. Social and political theorists must get their hands dirty and grapple with the ways in which movement activities are changing and with normative questions of good movement practice in the here and now. As black feminist theorist Sheila Radford-Hill reminds us:

> All social change is based in struggle; this struggle is both from within the
> movement itself . . . and outside the movement, based on resistance to

change. Mobilization tactics must be fashioned to the strength of the people whose struggle it is. . . . As the current state of feminist theory and practice would indicate, we must dig in for the long haul and accept the challenges of our history. The struggle continues, begins anew. (Radford-Hill 1986: 166–167, 171)

References

Afkhami, Mahnaz, and Erika Friedl. 1997. "Introduction." In Mahnaz Afkhami and Erika Friedl, eds. *Muslim Women and the Politics of Participation: Implementing the Beijing Platform.* Syracuse: Syracuse University Press.

Afshar, Haleh. 1989. "Women and Reproduction in Iran." In Nira Yuval-Davis and Floya Anthias, eds. *Woman-Nation-State.* Basingstoke, UK: Macmillan.

Agarwal, Bina. 1988. "Patriarchy and the 'Modernising' State." In Bina Agarwal, ed. *Structures of Patriarchy: The State, the Community and the Household.* London: Zed Books.

Agnew, John. 1994. "The Territorial Trap: The Geographical Assumptions of International Relations Theory." *Review of International Political Economy* 1/1: 53–80.

Agnew, Vijay. 1993. "Canadian Feminism and Women of Colour." *Women's Studies International Forum* 16/3: 217–227.

Alarcón, Norma. 1990. "The Theoretical Subject of *This Bridge Called My Back* and Anglo-American Feminism." In Gloria Anzaldúa, ed. *Making Face, Making Soul/Haciendo Caras: Creative and Critical Perspectives by Feminists of Color.* San Francisco: Aunt Lute Books.

Alexander, M. Jacqui, and Chandra Talpade Mohanty. 1997. "Genealogies, Legacies, Movements." In M. Jacqui Alexander and Chandra Talpade Mohanty, eds. *Feminist Genealogies, Colonial Legacies, Democratic Futures.* London: Routledge.

Alger, Chadwick. 1994. "Citizens and the UN System in a Changing World." In Yoshikazu Sakamoto, ed. *Global Transformation: Challenges to the State System.* Tokyo: United Nations University Press.

_____. 1992. "Local Responses to Global Intrusions." In Zdravko Mlinar, ed. *Globalization and Territorial Identities.* Aldershot, UK: Avebury.

Allen, John. 1992a. "Fordism and Modern Industry." In John Allen, Peter Braham, and Paul Lewis, eds. *Political and Economic Forms of Modernity.* Cambridge: Polity Press in association with the Open University.

_____. 1992b. "Post-Industrialism and Post-Fordism." In Stuart Hall, David Held, and Tony McGrew, eds. *Modernity and Its Futures.* Cambridge: Polity Press in association with the Open University.

Allen, Judith. 1990. "Does Feminism Need a Theory of 'The State'?" In Sophie Watson, ed. *Playing the State: Australian Feminist Interventions.* London: Verso.

Amos, Valerie, and Pratibha Parmar. 1984. "Challenging Imperial Feminism." *Feminist Review* 17: 3–19.

Anderson, Benedict. 1991. *Imagined Communities: Reflections on the Origin and Spread of Nationalism.* 2d ed. London: Verso.

Anthias, Floya, and Nira Yuval-Davis, in association with Harriet Cain. 1992. *Racialized Boundaries: Race, Nation, Gender, Colour and Class and the Anti-Racist Struggle.* London: Routledge.

Anzaldúa, Gloria. 1990a. "Haciendo Caras: Una Entrada." In Gloria Anzaldúa, ed. *Making Face, Making Soul/Haciendo Caras: Creative and Critical Perspectives by Feminists of Color.* San Francisco: Aunt Lute Books.

_____. 1990b. "La Conciencia de la Mestiza: Toward a New Consciousness." In Gloria Anzaldúa, ed. *Making Face, Making Soul/Haciendo Caras: Creative and Critical Perspectives by Feminists of Color.* San Francisco: Aunt Lute Books.

_____. 1987. *Borderlands/La Frontera: The New Mestiza.* San Francisco: Aunt Lute Books.

Apter, David E. 1992. "Democracy and Emancipatory Movements: Notes for a Theory of Inversionary Discourse." In Jan Nederveen Pieterse, ed. *Emancipations, Modern and Postmodern.* London and New Delhi: SAGE.

_____. 1970. "The Old Anarchism and the New—Some Comments." *Government and Opposition* 5/4: 397–409.

Arrighi, Giovanni, Terence K. Hopkins, and Immanuel Wallerstein. 1989. *Antisystemic Movements.* London: Verso.

Ashley, Richard K. 1988. "Untying the Sovereign State: A Double Reading of the Anarchy Problematique." *Millennium: Journal of International Studies* 17/2: 227–262.

Ashworth, Georgina. 1995. "Introduction." In Georgina Ashworth, ed. *A Diplomacy of the Oppressed: New Directions in International Feminism.* London: Zed Books.

Attwood, Lynne. 1997. 'She Was Asking for It: Rape and Domestic Violence Against Women." In Mary Buckley, ed. *Post-Soviet Women: From the Baltic to Central Asia.* Cambridge: Cambridge University Press.

Baden, Sally, and Anne Marie Goetz. 1998. "Who Needs [Sex] When You Can Have [Gender]? Conflicting Discourses on Gender at Beijing." In Cecile Jackson and Ruth Pearson, eds. *Feminist Visions of Development: Gender Analysis and Policy.* London: Routledge.

Bakunin, Michael. 1977. "The Illusion of Universal Suffrage." In George Woodcock, ed. *The Anarchist Reader.* Hassocks, UK: Harvester Press.

Balbo, Laura. 1987. "Crazy Quilts: Rethinking the Welfare State from the Woman's Point of View." In Anne Showstack Sassoon, ed. *Women and the State: The Shifting Boundaries of Public and Private.* London: Routledge.

Bandarage, Asoka. 1991. "In Search of a New World Order." *Women Studies International Forum* 14/4: 345–355.

Banks, Olive. 1986. *Faces of Feminism: A Study of Feminism as a Social Movement.* Oxford: Basil Blackwell.

Barbalet, J. M. 1988. *Citizenship: Rights, Struggles and Class Inequality.* Milton Keynes, UK: Open University Press.

Barber, Benjamin. 1984. *Strong Democracy: Participatory Politics for a New Age.* Berkeley, Los Angeles, and London: University of California Press.

Bartholomew, Amy, and Margit Mayer. 1992. "Nomads of the Present: Melucci's Contribution to 'New Social Movement' Theory." *Theory, Culture and Society* 9: 141–159.

Basu, Amrita. 1995. "Introduction." In Amrita Basu, ed. *The Challenge of Local Feminisms: Women's Movements in Global Perspective*. Boulder, CO: Westview Press.

Baumgartner, Frank R., and Beth L. Leech. 1998. *Basic Interests: The Importance of Groups in Politics and Political Science*. Princeton: Princeton University Press.

Baxter, Sandra, and Marjorie Lansing. 1983. *Women and Politics: The Visible Majority*. Rev. ed. Ann Arbor: University of Michigan Press.

Bayer, Marina. 1992. "The Situation of East German Women in Postunification Germany." *Women's Studies International Forum* 15/1: 111–114.

Beck, Ulrich. 1992. *Risk Society: Towards a New Modernity*. London and New Delhi: SAGE.

Beechey, Veronica. 1979. "On Patriarchy." *Feminist Review* 3: 67–82.

Benhabib, Seyla. 1996a. "Introduction: The Democratic Moment and the Problem of Difference." In Seyla Benhabib, ed. *Democracy and Difference: Contesting the Boundaries of the Political*. Princeton: Princeton University Press.

_____. 1996b. "Toward a Deliberative Model of Democratic Legitimacy." In Seyla Benhabib, ed. *Democracy and Difference: Contesting the Boundaries of the Political*. Princeton: Princeton University Press.

_____. 1992. *Situating the Self: Gender, Community and Postmodernism in Contemporary Ethics*. Cambridge: Polity Press.

Benhabib, Seyla, and Drucilla Cornell. 1987. "Introduction: Beyond the Politics of Gender." In Seyla Benhabib and Drucilla Cornell, eds. *Feminism as Critique: Essays on the Politics of Gender in Late-Capitalist Societies*. Cambridge: Polity Press.

Berki, R. N. 1971. "On Marxian Thought and the Problem of International Relations." *World Politics* 24/1: 80–105.

Bernard, Jessie. 1987. *The Female World from a Global Perspective*. Bloomington: Indiana University Press.

Bhattacharjee, Anannya. 1997. "The Public/Private Mirage: Mapping Homes/ Undomesticating Violence Work in the South Asian Immigrant Community." In M. Jacqui Alexander and Chandra Talpade Mohanty, eds. *Feminist Genealogies, Colonial Legacies, Democratic Futures*. London: Routledge.

Bhavnani, Kum-Kum. 1993. "Towards a Multicultural Europe? 'Race,' Nation and Identity in 1992 and Beyond." *Feminist Review* 45: 30–45.

Bocock, Robert. 1992. "The Cultural Formations of Modern Society." In Stuart Hall and Bram Gieben, eds. *Formations of Modernity*. Cambridge: Polity Press in association with the Open University.

Boggs, Carl. 1995. *The Socialist Tradition: From Crisis to Decline*. London: Routledge.

Bookchin, Murray. 1989. "New Social Movements: The Anarchic Dimension." In David Goodway, ed. *For Anarchism: History, Theory, and Practice*. London: Routledge.

Bordo, Susan. 1990. "Feminism, Postmodernism and Gender-Scepticism." In Linda J. Nicholson, ed. *Feminism/Postmodernism*. London: Routledge.

Böröcz, József, and Katherine Verdery. 1994. "Gender and Nation." *East European Politics and Society* Spring, 8/2: 223–224.

Boserup, Ester. 1989. *Women's Role in Economic Development*. 2d ed. London: Earthscan.

Bourne, Randolph. 1977. "War Is the Health of the State." In George Woodcock, ed. *The Anarchist Reader*. Hassocks, UK: Harvester Press.

Boutros-Ghali, Boutros. 1996. "Introduction: Translating the Momentum of Beijing into Action." In *The Beijing Declaration and the Platform for Action*. New York: United Nations Department of Public Information.

Bowker-Sauer. 1991. *Who's Who of Women in World Politics*. London: Bowker-Sauer.

Bradley, Harriet. 1992. "Changing Social Structures: Class and Gender." In Stuart Hall and Bram Gieben, eds. *Formations of Modernity*. Cambridge: Polity Press in association with the Open University.

Braidotti, Rosi. 1994. *Nomadic Subjects: Embodiment and Sexual Difference in Contemporary Feminist Theory*. New York: Columbia University Press.

Braidotti, Rosi, Ewa Charkiewicz, Sabine Häusler, and Saskia Wieringa. 1994. *Women, the Environment and Sustainable Development: Toward a Theoretical Synthesis*. London: Zed Books.

Brecher, Jeremy, John Brown Childs, and Jill Cutler. 1993. "Introduction: Globalization from Below." In Jeremy Brecher, John Brown Childs, and Jill Cutler, eds. *Global Visions: Beyond the New World Order*. Boston: South End Press.

Breines, Wini. 1989. *Community and Organization in the New Left, 1962–1968: The Great Refusal*. 2d ed. New Brunswick, NJ: Rutgers University Press.

Bretherton, Charlotte. 1996. "Contemporary Sources of Armed Conflict." In Charlotte Bretherton and Geoffrey Ponton, eds. *Global Politics: An Introduction*. Oxford: Blackwell.

Briskin, Linda. 1990. "Identity Politics and the Hierarchy of Oppression: A Comment." *Feminist Review* 35: 102–108.

Brodie, Janine. 1994. "Shifting the Boundaries: Gender and the Politics of Restructuring." In Isabella Bakker, ed. *The Strategic Silence: Gender and Economic Policy*. London: Zed Books.

Brown, Chris. 1994. "Turtles All the Way Down: Antifoundationalism, Critical Theory and International Relations." *Millennium: Journal of International Studies* 23/2: 213–236.

———. 1992. *International Relations Theory: New Normative Approaches*. Hemel Hempstead, UK: Harvester Wheatsheaf.

Brown, Phil, and Faith I. T. Ferguson. 1995. "Making a Big Stink: Women's Work, Women's Relationships and Toxic Waste Activism." *Gender and Society* 9/2: 145–172.

Brown, Wendy. 1995. *States of Injury: Power and Freedom in Late Modernity*. Princeton: Princeton University Press.

Budge, Ian. 1996. *The New Challenge of Direct Democracy*. Cambridge: Polity Press.

Budge, Ian, Ivor Crewe, David McKay, and Ken Newton. 1998. *The New British Politics*. Harlow, UK: Addison Wesley Longman.

Bujra, Janet M. 1978. "Introduction: Female Solidarity and the Sexual Division of Labour." In Patricia Caplan and Janet M. Bujra, eds. *Women United, Women Divided: Cross-Cultural Perspectives on Female Solidarity*. London: Tavistock.

Bulbeck, Chilla. 1988. *One World Women's Movement*. London: Pluto Press.

Bunch, Charlotte. 1987. *Passionate Politics: Feminist Theory in Action*. New York: St Martin's Press.

Burnheim, John. 1986. "Democracy, Nation-States and the World-System." In David Held and Christopher Pollitt, eds. *New Forms of Democracy*. London: SAGE.

_____. 1985. *Is Democracy Possible? The Alternative to Electoral Politics*. Cambridge: Polity Press.

Butegwa, Florence. 1996. "NGO Transformation into Political Actors: Issues of Conceptualization and Accountability." In Eva Friedlander, ed. *Look at the World Through Women's Eyes: Plenary Speeches from the NGO Forum on Women, Beijing '95*. New York: Women, Ink.

Butler, Judith. 1998. "Merely Cultural." *New Left Review* 227: 33–44.

_____. 1993. *Bodies That Matter: On the Discursive Limits of "Sex."* London: Routledge.

_____. 1992. "Contingent Foundations: Feminism and the Question of Postmodernism." In Judith Butler and Joan W. Scott, eds. *Feminists Theorize the Political*. London: Routledge.

_____. 1990. *Gender Trouble: Feminism and the Subversion of Identity*. London: Routledge.

Bystydzienski, Jill M. 1992. "Introduction." In Jill M. Bystydzienski, ed. *Women Transforming Politics: Worldwide Strategies for Empowerment*. Indianapolis: Indiana University Press.

Çağatay, Nilüfer, Caren Grown, and Aida Santiago. 1986. "The Nairobi Women's Conference: Toward a Global Feminism?" *Feminist Studies* 12/2: 401–412.

Camilleri, Joseph A. 1990. "Rethinking Sovereignty in a Shrinking, Fragmented World." In R. B. J. Walker and Saul H. Mendlovitz, eds. *Contending Sovereignties: Redefining Political Community*. Boulder, CO: Lynne Rienner.

Caraway, Nancie. 1991. *Segregated Sisterhood: Racism and the Politics of American Feminism*. Knoxville: University of Tennessee Press.

Carby, Hazel. 1997. "White Woman Listen! Black Feminism and the Boundaries of Sisterhood." In Heidi Safia Mirza, ed. *Black British Feminism: A Reader*. London: Routledge.

Carr, E. H. 1939. *The Twenty Year Crisis, 1919–1939*. London: Macmillan.

Carroll, Berenice A. 1989. "'Women Take Action!' Women's Direct Action and Social Change." *Women's Studies International Forum* 12/1: 3–24.

Carroll, William K., and R. S. Ratner. 1994. "Between Leninism and Radical Pluralism: Gramscian Reflections on Counter-Hegemony and the New Social Movements." *Critical Sociology* 20/2: 1–24.

Carter, April. 1973. *Direct Action and Liberal Democracy*. New York: Harper & Row.

Cassell, Joan. 1977. *A Group Called Women: Sisterhood and Symbolism in the Feminist Movement*. New York: David McKay.

Castells, Manuel. 1997. *The Power of Identity—The Information Age: Economy, Society and Culture II*. Oxford: Blackwell.

Chafetz, Janet Salzman, and Anthony Gary Dworkin. 1986. *Female Revolt: Women's Movements in World and Historical Perspective*. Totowa, NJ: Rowman & Allanheld.

Chai, Alice Yun, and Ho'oipo de Cambra. 1989. "Evolution of Global Feminism Through Hawaiian Feminist Politics: The Case of Wai'anae Women's Support Group." *Women's Studies International Forum* 12/1: 59–64.

(charles), Helen. 1997. "The Language of Womanism: Re-Thinking Difference." In Heidi Safia Mirza, ed. *Black British Feminism: A Reader*. London: Routledge.

Chowdhury, Geeta. 1995. "Engendering Development? Women in Development (WID) in International Development Regimes." In Marianne H. Marchand and Jane L. Parpart, eds. *Feminism/Postmodernism/Development*. London: Routledge.

Chowdhury, Najma, and Barbara J. Nelson, with Kathryn A. Carver, Nancy J. Johnson, and Paula L. O'Loughlin. 1994. "Redefining Politics: Patterns of Women's Political Engagement from a Global Perspective." In Barbara J. Nelson and Najma Chowdhury, eds. *Women and Politics Worldwide*. New Haven and London: Yale University Press.

Clark, Ian. 1989. *The Hierarchy of States: Reform and Resistance in the International Order*. Cambridge: Cambridge University Press.

Clark, John P. 1978. "What Is Anarchism?" In J. Roland Pennock and John W. Chapman, eds. *Anarchism*. New York: New York University Press.

Cohen, Jean. 1995. "Interpreting the Notion of Civil Society." In Michael Walzer, ed. *Toward a Global Civil Society*. Oxford: Berghahn Books.

_____. 1982. "Between Crisis Management and Social Movements: The Place of Institutional Reform." *Telos* Summer, 52: 21–40.

Cohen, Jean L., and Andrew Arato. 1992. *Civil Society and Political Theory*. Cambridge, MA: MIT Press.

Cohen, Joshua, and Joel Rogers. 1995. "Secondary Associations and Democratic Governance." In Joshua Cohen and Joel Rogers, eds. *Associations and Democracy*. London: Verso.

Colás, Alejandro. 1994. "Putting Cosmopolitanism into Practice: The Case of Socialist Internationalism." *Millennium: Journal of International Studies* 23/3: 513–534.

Cole, G. D. H. 1920. *Guild Socialism Restated*. London: Leonard Parsons.

Collins, Patricia Hill. 1997. "Comment on Hekman's 'Truth and Method: Feminist Standpoint Theory Revisited': Where's the Power?" *Signs: Journal of Women in Culture and Society* 22/2: 375–381.

_____. 1990. *Black Feminist Thought: Knowledge, Consciousness and the Politics of Empowerment*. London: Unwin Hyman.

Combahee River Collective. 1983. "The Combahee River Collective Statement." In Barbara Smith, ed. *Home Girls: A Black Feminist Anthology*. New York: Kitchen Table—Women of Color Press.

Commission on Global Governance (CGG). 1995. *Our Global Neighbourhood*. Oxford: Oxford University Press.

Connell, R. W. 1987. *Gender and Power: Society, the Person and Sexual Politics*. Cambridge: Polity Press.

Connolly, William E. 1991. "Democracy and Territoriality." *Millennium: Journal of International Studies* 20/3: 463–484.

_____. 1988. *Political Theory and Modernity*. Oxford: Basil Blackwell.

Conway, M. Margaret, Gertrude A Steuernagel, and David W. Ahern. 1997. *Women and Political Participation: Cultural Change in the Political Arena*. Washington, DC: Congressional Quarterly Press.

Costain, Anne N. 1992. *Inviting Women's Rebellion: A Political Process Interpretation of the Women's Movement*. Baltimore, MD: John Hopkins University Press.

Cox, Robert. 1999. "Civil Society at the Turn of the Millennium: Prospects for an Alternative World Order." *Review of International Studies* 25/1: 3–28.

_____. 1997. "Democracy in Hard Times: Economic Globalization and the Limits to Democracy." In Anthony McGrew, ed. *The Transformation of Democracy? Globalization and Territorial Democracy*. Cambridge: Polity Press.

_____. 1996. "Globalization, Multilateralism and Democracy." In Robert W. Cox with Timothy J. Sinclair. *Approaches to World Order*. Cambridge: Cambridge University Press.

_____. 1993. "Gramsci, Hegemony and International Relations: An Essay in Method." In Stephen Gill, ed. *Gramsci, Historical Materialism and International Relations*. Cambridge: Cambridge University Press.

_____. 1987. *Production, Power and World Order: Social Forces in the Making of History*. New York: Columbia University Press.

_____. 1986. "Social Forces, States and World Orders: Beyond International Relations Theory." In Robert O. Keohane, ed. *Neorealism and Its Critics*. New York: Columbia University Press.

Crowley, Helen. 1992. "Women and the Domestic Sphere." In Robert Bocock and Kenneth Thompson, eds. *Social and Cultural Forms of Modernity*. Cambridge: Polity Press in association with the Open University.

Dagnino, Evelina. 1993. "An Alternative World Order and the Meaning of Democracy." In Jeremy Brecher, John Brown Childs, and Jill Cutler, eds. *Global Visions: Beyond the New World Order*. Boston: South End Press.

Dahl, Robert A. 1982. *Dilemmas of Pluralist Democracy: Autonomy Versus Control*. New Haven and London: Yale University Press.

D'Anieri, Paul, Claire Ernst, and Elizabeth Kier. 1990. "New Social Movements in Historical Perspective." *Comparative Politics* 22: 445–458.

Declaration from the Founder Members' Meeting of the Independent Women's Democratic Initiative. 1991. "Democracy Without Women Is No Democracy!" *Feminist Review* 39: 127–132.

De Lauretis, Teresa. 1990. "Eccentric Subjects: Feminist Theory and Historical Consciousness." *Feminist Studies* 16/1: 115–150.

Delmar, Rosalind. 1986. "What Is Feminism?" In Juliet Mitchell and Ann Oakley, eds. *What Is Feminism?* Oxford: Blackwell.

Dickenson, Donna. 1997. "Counting Women In: Globalization, Democratization and the Women's Movement." In Anthony McGrew, ed. *The Transformation of Democracy? Globalization and Territorial Democracy*. Cambridge: Polity Press.

Dietz, Mary. 1992. "Context Is All: Feminism and Theories of Citizenship." In Chantal Mouffe, ed. *Dimensions of Radical Democracy: Pluralism, Citizenship, Community*. London: Verso.

DiQuinzio, Patrice. 1995. "Feminist Theory and the Question of Citizenship: A Response to Dietz' Critique of Maternalism." *Women and Politics* 15/3: 23–42.

Donaldson, Laura E. 1992. *Decolonizing Feminisms: Race, Gender and Empire Building*. London: Routledge.

Donaldson, Thomas. 1992. "Kant's Global Rationalism." In Terry Nardin and David R. Mapel, eds. *Traditions of International Ethics*. Cambridge: Cambridge University Press.

Doyle, Michael W. 1986. "Liberalism and World Politics." *American Political Science Review* 80/4: 1151–1163.

_____. 1983. "Kant, Liberal Legacies and Foreign Affairs 1." *Philosophy and Public Affairs* 12/3: 205–235.

Drakulic, Slavenka. 1993. "Women and the New Democracy in the Former Yugoslavia." In Nanette Funk and Magda Mueller, eds. *Gender Politics and Post-Communism—Reflections from Eastern Europe and the Former Soviet Union.* London: Routledge.

Dunleavy, Patrick, and Brendan O'Leary. 1987. *Theories of the State: The Politics of Liberal Democracy.* Basingstoke, UK: Macmillan.

Dunn, John. 1992. "Conclusion." In John Dunn, ed. *Democracy: The Unfinished Journey—508 BC to AD 1993.* Oxford: Oxford University Press.

Eduards, Maud L. 1994. "Women's Agency and Collective Action." *Women's Studies International Forum* 17/2–3: 181–186.

Einhorn, Barbara. 1993. *Cinderella Goes to Market: Citizenship, Gender and Women's Movements in East Central Europe.* London: Verso.

Eisenstein, Zillah. 1997. "Women's Publics and the Search for New Democracies." *Feminist Review* 57: 140–167.

_____. 1994. *The Color of Gender: Reimaging Democracy.* Los Angeles: University of California Press.

Elliot, Faith Robertson. 1986. *The Family: Change and Continuity.* Basingstoke, UK: Macmillan.

Ellis, Anthony. 1992. "Utilitarianism and International Ethics." In Terry Nardin and David R. Mapel, eds. *Traditions of International Ethics.* Cambridge: Cambridge University Press.

Elshtain, Jean Bethke. 1993. *Public Man, Private Woman: Women in Social and Political Thought.* 2d ed. Princeton: Princeton University Press.

_____. 1990. *Power Trips and Other Journeys: Essays in Feminism as Civic Discourse.* Madison: University of Wisconsin Press.

_____. 1982. "Feminism, Family and Community." *Dissent* Fall: 442–449.

Enloe, Cynthia. 1988. *Does Khaki Become You? The Militarization of Women's Lives.* 2d ed. London: Pandora Press.

Evans, Sara. 1979. *Personal Politics: The Roots of Women's Liberation in the Civil Rights Movement and the New Left.* New York: Vintage Books.

Falk, Richard A. 1995a. "The World Order Between Inter-State Law and the Law of Humanity." In Daniele Archibugi and David Held, eds. *Cosmopolitan Democracy: An Agenda for a New World Order.* Cambridge: Polity Press.

_____. 1995b. "Liberalism at the Global Level: The Last of the Independent Commissions?" *Millennium: Journal of International Studies* 24/3: 563–576.

_____. 1993. "The Pathways of Global Constitutionalism." In Richard A. Falk, Robert C. Johansen, and Samuel S. Kim, eds. *The Constitutional Foundations of World Peace.* Albany: State University of New York Press.

_____. 1987a. "The Global Promise of Social Movements: Explorations at the Edge of Time." *Alternatives* XII: 173–196.

_____. 1987b. "The States-System and Contemporary Social Movements." In Saul H. Mendlovitz and R. B. J. Walker, eds. *Towards a Just World Peace: Perspectives from Social Movements.* London: Butterworths.

_____. 1978. "Anarchism and World Order." In J. Roland Pennock and John W. Chapman, eds. *Anarchism.* New York: New York University Press.

Feagin, Joe R., and Hernán Vera. 1995. *White Racism*. New York and London: Routledge.

Feijoó, Maria del Carmen, and Mónica Gogna. 1990. "Women in the Transition to Democracy." In Elizabeth Jelin, ed. *Women and Social Change in Latin America.* London: Zed Books.

Femia, Joseph V. 1993. *Marxism and Democracy*. Oxford: Clarendon Press.

Ferguson, Kathy E. 1993. *The Man Question: Visions of Subjectivity in Feminist Theory.* Berkeley: University of California Press.

Ferree, Myra Marx, and Beth B. Hess. 1994. *Controversy and Coalition: The New Feminist Movement Across Three Decades of Change.* New York: Twayne.

Fireman, Bruce, and William A. Gamson. 1988. "Utilitarian Logic in the Resource Mobilization Perspective." In Mayer N. Zald and John D. McCarthy, eds. *The Dynamics of Social Movements: Resource Mobilization, Social Control and Tactics.* Lanham, MD: University Press of America.

Fishkin, James S. 1991. *Democracy and Deliberation: New Directions for Democratic Reform.* New Haven and London: Yale University Press.

Flax, Jane. 1990a. "Postmodernism and Gender Relations in Feminist Theory." In Linda J. Nicholson, ed. *Feminism/Postmodernism.* London: Routledge.

_____. 1990b. *Thinking Fragments: Psychoanalysis, Feminism and Postmodernism in the Contemporary West.* Berkeley, Los Angeles, and London: University of California Press.

Ford, Lucy. 1998. "The Global Enclosure: Social Movements and the Globalisation of Environmental Management." Paper presented at the Annual Conference of the International Studies Association, 18–21 March, Minneapolis, MN.

Ford-Smith, Honor. 1997. "Ring Ding in a Tight Corner: Sistren, Collective Democracy and the Organization of Cultural Production." In M. Jacqui Alexander and Chandra Talpade Mohanty, eds. *Feminist Genealogies, Colonial Legacies, Democratic Futures.* London: Routledge.

Foucault, Michel. 1986. "Disciplinary Power and Subjection." In Steven Lukes, ed. *Power.* Oxford: Blackwell.

Foweraker, Joe. 1995. *Theorizing Social Movements.* London: Pluto Press.

Frank, Andre Gunder, and Martha Fuentes. 1990. "Civil Democracy: Social Movements in World History." In Samir Amin, Giovanni Arrighi, Andre Gunder Frank, and Immanuel Wallerstein, eds. *Transforming the Revolution: Social Movements and the World System.* New York: Monthly Review Press.

Frankenberg, Ruth. 1997. "Introduction: Local Whitenesses, Localizing Whiteness." In Ruth Frankenburg, ed. *Displacing Whiteness: Essays in Social and Cultural Criticism.* Durham, NC, and London: Duke University Press.

Frankenberg, Ruth, and Lata Mani. 1996. "Crosscurrents, Crosstalk: Race, 'Postcoloniality' and the Politics of Location." In Padmini Mongia, ed. *Contemporary Postcolonial Theory: A Reader.* London: Arnold.

Fraser, Nancy. 1987. "What's Critical About Critical Theory? The Case of Habermas and Gender." In Seyla Benhabib and Drucilla Cornell, eds. *Feminism as Critique: Essays on the Politics of Gender in Late-Capitalist Societies.* Cambridge: Polity Press.

Fraser, Nancy, and Linda Nicholson. 1990. "Social Criticism Without Philosophy? An Encounter Between Feminism and Postmodernism." In Linda J. Nicholson, ed. *Feminism/Postmodernism.* London: Routledge.

Frazer, Elisabeth. 1997. "Capitalism and Communitarianism." Paper presented at the Graduate and Faculty Seminar of the Social and Political Thought Programme, 16 January, University of Sussex, UK.

Freeman, Jo. 1984. "The Tyranny of Structurelessness." In *Untying the Knot: Feminism, Anarchism and Organisation*. London: Dark Star/Rebel Press.

French, Marilyn. 1985. *Beyond Power: On Women, Men and Morals*. New York: Summit Books.

Friedan, Betty. 1965. *The Feminine Mystique*. London: Penguin.

Frost, Mervyn. 1996. "Global Civil Society: Taking Rights Seriously." Paper presented at the *Millennium: Journal of International Studies* 25th Anniversary Conference, 17–19 October, London School of Economics, London.

Fukuyama, Francis. 1989. "The End of History?" *National Interest* Summer: 3–18.

Gabriel, Christina, and Laura Macdonald. 1994. "NAFTA, Women and Organising in Canada and Mexico: Forging a Feminist Internationality." *Millennium: Journal of International Studies* 23/3: 535–556.

Gelb, Joyce. 1989. *Feminism and Politics: A Comparative Perspective*. Berkeley and Los Angeles: University of California Press.

Gerlach, Luther P., and Virginia H. Hine. 1970. *People, Power, Change: Movements of Social Transformation*. Indianapolis and New York: Bobbs Merrill.

Giddens, Anthony. 1994. *Beyond Left and Right: The Future of Radical Politics*. Cambridge: Polity Press.

_____. 1990. *The Consequences of Modernity*. Cambridge: Polity Press.

_____. 1985. *The Nation-State and Violence*. Berkeley and Los Angeles: University of California Press.

Gilbert, Alan. 1992. "Must Global Politics Constrain Democracy? Realism, Regimes and Democratic Internationalism." *Political Theory* 20/1: 8–37.

Gill, Stephen. 1997. "Finance, Production and Panopticism: Inequality, Risk and Resistance in an Era of Disciplinary Neo-Liberalism." In Stephen Gill, ed. *Globalization, Democratization and Multilateralism*. Tokyo: United Nations Press, and Basingstoke, UK: Macmillan.

_____. 1995. "Globalisation, Market Civilisation and Disciplinary Neo-Liberalism." *Millennium: Journal of International Studies* 24/3: 399–423.

_____. 1993. "Gramsci and Global Politics: Towards a Post-Hegemonic Research Agenda." In Stephen Gill, ed. *Gramsci, Historical Materialism and International Relations*. Cambridge: Cambridge University Press.

Gilligan, Carol. 1982. *In a Different Voice: Psychological Theory and Women's Development*. Cambridge, MA, and London: Harvard University Press.

Gilmartin, Patricia, and Stanley D. Brunn. 1998. "The Representation of Women in Political Cartoons of the 1995 World Conference on Women." *Women's Studies International Forum* 21/5: 535–549.

Gilpin, Robert G. 1986. "The Richness of the Tradition of Political Realism." In Robert O. Keohane, ed. *Neorealism and Its Critics*. New York: Columbia University Press.

_____. 1981. *War and Change in World Politics*. Cambridge: Cambridge University Press.

Goetz, Anne Marie. 1988. "Feminism and the Claim to Know: Contradictions in Feminist Approaches to Women in Development." *Millennium: Journal of International Studies* 17/3: 477–496.

Goldman, Emma. 1970. *The Traffic in Women and Other Essays on Feminism.* Ojai, CA: Times Change Press.

Graham, B. D. 1993. *Representation and Party Politics.* Oxford: Blackwell.

Grant, Wyn. 1995. *Pressure Groups, Politics and Democracy in Britain.* 2d ed. Hemel Hempstead, UK: Harvester Wheatsheaf.

Greer, Germaine. 1971. *The Female Eunuch.* London: Paladin.

Grewal, Inderpal. 1994. "Autobiographic Subjects and Diasporic Locations: *Meatless Days* and *Borderlands.*" In Inderpal Grewal and Caren Kaplan, eds. *Scattered Hegemonies: Postmodernities and Transnational Feminist Practices.* London and Minneapolis: University of Minnesota Press.

Guérin, Daniel. 1989. "Marxism and Anarchism." In David Goodway, ed. *For Anarchism: History, Theory and Practice.* London: Routledge.

Gullickson, Gay L. 1989. "Feminists and Suffragists: The British and French Experiences." *Feminist Studies* 15/3: 591–602.

Habermas, Jürgen. 1996. "Three Models of Democracy." In Seyla Benhabib, ed. *Democracy and Difference: Contesting the Boundaries of the Political.* Princeton: Princeton University Press.

_____. 1990. *Moral Consciousness and Communicative Action.* Translated by Christian Lenhardt and Shierry Weber Nicholsen. Cambridge, MA: MIT Press.

_____. 1985. "Modernity—An Incomplete Project." In Hal Foster, ed. *Postmodern Culture.* London: Pluto Press.

_____. 1981. "New Social Movements." *Telos* 49: 33–37

Hall, John A. 1985. *Powers and Liberties: The Causes and Consequences of the Rise of the West.* Oxford: Basil Blackwell.

Hall, Stuart. 1997. *Representation: Cultural Representation and Signifying Practices.* London: SAGE.

_____. 1992. "Introduction." In Stuart Hall and Bram Gieben, eds. *Formations of Modernity.* Cambridge: Polity Press in association with the Open University.

_____. 1989. "The Meaning of New Times." In Stuart Hall and Martin Jacques, eds. *New Times: The Changing Face of Politics in the 1990s.* London: Lawrence and Wishart.

Hall, Stuart, and David Held. 1989. "Citizens and Citizenship." In Stuart Hall and Martin Jacques, eds. *New Times: The Changing Face of Politics in the 1990s.* London: Lawrence and Wishart.

Halliday, Fred. 1994. *Rethinking International Relations.* Basingstoke, UK: Macmillan.

Hamilton, Peter. 1992. "The Enlightenment and the Birth of Social Science." In Stuart Hall and Bram Gieben, eds. *Formations of Modernity.* Cambridge: Polity Press in association with the Open University.

Hammonds, Evelynn, M. 1997. "Toward a Genealogy of Black Female Sexuality: The Problematic of Silence." In M. Jacqui Alexander and Chandra Talpade Mohanty, eds. *Feminist Genealogies, Colonial Legacies, Democratic Futures.* London: Routledge.

Hannerz, Ulf. 1990. "Cosmopolitans and Locals in World Culture." In Mike Featherstone, ed. *Global Culture: Nationalism, Globalization and Modernity*. London: SAGE.

Hansen, Lene. 1997. "R. B. J. Walker and International Relations: Deconstructing a Discipline." In Iver B. Neumann and Ole Waever, eds. *The Future of International Relations: Masters in the Making?* London: Routledge.

Harding, Sandra. 1997. "Comment on Hekman's 'Truth and Method: Feminist Standpoint Theory Revisited': Whose Standpoint Needs the Regimes of Truth and Reality?" *Signs: Journal of Women in Culture and Society* 22/2: 382–389.

_____. 1987a. "Introduction: Is There a Feminist Method?" In Sandra Harding, ed. *Feminism and Methodology: Social Science Issues*. Bloomington: Indiana University Press.

_____. 1987b. "Conclusion: Epistemological Questions." In Sandra Harding, ed. *Feminism and Methodology: Social Science Issues*. Bloomington: Indiana University Press.

Hartsock, Nancy C. M. 1997. "Comment on Hekman's 'Truth and Method: Feminist Standpoint Theory Revisited'—Truth or Justice?" *Signs: Journal of Women in Culture and Society* 22/2: 367–374.

_____. 1987. "The Feminist Standpoint: Developing the Ground for a Specifically Feminist Historical Materialism." In Sandra Harding, ed. *Feminism and Methodology: Social Science Issues*. Bloomington: Indiana University Press.

Harvey, David. 1989. *The Condition of Postmodernity: An Enquiry into the Origins of Cultural Change*. Oxford: Blackwell Publishers.

Hebdige, Dick. 1989. "After the Masses." In Stuart Hall and Martin Jacques, eds. *New Times: The Changing Face of Politics in the 1990s*. London: Lawrence and Wishart.

Heinen, Jacqueline. 1992. "Polish Democracy Is a Masculine Democracy." *Women's Studies International Forum* 15/1: 129–138.

Hekman, Susan. 1997. "Truth and Method: Feminist Standpoint Theory Revisited." *Signs: Journal of Women in Culture and Society* 22/2: 341–365.

_____. 1995. *Moral Voices, Moral Selves: Carol Gilligan and Feminist Moral Theory*. Cambridge: Polity Press.

Held, David. 1996. *Models of Democracy*. 2d ed. Cambridge: Polity Press.

_____. 1995. *Democracy and the Global Order*. Cambridge: Polity Press.

_____. 1993. "Nothing But a Dog's Life? Further Comments on Fukuyama, Callinicos and Giddens." *Theory and Society* 22: 293–304.

_____. 1992a. "The Development of the Modern State." In Stuart Hall and Bram Gieben, eds. *Formations of Modernity*. Cambridge: Polity Press in association with the Open University.

_____. 1992b. "Liberalism, Marxism and Democracy." In Stuart Hall, David Held, and Tony McGrew, eds. *Modernity and Its Futures*. Cambridge: Polity Press in association with the Open University.

_____. 1991. "Democracy, the Nation-State and the Global System." *Economy and Society* 20/2: 138–172.

Held, Virginia. 1993. *Feminist Morality: Transforming Culture, Society and Politics*. Chicago: University of Chicago Press.

Helman, Sara, and Tamar Rapoport. 1997. "Women in Black: Challenging Israel's Gender and Socio-Political Orders." *British Journal of Sociology* 48/4: 681–700.

Heng, Geraldine. 1997. "'A Great Way to Fly': Nationalism, the State and the Varieties of Third-World Feminism." In M. Jacqui Alexander and Chandra Talpade Mohanty, eds. *Feminist Genealogies, Colonial Legacies, Democratic Futures*. London: Routledge.

Hewitt, Marsha. 1986. "Emma Goldman: The Case for Anarcho-Feminism." In Dimitrios I. Roussopoulos, ed. *The Anarchist Papers 1*. Montreal: Black Rose Books.

Hindess, Barry. 1980. "Marxism and Parliamentary Democracy." In Alan Hunt, ed. *Marxism and Democracy*. London: Lawrence and Wishart.

Hirst, Paul. 1995. "Can Secondary Associations Enhance Democratic Governance?" In Joshua Cohen and Joel Rogers, eds. *Associations and Democracy*. London: Verso.

_____. 1994. *Associative Democracy: New Forms of Economic and Social Governance*. Cambridge: Polity Press.

_____. 1990. *Representative Democracy and Its Limits*. Cambridge: Polity Press.

_____. 1986. Review of John Burnheim's *Is Democracy Possible? The Alternative to Electoral Politics*. *The Sociological Review* 34/3: 669–673.

Hirst, Paul, and Grahame Thompson. 1996. *Globalization in Question: The International Economy and the Possibility of Governance*. Cambridge: Polity Press.

Hoare, Quentin, and Geoffrey Nowell Smith, eds. 1971. *Selections from the Prison Notebooks of Antonio Gramsci*. London: Lawrence and Wishart.

Hobsbawm, E. J. 1990. *Nations and Nationalism Since 1780: Programme, Myth, Reality*. Cambridge: Canto.

Holden, Barry. 1993. *Understanding Liberal Democracy*. 2d ed. Hemel Hempstead, UK: Harvester Wheatsheaf.

hooks, bell. 1991. *Yearning: Race, Gender and Cultural Politics*. London: Turnaround.

_____. 1984. *Feminist Theory: From Margin to Center*. Boston: South End Press.

Howell, Jude. 1997. "Post-Beijing Reflections: Creating Ripples, but Not Waves in China." *Women's Studies International Forum* 20/2: 235–252.

Hunt, Alan. 1980. "Taking Democracy Seriously." In Alan Hunt, ed. *Marxism and Democracy*. London: Lawrence and Wishart.

Huntington, Samuel P. 1991. *The Third Wave: Democratization in the Late Twentieth Century*. Norman: University of Oklahoma Press.

_____. 1975. "The United States." In Michael Crozier, Samuel P. Huntington, and Joui Watanuki. *The Crisis of Democracy: Report on the Governability of Democracies to the Trilateral Commission*. New York: New York University Press.

Hurrell, Andrew, and Ngaire Woods. 1995. "Globalisation and Inequality." *Millennium: Journal of International Studies* 24/3: 447–470.

Hutchings, Kimberly. 1998. "Political Theory and Cosmopolitan Citizenship." In Kimberly Hutchings and Roland Dannreuther, eds. *Cosmopolitan Citizenship*. Basingstoke, UK: Macmillan.

Ichiyo, Muto. 1993. "For an Alliance of Hope." In Jeremy Brecher, John Brown Childs, and Jill Cutler, eds. *Global Visions: Beyond the New World Order*. Boston: South End Press.

Imam, Ayesha M. 1997. "The Dynamics of WINning: An Analysis of Women in Nigeria (WIN)." In M. Jacqui Alexander and Chandra Talpade Mohanty, eds. *Feminist Genealogies, Colonial Legacies, Democratic Futures.* London: Routledge.

Jaggar, Alison. 1989. "Love and Knowledge: Emotion in Feminist Epistemology." In Ann Garry and Marilyn Pearsall, eds. *Women, Knowledge and Reality: Explorations in Feminist Philosophy.* London: Unwin Hyman.

_____. 1988. *Feminist Politics and Human Nature.* Totowa, NJ: Rowman & Littlefield.

Janova, Mira, and Mariette Sineau. 1992. "Women's Participation in Political Power in Europe: An Essay in East-West Comparison." *Women's Studies International Forum* 11/1: 115–128.

Jaquette, Jane S. 1997. "Women in Power: From Tokenism to Critical Mass." *Foreign Policy* 108: 23–37.

_____. 1994a. "Introduction: From Transition to Participation—Women's Movements and Democratic Politics." In Jane Jaquette, ed. *The Women's Movement in Latin America: Participation and Democracy.* Boulder, CO: Westview Press.

_____. 1994b. "Conclusion: Women's Political Participation and the Prospects for Democracy." In Jane Jaquette, ed. *The Women's Movement in Latin America: Participation and Democracy.* Boulder, CO: Westview Press.

Jayaratne, Toby Epstein, and Abigail J. Stewart. 1992. "Quantitative and Qualitative Methods in the Social Sciences: Current Feminist Issues and Practical Strategies." In Mary Margaret Fonow and Judith A. Cook, eds. *Beyond Methodology: Feminist Scholarship as Lived Research.* Bloomington: Indiana University Press.

Jayawaradena, Kumari. 1986. *Feminism and Nationalism in the Third World.* London: Zed Books.

Jelin, Elizabeth. 1990. "Introduction." In Elizabeth Jelin, ed. *Women and Social Change in Latin America.* London: Zed Books.

Johnson-Odim, Cheryl. 1991. "Common Themes, Different Contexts: Third World Women and Feminism." In Chandra Talpade Mohanty, Ann Russo, and Lourdes Torres, eds. *Third World Women and the Politics of Feminism.* Bloomington: Indiana University Press.

Jones, Kathleen B. 1990. "Citizenship in a Woman Friendly Polity." *Signs: Journal of Women, Culture and Society* 15/4: 781–812.

Kaplan, Caren. 1994. "The Politics of Location as Transnational Feminist Critical Practice." In Inderpal Grewal and Caren Kaplan, eds. *Scattered Hegemonies: Postmodernities and Transnational Feminist Practices.* London/Minneapolis: University of Minnesota Press.

Katzenstein, Mary Fainsod. 1987. "Comparing the Feminist Movements of the United States and Western Europe: An Overview." In Mary Fainsod Katzenstein and Carol McClurg Mueller, eds. *The Women's Movement of the United States and Western Europe: Consciousness, Political Opportunity and Public Policy.* Philadelphia: Temple University Press.

Keane, John. 1988. *Democracy and Civil Society: On the Predicaments of European Socialism, The Prospects for Democracy and the Problem of Controlling State Power.* London: Verso.

Keane, John, and Paul Mier. 1989. "Editors' Preface." In Alberto Melucci, *Nomads of the Present: Social Movements and Individual Needs in Contemporary Society.* Edited by John Keane and Paul Mier. London: Radius.

Keysers, Loes, and Ines Smyth. 1992. "Reflections on Global Solidarity for Women's Health and Reproductive Rights." *Vena Journal* 3/1: 26–31.

King, Deborah K. 1988. "Multiple Jeopardy, Multiple Consciousness: The Context of a Black Feminist Ideology." *Signs: Journal of Women in Culture and Society* 14/1: 42–72.

Klandermans, Bert. 1992. "The Social Construction of Protest and Multiorganizational Fields." In Aldon D. Morris and Carol McClurg Mueller, eds. *Frontiers in Social Movement Theory.* New Haven and London: Yale University Press.

Klimenkova, Tatania. 1994. "What Does Our New Democracy Offer Society?" In Anastasia Posadskaya, ed. *Women in Russia: A New Era in Russian Feminism.* London: Verso.

Konstantinova, Valentina. 1994. "No Longer Totalitarianism but Not Yet Democracy: The Emergence of an Independent Women's Movement in Russia." In Anastasia Posadskaya, ed. *Women in Russia: A New Era in Russian Feminism.* London: Verso.

Kramarae, Cheris, and Paula A. Trechler. 1992. *Amazons, Bluestockings and Crones: A Feminist Dictionary.* London: Pandora.

Kumar, Krishan. 1993. "Civil Society: An Inquiry into the Usefulness of an Historical Term." *British Journal of Sociology* 44/3: 375–395.

Kymlicka, Will. 1990. *Contemporary Political Philosophy: An Introduction.* Oxford: Clarendon Press.

Laclau, Ernesto, and Chantal Mouffe. 1998. "Post-Marxism Without Apologies." In Stuart Sim, ed. *Post-Marxism: A Reader.* Edinburgh: Edinburgh University Press.

_____. 1985. *Hegemony and Socialist Strategy: Towards a Radical Democracy.* London: Verso.

Larochelle, Gilbert. 1992. "Interdependence, Globalization and Fragmentation." In Zdravko Mlinar, ed. *Globalization and Territorial Identities.* Aldershot, UK: Avebury.

Laxer, Gordon. 1995. "Social Solidarity, Democracy and Global Capitalism." *Canadian Review of Sociology and Anthropology* 32/2: 287–313.

Lerner, Michael. 1970. "Anarchism and the American Counter-Culture." *Government and Opposition* 5/4: 430–451.

Levine, Cathy. 1984. "The Tyranny of Tyranny." In *Untying the Knot: Feminism, Anarchism and Organisation.* London: Dark Star/Rebel Press.

Lewis, Paul G. 1997a. "Democratization in Eastern Europe." In David Potter, David Goldblatt, Margaret Kiloh, and Paul Lewis, eds. *Democratization.* Cambridge: Polity Press in association with the Open University.

_____. 1997b. "Political Participation in Post-Communist Democracies." In David Potter, David Goldblatt, Margaret Kiloh, and Paul Lewis, eds. *Democratization.* Cambridge: Polity Press in association with the Open University.

_____. 1992. "Democracy in Modern Societies." In John Allen, Peter Braham, and Paul Lewis, eds. *Political and Economic Forms of Modernity.* Cambridge: Polity Press in association with the Open University.

Linklater, Andrew. 1990. *Men and Citizens in the Theory of International Relations*. 2d ed. Basingstoke, UK: Macmillan.

Linklater, Andrew, and John Macmillan. 1995. "Introduction: Boundaries in Question." In Andrew Linklater and John Macmillan, eds. *Boundaries in Question: New Directions in International Relations*. London: Pinter.

Lipovskaya, Olga. 1997. "Women's Groups in Russia." In Mary Buckley, ed. *Post-Soviet Women: From the Baltic to Central Asia*. Cambridge: Cambridge University Press.

Lipschutz, Ronnie D. 1992. "Reconstructing World Politics: The Emergence of Global Civil Society." *Millennium: Journal of International Studies* 21/3: 389–420.

Lister, Ruth. 1997. *Citizenship: Feminist Perspectives*. Basingstoke, UK: Macmillan.

_____. 1995. "Dilemmas in Engendering Citizenship." *Economy and Society* 24/1: 1–40.

Lloyd, Genevieve. 1989. "The Man of Reason." In Ann Garry and Marilyn Pearsall, eds. *Women, Knowledge and Reality: Explorations in Feminist Philosophy*. London: Unwin Hyman.

Lorde, Audre. 1983. "An Open Letter to Mary Daly." In Cherríe Moraga and Gloria Anzaldúa, eds. *This Bridge Called My Back: Writings by Radical Women of Color*. 2d ed. New York: Kitchen Table—Women of Color Press.

Luard, Evan. 1990. *The Globalization of Politics: The Changed Focus of Political Action in the Modern World*. Basingstoke, UK: Macmillan.

Luckham, Robin. 1996. "Faustian Bargains: Democratic Control over Military and Security Establishments." In Robin Luckham and Gordon White, eds. *Democratization in the South: The Jagged Wave*. Manchester, UK: Manchester University Press.

Luckham, Robin, and Gordon White. 1996. "Introduction: Democratizing the South." In Robin Luckham and Gordon White, eds. *Democratization in the South: The Jagged Wave*. Manchester, UK: Manchester University Press.

Lugones, María. 1990. "Playfulness, World-Travelling and Loving Perception." In Gloria Anzaldúa, ed. *Making Face, Making Soul/Haciendo Caras: Creative and Critical Perspectives by Feminists of Color*. San Francisco: Aunt Lute Books.

Lugones, María C., and Elizabeth V. Spelman. 1983. "Have We Got a Theory for You! Feminist Theory, Cultural Imperialism and the Demand for 'the Woman's Voice.'" *Women's Studies International Forum* 6/6: 573–581.

Lynch, Celia. 1994. "E. H. Carr, International Relations Theory, and the Societal Origins of International Legal Norms." *Millennium: Journal of International Studies* 23/3: 589–619.

Macdonald, Laura. 1994. "Globalising Civil Society: Interpreting International NGOs in Central America." *Millennium: Journal of International Studies* 23/2: 267–85.

Mackinnon, Catherine A. 1989. *Toward a Feminist Theory of the State*. Cambridge, MA: Harvard University Press.

Mackintosh, Maureen. 1981. "Gender and Economics: The Sexual Division of Labour and the Subordination of Women." In Kate Young, Carol Wolkowitz, and Roslyn McCullagh, eds. *Woman, Marriage and the Market: Women's Subordination Internationally and Its Lessons*. London: Routledge.

Macpherson, C. B. 1977. *The Life and Times of Liberal Democracy*. Oxford: Oxford University Press.

———. 1972. *The Real World of Democracy*. Oxford: Oxford University Press.

Magnusson, Warren. 1993. "Social Movements and the State: Presentation and Representation." In Gregory Albo, David Langulle, and Leo Panitch, eds. *A Different Kind of State? Popular Power and Democratic Administration*. Toronto: Oxford University Press.

Maiguashca, Bice. 1994. "The Transnational Indigenous Movement in a Changing World Order." In Yoshikazu Sakamoto, ed. *Global Transformation: Challenges to the State System*. Tokyo: United Nations University Press.

Malatesta, Ernesto. 1977. "Syndicalism: An Anarchist Critique." In George Woodcock, ed. *The Anarchist Reader*. Hassocks, UK: Harvester Press.

Malti-Douglas, Fedwa. 1996. "As the World (or Dare I Say the Globe?) Turns: Feminism and Transnationalism." *Indiana Journal of Global Legal Studies* 4/1: 137–144.

Mani, Lati. 1990. "Multiple Mediations: Feminist Scholarship in the Age of Multinational Reception." *Feminist Review* 35: 24–41.

Mansbridge, Jane. 1998. "Feminism and Democracy." In Anne Phillips, ed. *Feminism and Politics*. Oxford: Oxford University Press.

———. 1996. "Using Power/Fighting Power: The Polity." In Seyla Benhabib, ed. *Democracy and Difference: Contesting the Boundaries of the Political*. Princeton: Princeton University Press.

Marshall, Peter. 1993. *Demanding the Impossible: A History of Anarchism*. London: Fontana Press.

———. 1989. "Human Nature and Anarchism." In David Goodway, ed. *For Anarchism: History, Theory and Practice*. London: Routledge.

Martell, Luke, and Neil Stammers. 1996. "The Study of 'Solidarity' and the Social Theory of Alain Touraine." In Jon Clark and Marco Diani, eds. *Alain Touraine*. London and Washington, DC: Falmer Press.

Martin, Thomas S. 1989. "Unhinging All Government: The Defects of Political Representation." In Dimitrios Roussopoulos, ed. *The Anarchist Papers 1*. Montreal: Black Rose Books.

Marx, Karl. 1977. *Selected Writings*. Edited by David McLellan. Oxford: Oxford University Press.

McCarthy, John D., and Mayer N. Zald. 1977. "Resource Mobilisation and Social Movements: A Partial Theory." *American Journal of Sociology* 82/6: 1212–1241.

McCarthy, Michael. 1989. "Introduction: The Boundaries of Welfare." In Michael McCarthy, ed. *The New Politics of Welfare: An Agenda for the 1990s?* Basingstoke, UK: Macmillan.

McGrew, Anthony. 1997a. "Globalisation and Territorial Democracy: An Introduction." In Anthony McGrew, ed. *The Transformation of Democracy? Globalization and Territorial Democracy*. Cambridge: Polity Press.

———. 1997b. "Democracy Beyond Borders? Globalization and the Reconstruction of Democratic Theory and Politics." In Anthony McGrew, ed. *The Transformation of Democracy? Globalization and Teritorial Democracy*. Cambridge: Polity Press.

_____. 1992a. "A Global Society?" In Stuart Hall, David Held, and Tony Mc-Grew, eds. *Modernity and Its Futures*. Cambridge: Polity Press in association with the Open University.

_____. 1992b. "The State in Advanced Capitalist Societies." In John Allen, Peter Braham, and Paul Lewis, eds. *Political and Economic Forms of Modernity*. Cambridge: Polity Press in association with the Open University.

McLennan, Gregor. 1992. "The Enlightenment Project Revisited." In Stuart Hall, David Held, and Tony McGrew, eds. *Modernity and Its Futures*. Cambridge: Polity Press in association with the Open University.

McRobbie, Angela. 1994. *Postmodernism and Popular Culture*. London: Routledge.

Melucci, Alberto. 1996a. *Challenging Codes: Collective Action in the Information Age*. Cambridge: Cambridge University Press.

_____. 1996b. "An End to Social Movements? A Reassessment from the 1990s." Paper presented at the Second European Conference on Social Movements, 2–5 October, Vitoria-Gasteiz, Spain.

_____. 1992. "Liberation or Meaning? Social Movements, Culture and Democracy." In Jan Nederveen Pieterse, ed. *Emancipations, Modern and Postmodern*. London: SAGE.

_____. 1989. *Nomads of the Present: Social Movements and Individual Needs in Contemporary Society*. Edited by John Keane and Paul Mier. London: Radius.

Mendus, Susan. 1992. "Losing the Faith: Feminism and Democracy." In John Dunn, ed. *Democracy: The Unfinished Journey—508 BC to AD 1993*. Oxford: Oxford University Press.

Mezei, Smaranda. 1994. "Gendering the Social Body in Postcommunist Romania—From 'Homogenization' to Diversity: New Discourses, Old Practices." *Women's Studies International Forum* 17/2–3: 313–314.

Mies, Maria. 1998. *Patriarchy and Accumulation on a World Scale: Women in the International Division of Labour*. 2d ed. London: Zed Books.

Miles, Angela. 1996. *Integrative Feminisms: Building Global Visions 1960s–1990s*. London: Routledge.

Miliband, Ralph. 1989. "Marx and the State." In Graeme Duncan, ed. *Democracy and the Capitalist State*. Cambridge: Cambridge University Press.

Miller, David. 1998. "Bounded Citizenship." In Kimberly Hutchings and Roland Dannreuther, eds. *Cosmopolitan Citizenship*. Basingstoke, UK: Macmillan.

_____. 1984. *Anarchism*, London: J. M. Dent & Sons.

Miller, David, Janet Coleman, William Connolly, and Alan Ryan, eds. 1991. *The Blackwell Encyclopaedia of Political Thought*. Paper ed. Oxford: Blackwell.

Mirza, Heidi Safia. 1997. "Introduction: Mapping a Genealogy of Black British Feminism." In Heidi Safia Mirza, ed. *Black British Feminism: A Reader*. London: Routledge.

Mittelman, James H. 1994. "The Global Restructuring of Production and Migration." In Yoshikazu Sakamoto, ed. *Global Transformation: Challenges to the State System*. Tokyo: United Nations University Press.

Mitter, Swasti. 1986. *Common Fate, Common Bond: Women in the Global Economy*. London: Pluto Press.

Mlinar, Zdravko. 1992. "Individuation and Globalization: The Transformation of Territorial Social Organization." In Zdravko Mlinar, ed. *Globalization and Territorial Identities*. Aldershot, UK: Avebury.

Moghadam, Valentine M. 1993. "Bringing the Third World In: A Comparative Analysis of Gender and Restructuring." In Valentine M. Moghadam, ed. *Democratic Reform and the Position of Women in Transitional Economies*. Oxford: Clarendon Press.

Mohanty, Chandra Talpade. 1998. "Feminist Encounters: Locating the Politics of Experience." In Anne Phillips, ed. *Feminism and Politics*. Oxford: Oxford University Press.

_____. 1997. "Women Workers and Capitalist Scripts: Ideologies of Domination, Common Interests and the Politics of Solidarity." In M. Jacqui Alexander and Chandra Talpade Mohanty, eds. *Feminist Genealogies, Colonial Legacies, Democratic Futures*. London: Routledge.

_____. 1991a. "Cartographies of Struggle: Third World Women and the Politics of Feminism." In Chandra Talpade Mohanty, Ann Russo, and Lourdes Torres, eds. *Third World Women and the Politics of Feminism*. Bloomington: Indiana University Press.

_____. 1991b. "Under Western Eyes: Feminist Scholarship and Colonial Discourses." In Chandra Talpade Mohanty, Ann Russo, and Lourdes Torres, eds. *Third World Women and the Politics of Feminism*. Bloomington: Indiana University Press.

Molyneux, Maxine. 1998. "Analysing Women's Movements." In Cecile Jackson and Ruth Pearson, eds. *Feminist Visions of Development: Gender Analysis and Policy*. London: Routledge.

_____. 1985. "Mobilisation Without Emancipation? Women's Interests, the State and Revolution in Nicaragua." *Feminist Studies* 11/2: 227–255.

Mongia, Padmini. 1996. "Introduction." In Padmini Mongia, ed. *Contemporary Postcolonial Theory: A Reader*. London: Arnold.

Morgan, Robin. 1985. "Planetary Feminism: The Politics of the 21st Century." In Robin Morgan, ed. *Sisterhood Is Global: The International Women's Movement Anthology*. Harmondsworth, UK: Penguin Books.

_____. ed. 1970. *Sisterhood Is Powerful: An Anthology of Writings from the Women's Liberation Movement*. New York: Vintage.

Morgen, Sandra, and Ann Bookman. 1988. "Rethinking Women and Politics: An Introductory Essay." In Ann Bookman and Sandra Morgen, eds. *Women and the Politics of Empowerment*. Philadelphia: Temple University Press.

Morgenthau, Hans J. 1978. *Politics Among Nations: The Struggle for Power and Peace*. 5th ed. New York: Alfred A. Knopf.

Mouffe, Chantal. 1995. "Pluralism and the Left Identity." In Michael Walzer, ed. *Toward a Global Civil Society*. Oxford: Berghahn Books.

_____. 1993. *The Return of the Political*. London: Verso.

Moya, Paula. 1997. "Postmodernism, 'Realism' and the Politics of Identity: Cherríe Moraga and Chicana Feminism." In M. Jacqui Alexander and Chandra Talpade Mohanty, eds. *Feminist Genealogies, Colonial Legacies, Democratic Futures*. London: Routledge.

Mueller, Carol. 1994. "Conflict Networks and the Origins of Women's Libera-
tion." In Enrique Laraña, Hank Johnston, and Joseph R. Gusfield, eds. *New
Social Movements: From Ideology to Identity*. Philadelphia: Temple University
Press.

Nash, June. 1988. "Cultural Parameters of Sexism and Racism in the International
Division of Labour." In Joan Smith, Jane Collins, Terence K. Hopkins, and Ak-
bar Muhammad, eds. *Racism, Sexism and the World System*. Westport, CT:
Greenwood Press.

Nash, Kate. 1998. "Beyond Liberalism? Feminist Theories of Democracy." In
Vicky Randall and Georgina Waylen, eds. *Gender, Politics and the State*. London:
Routledge.

Nelson, Barbara J., and Najma Chowdhury, eds. 1994. *Women and Politics Worldwide*. New Haven and London: Yale University Press.

Newland, Kathleen. 1988. "From Transnational Relationships to International Relations: Women in Development and the International Decade for Women."
Millennium: Journal of International Studies 17/3: 507–516.

Obiora, L. Amede. 1997. "Feminism, Globalism and Culture: After Beijing." *Indiana Journal of Global Legal Studies* 4/2: 97–105.

Offe, Claus. 1995. "Some Sceptical Considerations on the Malleability of Representative Institutions." In Joshua Cohen and Joel Rogers, eds. *Associations and
Democracy*. London: Verso.

_____. 1985. "New Social Movements: Challenging the Boundaries of Institu-
tional Politics." *Social Research* 52/4: 817–869.

Olson, Mancur. 1993. "The Logic of Collective Action." In Jeremy J. Richardson,
ed. *Pressure Groups*. Oxford: Oxford University Press.

Ong, Aihwa. 1996. "Strategic Sisterhood or Sisters in Solidarity? Questions of
Communitarianism and Citizenship in Asia." *Indiana Journal of Global Legal
Studies* 4/1: 107–135.

Ostergaard, Geoffrey. 1989. "Indian Anarchism: The Curious Case of Vinoba
Bhave, Anarchist 'Saint of the Government.'" In David Goodway, ed. *For Anarchism: History, Theory and Practice*. London: Routledge.

Outhwaite, William. 1997. Review of David Held's *Democracy and the Global Order. Sociological Review* 45/1: 179–181.

Outhwaite, William, and Tom Bottomore, eds. 1994. *The Blackwell Dictionary of
Twentieth Century Social Thought*. Paper ed. Oxford: Blackwell.

Pak Po-Hi. 1996. "Opening Remarks." In Eva Friedlander, ed. *Look at the World
Through Women's Eyes: Plenary Speeches from the NGO Forum on Women, Beijing
'95*. New York: Women, Ink.

Panjabi, Kavita. 1997. "Probing 'Morality' and State Violence: Feminist Values
and Communicative Interaction in Prison Testimonios in India and Argentina." In M. Jacqui Alexander and Chandra Talpade Mohanty, eds. *Feminist
Genealogies, Colonial Legacies, Democratic Futures*. London: Routledge.

Papandreou, Margerita Chant. 1988. "Global Feminism for the Year 2000." In
Daniela Gioseffi, ed. *Women on War: Essential Voices for the Nuclear Age*. New
York: Simon & Schuster/Touchstone.

Papic, Zarena. 1992. "Report on Women as Citizens in Yugoslavia." In Anna
Ward, Jeanne Gregory, and Nira Yuval-Davis, eds. *Women and Citizenship in Eu-*

rope—*Borders, Rights and Duties: Women's Differing Identities in a Europe of Contested Boundaries.* Stoke on Trent, UK: Trentham Books.

Parmar, Pratibha. 1989. "Other Kinds of Dreams." *Feminist Review* 31: 55–65.

Parpart, Jane L., and Marianne H. Marchand. 1995. "Exploding the Canon: An Introduction/Conclusion." In Marianne H. Marchand and Jane L. Parpart, eds. *Feminism/Postmodernism/Development.* London: Routledge.

Passerini, Luisa. 1994. "The Interpretation of Democracy in the Italian Women's Movement of the 1970s and 1980s." *Women's Studies International Forum* 17/2–3: 235–239

Pateman, Carole. 1992. "Equality, Difference, Subordination: The Politics of Motherhood and Women's Citizenship." In Gisela Bock and Susan James, eds. *Beyond Equality and Difference: Citizenship, Feminist Politics and Female Subjectivity.* London: Routledge.

_____. 1989. *The Disorder of Women: Democracy, Feminism and Political Theory.* Cambridge: Polity Press.

_____. 1988. *The Sexual Contract.* Cambridge: Polity Press.

_____. 1970. *Participation and Democratic Theory.* Cambridge: Cambridge University Press.

Pearson, Ruth, and Cecile Jackson. 1999. "Introduction—Interrogating Development: Feminism, Gender and Policy." In Cecile Jackson and Ruth Pearson, eds. *Feminist Visions of Development: Gender Analysis and Policy.* London: Routledge.

Pécault, Daniel. 1996. "Politics, the Political and the Theory of Social Movements." In Jon Clark and Marco Diani, ed. *Alain Touraine.* London: Falmer Press.

Peterson, V. Spike. 1996. "The Politics of Identification in the Context of Globalization." *Women's Studies International Forum* 19/1–2: 5–15.

_____. 1995. "Reframing the Politics of Identity: Democracy, Globalization and Gender." *Political Expressions* 1/1: 1–16.

_____. 1992a. "Transgressing Boundaries: Theories of Knowledge, Gender and International Relations." *Millennium: Journal of International Studies* 21/2: 182–306.

_____. 1992b. "Security and Sovereign States: What Is at Stake in Taking Feminism Seriously?" In V. Spike Peterson, ed. *Gendered States: Feminist Revisions of International Relations Theory.* Boulder, CO: Lynne Rienner.

Peterson, V. Spike, and Anne Sisson Runyan. 1999. *Global Gender Issues.* 2d ed. Boulder, CO: Westview Press.

Pettman, Jan Jindy. 1996. *Worlding Women: A Feminist International Politics.* London: Routledge.

Phillips, Anne. 2000. "Feminism and Republicanism: Is This a Plausible Alliance?" Paper presented at the Graduate and Faculty Seminar of the Social and Political Thought Programme, 17 February, University of Sussex, UK.

_____. 1996. "Dealing with Difference: A Politics of Ideas or a Politics of Presence?" In Seyla Benhabib, ed. *Democracy and Difference: Contesting the Boundaries of the Political.* Princeton: Princeton University Press.

_____. 1995. *The Politics of Presence.* Oxford: Clarendon Press.

_____. 1993. *Democracy and Difference.* Cambridge: Polity Press.

_____. 1992. "Universal Pretensions in Political Thought." In Michèle Barratt and Anne Phillips, eds. *Destabilizing Theory: Contemporary Feminist Debates*. Cambridge: Polity Press.

_____. 1991. *Engendering Democracy*. Cambridge: Polity Press.

Pieterse, Jan Nederveen. 1995. "Globalization as Hybridization." In Michael Featherstone, Scott Lash, and Roland Robertson, eds. *Global Modernities*. London: SAGE.

_____. 1992. "Emancipations, Modern and Postmodern." In Jan Nederveen Pieterse, ed. *Emancipations, Modern and Postmodern*. London: SAGE.

Pietilä, Hikka, and Jeanne Vickers. 1994. *Making Women Matter*. 2d ed. London: Zed Books.

Pitkin, Hannah Fenichel. 1967. *The Concept of Representation*. Berkeley and Los Angeles: University of California Press.

Posadskaya, Anastasia. 1994. "Introduction." In Anastasia Posadskaya, ed. *Women in Russia: A New Era in Russian Feminism*. London: Verso.

Potter, David. 1997. "Explaining Democratization." In David Potter, David Goldblatt, Margaret Kiloh, and Paul Lewis, eds. *Democratization*. Cambridge: Polity Press in association with the Open University.

Proudhon, Pierre-Joseph. 1977. "Parliamentary Isolation." In George Woodcock, ed. *The Anarchist Reader*. Hassocks, UK: Harvester Press.

Radford-Hill, Sheila. 1986. "Considering Feminism as a Model for Social Change." In Teresa De Lauretis, ed. *Feminist Studies/Critical Studies*. Basingstoke, UK: Macmillan.

Ram, Kalpana. 1993. "Too `Traditional' Once Again: Some Post-structuralists on the Aspirations of the Immigrant/Third World Female Subject." *Australian Feminist Studies* 17: 5–28.

Randall, Vicky. 1987. *Women and Politics: An International Perspective*. 2d ed. Basingstoke, UK: Macmillan.

Rapoport, Tamar, and Orna Sasson-Levy. 1997. "Men's Knowledge, Women's Body: A Story of Two Protest Movements." Paper presented at the First Regional Conference on Social Movements, 8–10 September, Tel Aviv, Israel.

Reagon, Bernice Johnson. 1983. "Coalition Politics: Turning the Century." In Barbara Smith, ed. *Home Girls: A Black Feminist Anthology*. New York: Kitchen Table—Women of Colour Press.

Reardon, Betty. 1993. "A Feminist Perspective on World Constitutional Order." In Richard A. Falk, Robert C. Johansen, and Samuel S. Kim, eds. *The Constitutional Foundations of World Peace*. Albany: State University of New York Press.

Rengger, N. J. 1994. "Towards a Culture of Democracy? Democratic Theory and Democratisation in Eastern and Central Europe." In Geoffrey Pridham, Eric Herring, and George Sandford, eds. *Building Democracy? The International Dimension of Democratisation in Eastern Europe*. London: Leicester University Press.

Rich, Adrienne. 1986. *Blood, Bread and Poetry: Selected Prose 1979–1985*. New York: W. W. Books.

Richardson, Jeremy J. 1993. "Introduction: Pressure Groups and Government." In Jeremy J. Richardson, ed. *Pressure Groups*. Oxford: Oxford University Press.

Riley, Denise. 1988. *"Am I That Name?" Feminism and the Category of "Women" in History.* Basingstoke, UK: Macmillan Press.

Robertson, Roland. 1992. *Globalization: Social Theory and Global Culture.* London: SAGE.

_____. 1990. "Mapping the Global Condition: Globalization as the Central Concept." In Mike Featherstone, ed. *Global Culture: Nationalism, Globalization and Modernity.* London: SAGE.

Rocker, Rudolf. 1969. "Anarcho-Syndicalism." In Priscilla Long, ed. *The New Left.* Boston: Extending Horizons Books.

Rosenau, James. 1990. *Turbulence in World Politics.* Princeton: Princeton University Press.

Rosenberg, Justin. 1994. *The Empire of Civil Society: A Critique of the Realist Theory of International Relations.* London: Verso.

Roseneil, Sasha. 1995. *Disarming Patriarchy: Feminism and Political Action at Greenham.* Milton Keynes, UK: Open University Press.

Rourke, John T., Richard P. Hiskes, and Cyrus Ernesto Zurakzadeh. 1992. *Direct Democracy and International Politics: Deciding International Issues Through Referendums.* Boulder, CO: Lynne Rienner.

Rowbotham, Sheila. 1992. *Women in Movement: Feminism and Social Action.* London: Routledge.

_____. 1986. "Feminism and Democracy." In David Held and Christopher Pollit, eds. *New Forms of Democracy.* London: SAGE in association with the Open University.

_____. 1981. "The Trouble with 'Patriarchy.'" In Feminist Anthology Collective, eds. *No Turning Back: Writings from the Women's Liberation Movement 1975–1980.* London: Women's Press.

_____. 1979. "The Women's Movement and Organising for Socialism." In Sheila Rowbotham, Lynn Segal, and Hilary Wainwright. *Beyond the Fragments: Feminism and the Making of Socialism.* London: Merlin Press

Ruddick, Sara. 1990. *Maternal Thinking: Towards a Politics of Peace.* London: Women's Press.

Ruggie, John Gerard. 1993. "Territoriality and Beyond: Problematising Modernity in International Relations." *International Organization* 47: 140–174.

Runyan, Anne Sisson. 1996. "The Places of Women in Trading Places: Gendered Global/Regional Regimes and Inter-nationalized Feminist Resistance." In Eleonore Kofman and Gillian Youngs, eds. *Globalization: Theory and Practice.* London: Pinter.

Rustin, Michael. 1989. "The Trouble with New Times." In Stuart Hall and Martin Jacques, eds. *New Times: The Changing Face of Politics in the 1990s.* London: Lawrence and Wishart.

Ryan, Barbara. 1992. *Feminism and the Women's Movement: Dynamics of Change in Social Movement Ideology and Activism.* London: Routledge.

Sahgal, Gita, and Nira Yuval-Davis. 1992. "Introduction: Fundamentalism, Multiculturalism and Women in Britain." In Gita Sahgal and Nira Yuval-Davis, eds. *Refusing Holy Orders: Women and Fundamentalism in Britain.* London: Virago.

Sakamoto, Yoshikazu. 1997. "Civil Society and Democratic World Order." In Stephen Gill and James H. Mittelman, eds. *Innovation and Transformation in International Studies*. Cambridge: Cambridge University Press.

Sakolsky, Ron. 1989. "Toward a Participatory Culture: Creating Democracy by Democratising Creativity." In Dimitrios I. Roussopoulos, ed. *The Anarchist Papers 2*. Montreal: Black Rose Books.

Sandilands, Catriona. 1995. "From Natural Identity to Radical Democracy." *Environmental Ethics* 17/1: 75–91.

Sandoval, Chéla. 1995. "Feminist Forms of Agency and Oppositional Consciousness: U.S. Third World Feminist Criticism." In Judith Kegan Gardiner, ed. *Provoking Agents: Gender and Agency in Theory and Practice*. Urbana and Chicago: University of Illinois Press.

_____. 1990. "Feminism and Racism: A Report on the 1981 National Women's Studies Association Conference." In Gloria Anzaldúa, ed. *Making Face, Making Soul/Haciendo Caras: Creative and Critical Perspectives by Feminists of Color*. San Francisco: Aunt Lute Books.

Sarvasy, Wendy. 1992. "Beyond the Difference Versus Equality Policy Debate: Postsuffrage Feminism, Citizenship and the Quest for a Feminist Welfare State." *Signs: Journal of Women, Culture and Society* 17/2: 329–362.

Sassen, Saskia. 1996. "Toward a Feminist Analytics of the Global Economy." *Indiana Journal of Global Legal Studies* 4/1: 7–41.

Saurin, Julian. 1995. "The End of International Relations? The State and International Theory in the Age of Globalization." In Andrew Linklater and John Macmillan, eds. *Boundaries in Question: New Directions in International Relations*. London: Pinter.

Sawicki, Jana. 1991. *Disciplining Foucault: Feminism, Power and the Body*. London: Routledge.

Sayer, Andrew. 1992. *Method in Social Science: A Realist Approach*. 2d ed. London: Routledge.

Schaeffer-Hegel, Barbar. 1992. "Makers and Victims of Unification: German Women and the Two Germanies." *Women's Studies International Forum* 15/1: 101–110.

Schecter, Darrow. 1994. *Radical Theories: Paths Beyond Marxism and Social Democracy*. Manchester: Manchester University Press.

Scholte, Jan Aart. 1996. "Beyond the Buzzword: Toward a Critical Theory of Globalization." In Eleonore Kofman and Gillian Youngs, eds. *Globalization: Theory and Practice*. London: Pinter.

_____. 1995a. "Constructions of Collective Identity in a Time of Globalisation." Paper presented at the Annual Convention of the International Studies Association, 21–25 February, Chicago.

_____. 1995b. "Governance and Democracy in a Globalised World." Paper presented at the ACUNS/ASIL Summer Workshop on International Organisation Studies, 16–28 July, The Hague.

Schumpeter, Joseph A. 1976. *Capitalism, Socialism and Democracy*. London: Allen & Unwin.

Scott, Alan. 1992. "Political Culture and Social Movements." In John Allen, Peter Braham, and Paul Lewis, eds. *Political and Economic Forms of Modernity*. Cambridge: Polity Press in association with the Open University.

_____. 1990. *Ideology and the New Social Movements*. London: Unwin Hyman.

Seager, Joni. 1997. *The State of Women in the World Atlas*. 2d ed. London: Penguin Reference.

Segal, Lynne. 1979. "A Local Experience." In Sheila Rowbotham, Lynn Segal, and Hilary Wainwright. *Beyond the Fragments: Feminism and the Making of Socialism*. London: Merlin Press

Sen, Gita, and Caren Grown. 1987. *Development Crises and Alternative Visions: Third World Women's Perspectives*. London: Earthscan.

Shaw, Martin. 1997. "Globalisation and Post-Military Democracy." In Anthony McGrew, ed. *The Transformation of Democracy? Globalization and Territorial Democracy*. Cambridge: Polity Press.

_____. 1996. *Civil Society and Media in Global Crises: Representing Distant Violence*. London: Pinter.

_____. 1994. "Civil Society and Global Politics: Beyond a Social Movements Approach." *Millennium: Journal of International Studies* 23/3: 647–667.

Shiva, Vandana. 1989. *Staying Alive: Women, Ecology and Development*. London: Zed Books.

Shohat, Ella. 1997. "Post-Third-Worldist Culture: Gender, Nation and the Cinema." In M. Jacqui Alexander and Chandra Talpade Mohanty, eds. *Feminist Genealogies, Colonial Legacies, Democratic Futures*. London: Routledge.

_____. 1996. "Notes on the Post-Colonial." In Padmini Mongia, ed. *Contemporary Postcolonial Theory: A Reader*. London: Arnold.

Sim, Stuart. 1998. "Spectres and Nostalgia: 'Post-*Marxism*' and '*Post*-Marxism.'" In Stuart Sim, ed. *Post-Marxism: A Reader*. Edinburgh: Edinburgh University Press.

Smart, Barry. 1994. "Sociology, Globalisation and Postmodernity: Comments on the 'Sociology for One World' Thesis." *International Sociology* 9/2: 149–159.

Smith, Anthony D. 1990. "Towards a Global Culture?" In Mike Featherstone, ed. *Global Culture: Nationalism, Globalization and Modernity*. London: SAGE.

Smith, Barbara. 1990. "Racism and Women's Studies." In Gloria Anzaldúa, ed. *Making Face, Making Soul/Haciendo Caras: Creative and Critical Perspectives by Feminists of Color*. San Francisco: Aunt Lute Books.

Smith, Martin J. 1993. *Pressure, Power and Policy: State Autonomy and Policy Networks in Britain and the United States*. Hemel Hempstead, UK: Harvester Wheatsheaf.

Smith, Michael. 1992. "Modernization, Globalization and the Nation-State." In Anthony McGrew and Paul G. Lewis, eds. *Global Politics: Globalization and the Nation-State*. Cambridge: Polity Press.

Smith, Michael Joseph. 1992. "Liberalism and International Reform." In Terry Nardin and David R. Mapel, eds. *Traditions of International Ethics*. Cambridge: Cambridge University Press.

Spelman, Elizabeth V. 1988. *Inessential Woman: Problems of Exclusion in Feminist Thought*. London: Woman's Press.

Spooner, Lysander. 1977. "The Indefensible Constitution." In George Woodcock, ed. *The Anarchist Reader*. Hassocks, UK: Harvester Press.

Squires, Judith. 1999. *Gender in Political Theory*. Cambridge: Polity Press.

Stafford, David. 1970. "Anarchists in Britain Today." *Government and Opposition* 5/4: 480–500.

Stammers, Neil. 1999. "Social Movements and the Challenge to Power." In Martin Shaw, ed. *Politics and Globalisation: Knowledge, Ethics and Agency*. London: Routledge.

_____. 1996. "Shadows from the East: The End of 'New Social Movements'? The Limits of a Civil Society Strategy." Paper presented at the Second European Conference on Social Movements, 2–5 October, Vitoria-Gasteiz, Spain.

Statement of Principles of the Vermont and New Hampshire Greens. 1989. "Toward a New Politics." In Dimitrios I. Roussopoulos, ed. *The Anarchist Papers 2*. Montreal: Black Rose Books.

Stefanik, Nancy. 1993. "Sustainable Dialogue/Sustainable Development: Developing Planetary Consciousness via Electronic Democracy." In Jeremy Brecher, John Brown Childs, and Jill Cutler, eds. *Global Visions: Beyond the New World Order*. Boston: South End Press.

Stiehm, Judith Hicks. 1983. "The Protector, the Protected, the Defender." In Judith Hicks Stiehm, ed. *Women and Men's Wars*. Oxford: Pergamon.

_____. 1981. "Women and Citizenship: Mobilisation, Participation, Representation." In Margherita Rendel, ed. *Women, Power and Political Systems*. London: Croon Helm.

Stienstra, Deborah. 1995. "Organising for Change: International Women's Movements and World Politics." In Francine D'Amico and Peter R. Beckman, eds. *Women in World Politics: An Introduction*. Westport, CT: Bergin & Garvey.

_____. 1994. *Women's Movements and International Organizations*. Basingstoke, UK: Macmillan.

Strange, Susan. 1994. "The Structure of Finance in the World System." In Yoshikazu Sakamoto, ed. *Global Transformation: Challenges to the State System*, Tokyo: United Nations University Press.

Sturgeon, Noël. 1997. *Ecofeminist Natures: Race, Gender, Feminist Theory and Political Action*. London: Routledge.

Suleri, Sara. 1996. "Woman Skin Deep: Feminism and the Postcolonial Condition." In Padmini Mongia, ed. *Contemporary Postcolonial Theory: A Reader*. London: Arnold.

Sylvester, Christine. 1998. "Homeless in International Relations? 'Women's' Place in Canonical Texts and Feminist Reimaginings." In Anne Phillips, ed. *Feminism and Politics*. Oxford: Oxford University Press.

_____. 1995. "African and Western Feminisms: World-Travelling the Possibilities." *Signs: Journal of Women in Culture and Society* 20/4: 941–969.

_____. 1994. *Feminist Theory and International Relations in a Postmodern Era*. Cambridge: Cambridge University Press.

Szasz, Andrew. 1995. "Progress Through Mischief: The Social Movement Alternative to Secondary Associations." In Joshua Cohen and Joel Rogers, eds. *Associations and Democracy*. London: Verso.

Tahir, Sharifah. 1997. "Leadership Development for Young Women: A Model." In Mahnaz Afkhami and Erika Friedl, eds. *Muslim Women and the Politics of Participation: Implementing the Beijing Platform.* Syracuse: Syracuse University Press.

Tang Nain, Gemma. 1991. "Black Women, Sexism and Racism: Black or Anti-Racist Feminism?" *Feminist Review* 37: 1–22.

Tarrow, Sidney. 1998. *Power in Movement: Social Movements and Contentious Politics.* 2d ed. Cambridge: Cambridge University Press.

Taylor, Verta. 1995. "Watching for Vibes: Bringing Emotions into the Study of Feminist Organizations." In Myra Marx Ferree and Patricia Yancey Martin, eds. *Feminist Organizations: Harvest of the Women's Movement.* Philadelphia: Temple University Press.

_____. 1983. "The Future of Feminism in the 1980s: A Social Movement Analysis." In Laurel Richardson and Verta Taylor, eds. *Feminist Frontiers: Rethinking Gender and Society.* Reading, MA: Addison-Wesley.

Taylor, Verta, and Leila J. Rupp. 1993. "Women's Culture and Lesbian Feminist Activism: A Reconsideration of Cultural Feminism." *Signs: Journal of Women in Culture and Society* 19/1: 32–61.

Thiele, Leslie Paul. 1993. "Making Democracy Safe for the World: Social Movements and Global Politics." *Alternatives* 8/3: 273–305.

Thompson, Janna. 1986. "Women and Political Rationality." In Carole Pateman and Elizabeth Gross, eds. *Feminist Challenges: Social and Political Theory.* London: Allen & Unwin.

Thompson, Kenneth. 1992. "Social Pluralism and Post-Modernity." In Stuart Hall, David Held, and Tony McGrew, eds. *Modernity and Its Futures.* Cambridge: Polity Press in association with the Open University.

Thoreau, Henry David. 1977. "Civil Disobedience." In George Woodcock, ed. *The Anarchist Reader.* Hassocks, UK: Harvester Press.

Tickner, J. Ann. 1992. *Gender in International Relations: Feminist Perspectives on Achieving Global Security.* New York: Columbia University Press.

Tijerina, Alética. 1990. "Notes on Oppression and Violence." In Gloria Anzaldúa, ed. *Making Face, Making Soul/Haciendo Caras: Creative and Critical Perspectives by Feminists of Color.* San Francisco: Aunt Lute Books.

Timothy, Kristen. 1995. "Women as Insiders: The Glass Ceiling at the United Nations." In Francine D'Amico and Peter R Beckman, eds. *Women in World Politics: An Introduction.* Westport, CT: Bergin & Garvey.

Tinker, Irene. 1981. "A Feminist View of Copenhagen." *Signs: Journal of Women and Culture* 6/3: 531–535.

Tinker, Irene, and Jane Jaquette. 1987. "UN Decade for Women: Its Impact and Legacy." *World Development* 15/3: 419–427.

Tolstoy, Leo. 1977. "The Violence of Laws." In George Woodcock, ed. *The Anarchist Reader.* Hassocks, UK: Harvester Press.

Tong, Rosemarie. 1989. *Feminist Thought: A Comprehensive Introduction.* London: Routledge.

Touraine, Alain. 1997. *What Is Democracy?* Translated by David Macey. Boulder, CO: Westview Press.

_____. 1995. *Critique of Modernity*. Translated by David Macey. Oxford: Basil Blackwell.

_____. 1985. "An Introduction to the Study of Social Movements." *Social Research* 52/4: 749–787.

_____. 1974. *The Post-Industrial Society—Tomorrow's Social History Today: Classes, Conflicts and Cultures in the Programmed Society*. London: Wildwood House.

Tucker, Kenneth H. 1991. "How New Are the New Social Movements?" *Theory, Culture and Society* 8: 75–98.

Uberoi, Patricia. 1995. "Problems with Patriarchy: Conceptual Issues in Anthropology and Feminism." *Sociological Bulletin* 44/2: 195–221.

Uttal, Lynet. 1990. "Inclusion Without Influence: The Continuing Tokenism of Women of Color." In Gloria Anzaldúa, ed. *Making Face, Making Soul/Haciendo Caras: Creative and Critical Perspectives by Feminists of Color*. San Francisco: Aunt Lute Books.

Verdery, Katherine. 1994. "From Parent-State to Family Patriarchs: Gender and Nation in Contemporary Eastern Europe." *Eastern European Politics and Society* Spring, 8/2: 225–255.

Voronina, Olga. 1994. "The Mythology of Women's Emancipation in the USSR as the Foundation for a Policy of Discrimination." In Anastasia Posadskaya, ed. *Women in Russia: A New Era in Russian Feminism*. London: Verso.

Walby, Sylvia. 1990a. *Theorizing Patriarchy*. Oxford: Basil Blackwell.

_____. 1990b. "Women's Employment and the Historical Periodisation of Patriarchy." In Helen Corr and Lynn Jamieson, eds. *Politics of Everyday Life: Continuity and Change in Work and the Family*. Basingstoke, UK: Macmillan.

Walker, Alice. 1990. "Definition of Womanist." In Gloria Anzaldúa, ed. *Making Face, Making Soul/Haciendo Caras: Creative and Critical Perspectives by Feminists of Color*. San Francisco: Aunt Lute Books.

Walker, R. B. J. 1998. "Citizenship After the Modern Subject." In Kimberly Hutchings and Roland Dannreuther, eds. *Cosmopolitan Citizenship*. Basingstoke, UK: Macmillan.

_____. 1995. "International Relations and the Concept of the Political." In Ken Booth and Steve Smith, eds. *International Relations Theory Today*. Cambridge: Polity Press.

_____. 1994. "Social Movements/World Politics." *Millennium: Journal of International Studies* 23/3: 669–700.

_____. 1993. *Inside/Outside: International Relations as Political Theory*. Cambridge: Cambridge University Press.

_____. 1992. "Gender and Critique in the Theory of International Relations." In V. Spike Peterson, ed. *Gendered States: Feminist Revisions of International Relations Theory*. Boulder, CO: Lynne Rienner.

_____. 1990. "Sovereignty, Identity, Community: Reflections on the Horizons of Contemporary Political Practice." In R. B. J. Walker and Saul H. Mendlovitz, eds. *Contending Sovereignties: Redefining Political Community*. Boulder, CO: Lynne Rienner.

_____. 1988. *One World, Many Worlds: Struggles for a Just World Peace*. Boulder CO: Lynne Rienner.

Walker, R. B. J., and Saul H. Mendlovitz. 1990. "Interrogating State Sovereignty." In Saul H. Mendlovitz and R. B. J. Walker, eds. *Contending Sovereignties: Redefining Political Community.* Boulder, CO: Lynne Rienner.

Wallerstein, Immanuel. 1990. "Antisystemic Movements: History and Dilemmas." In Samir Amin, Giovanni Arrighi, Andre Gunder Frank, and Immanuel Wallerstein. *Transforming the Revolution: Social Movements and the World System.* New York: Monthly Review Press.

———. 1986. "Societal Development, or Development of the World-System?" *International Sociology* 1/1: 3–17.

Waltz, Kenneth. 1979. *Theory of International Politics.* Reading, MA: Addison-Wesley.

———. 1959. *Man, the State and War: A Theoretical Analysis.* New York: Columbia University Press.

Wapner, Paul. 1995. "Politics Beyond the State: Environmental Activism and World Civic Politics." *World Politics* 47: 311–340.

Ward, Kathryn B. 1993. "Reconceptualizing World System Theory to Include Women." In Paula England, ed. *Theory on Gender/Feminism on Theory.* New York: Aldine de Gruyter.

———. 1988. "Female Resistance to Marginalization: The Igbo Women's War of 1929." In Joan Smith, Jane Collins, Terence K. Hopkins, and Akbar Muhammad, eds. *Racism, Sexism and the World System.* Westport, CT: Greenwood Press.

Ware, Vron. 1992. *Beyond the Pale: White Women, Racism and History.* London: Verso.

Warren, Mark. 1992. "Democratic Theory and Self-Transformation." *American Political Science Review* 86/1: 8–23.

Waterman, Peter. 1998. *Globalization, Social Movements and the New Internationalisms.* London: Mansell.

Waters, Malcolm. 1995. *Globalization.* London: Routledge.

Watson, Adam. 1984. "European International Society and Its Expansion." In Hedley Bull and Adam Watson, eds. *The Expansion of International Society.* Oxford: Clarendon Press.

Watson, Peggy. 1993. "The Rise of Masculinism in Eastern Europe." *New Left Review* 198: 71–82.

Watson, Sophie. 1990. "The State of Play: An Introduction." In Sophie Watson, ed. *Playing the State: Australian Feminist Interventions.* London: Verso.

Waylen, Georgina. 1998. "Gender, Feminism and the State: An Overview." In Vicky Randall and Georgina Waylen, eds. *Gender, Politics and the State.* London: Routledge.

———. 1994. "Women and Democratization: Conceptualizing Gender Relations in Transition Politics." *World Politics* 46/3: 327–354.

Weeks, Jeffrey. 1981. *Sex, Politics and Society: The Regulation of Sexuality Since 1800.* London and New York: Longman.

Wekker, Gloria. 1997. "One Finger Does Not Drink Okra Soup: Surinamese Women and Critical Agency." In M. Jacqui Alexander and Chandra Talpade Mohanty, eds. *Feminist Genealogies, Colonial Legacies, Democratic Futures.* London: Routledge.

West, Guida, and Rhoda Lois Blumberg. 1990. "Reconstructing Social Protest from a Feminist Perspective." In Guida West and Rhoda Lois Blumberg, eds. *Women and Social Protest*. Oxford: Oxford University Press.

West, Lois A. 1992. "Feminist Nationalist Social Movements: Beyond Universalism and Towards a Gendered Cultural Relativism." *Women's Studies International Forum* 15/5–6: 563–579.

Wexler, Alice Ruth. 1986. "Emma Goldman and Women." In Dimitrios I. Roussopoulos, ed. *The Anarchist Papers 1*. Montreal: Black Rose Books.

Whitehead, Laurence. 1996. "Concerning International Support for Democracy in the South." In Robin Luckham and Gordon White, eds. *Democratization in the South: The Jagged Wave*. Manchester: Manchester University Press.

Whitworth, Sandra. 1989. "Gender in the Interparadigm Debate." *Millennium: Journal of International Studies* 18/2: 265–272.

Wieringa, Sasha. 1994. "Women's Interests and Empowerment: Gender Planning Reconsidered." *Development and Change* 25/4: 829–848.

Willetts, Peter. 1982a. "Pressure Groups as Transnational Actors." In Peter Willetts, ed. *Pressure Groups in the Global System: The Transnational Relations of Issue-Oriented, Non-Governmental Organisations*. London: Pinter.

_____. 1982b. "The Impact of Promotional Pressure Groups on Global Politics." In Peter Willetts, ed. *Pressure Groups in the Global System: The Transnational Relations of Issue-Oriented, Non-Governmental Organisations*. London: Pinter.

Wilson, Graham K. 1981. *Interest Groups in the United States*. Oxford: Clarendon Press.

Wolin, Sheldon. 1996. "Fugitive Democracy." In Seyla Benhabib, ed. *Democracy and Difference: Contesting the Boundaries of the Political*. Princeton: Princeton University Press.

Wood, Ellen Mieskins. 1995. *Democracy Against Capitalism: Renewing Historical Materialism*. Cambridge: Cambridge University Press.

_____. 1990. "The Uses and Abuses of Civil Society." In Ralph Miliband, Lee Panitch, and John Saville, eds. *The Socialist Register*. London: Merlin Press.

Woodcock, George. 1977. "Syndicalism Defined." In George Woodcock, ed. *The Anarchist Reader*. Hassocks, UK: Harvester Press.

_____. 1968. "Anarchism Revisited." *Commentary* 46/2: 54–60.

Woolf, Virginia. 1938. *Three Guineas*. London: Hogarth Press.

Young, Iris Marion. 1996. "Communication and the Other: Beyond Deliberative Democracy." In Seyla Benhabib, ed. *Democracy and Difference: Contesting the Boundaries of the Political*. Princeton: Princeton University Press.

_____. 1995. "Social Groups in Associative Democracy." In Joshua Cohen and Joel Rogers, eds. *Associations and Democracy*. London: Verso.

_____. 1994. "Gender as Seriality: Thinking About Women as a Social Collective." *Signs: Journal of Women, Culture and Society* 19/3: 713–738.

_____. 1990. *Justice and the Politics of Difference*. Princeton: Princeton University Press.

_____. 1987. "Impartiality and the Civic Public: Some Implications of Feminist Critiques of Moral and Political Theory." In Seyla Benhabib and Drucilla Cornell, eds. *Feminism as Critique: Essays on the Politics of Gender in Late-Capitalist Societies*. Cambridge: Polity Press.

Yuval-Davis, Nira. 1997a. "Women, Citizenship and Difference." *Feminist Review* 57: 4–27

_____. 1997b. *Gender and Nation*. London: SAGE.

Zalewski, Marysia. 1994. "The Women/'Women' Question in International Relations." *Millennium: Journal of International Studies* 23/2: 407–423.

Zinn, Maxine Baca, Lynn Weber Cannen, Elizabeth Higginbotham, and Bonnie Thornton Dill. 1990. "The Costs of Exclusionary Practices in Women's Studies." In Gloria Anzaldúa, ed. *Making Face, Making Soul/Haciendo Caras: Creative and Critical Perspectives by Feminists of Color*. San Francisco: Aunt Lute Books.

Zook, Kristal Brent. 1990. "Light Skinned-ded Naps." In Gloria Anzaldúa, ed. *Making Face, Making Soul/Haciendo Caras: Creative and Critical Perspectives by Feminists of Color*. San Francisco: Aunt Lute Books.

Index

Printed in the United States
32754LVS00016B/81